DAVID DOUGLAS

DAVID DOUGLAS

Explorer and Botanist

Ann Lindsay Mitchell
and Syd House

AURUM PRESS

First published in Great Britain
1999 by Aurum Press Ltd
25 Bedford Avenue, London WC1B 3AT

ISBN 1 85410 591 4

1   3   5   7   9   10   8   6   4   2
1999   2001   2003   2002   2000

Edited by Christopher Pick
Text design and maps by Don Macpherson
Typeset by Action Publishing Technology Ltd, Gloucester
Printed and bound by in Great Britain by
MPG Books Ltd, Bodmin

CONTENTS

ACKNOWLEDGEMENTS

Writing a book is no way to spend time! After two years of graft we feel as if we have travelled almost as far as David Douglas did on his adventures.

There are a great many people to whom both Ann Lindsay Mitchell and I owe our thanks for their help and guidance in getting this book into print. Many past and current friends and colleagues in the Forestry Commission have contributed information, ideas and support. They include John Davies and Archie Smith, both experts and writers on Douglas, who have kept the candle lit and have passed it on to others. Thanks also go to Alan Fletcher, for advice on the source of surviving 'Douglas' trees and photographs of his trips to the Pacific North West; James Ogilvie, for photographs and advice on the 'Douglas trail'; Alan Chalmers, for cartographic expertise; Douglas Green, for his photographs; and David Henderson-Howat for his understanding. Particular thanks are due to Sir Peter Hutchison, Chairman of the Forestry Commission, for his advice and contacts and for the loan of his precious original copies of Douglas' journal and Hooker's 'Brief Memoir'. Many other people have assisted, and so further thanks go to David Knott, Curator of Dawyck Gardens, for his enthusiasm and photographs; the Duke of Buccleuch and Graham Booth, his Forest Manager; Jeremy Duncan, Head Librarian at Perth Library, for access to the records and the work of Magnus Jackson, Victorian photographer of trees; Morag Norris, archivist at Scone Palace, Perth; Paul Adair, Perth and Kinross Museum; Remy Claire of France; Christine McLaren-Dow, gardener at Scone; Paul Matthews, Curator, Glasgow Botanic Gardens; Jim Paterson of the Tree Register of the British Isles; Leslie Price, Archivist at Kew Gardens; Peter and Kate Drummond-Hay; the staff at the Lindley Library of the Royal Horticultural Society in London; Piers Burnett, Editorial Director of Aurum Press for his great patience; and the various members of the David Douglas Society in Scone, especially Jean Stewart, for help and encouragement.

Finally, I would like to thank my wife, Katie, and my sons, Andrew and Euan, for indulging 'the Old Man' by walking to see trees, forests and monuments and visiting botanic gardens, and for generally putting up with two years of constant remarks on the lines of 'Did you know that Douglas visited here?' and 'That's a Douglas introduction'! And that's not counting the evenings, weekends and holidays spent at the AppleMac. Thank you.

Syd House

As well as working with Syd on the research and writing here in Scotland, I also visited Vancouver, where I enjoyed a crash course on David Douglas, viewing the great trees for which he is famed and visiting Vancouver Island to research the flowers he found. Here I was much assisted by Andy McKinnon and Robert Parish of the British Columbia Forest Service. In and around Vancouver, we offer great thanks to Clive Justice, forester and energetic correspondent, whose masterly account of Douglas' journey, especially around the Red River area, we have drawn on extensively. Gordon and Christy Stewart supplied much information, and J.T. (Roli) Parker helped develop my understanding of the native peoples and cultures; at the Museum of Anthropology, University of British Columbia, Vancouver, I was considerably assisted by Deborah Tibbel. Bill Young conducted me round Vancouver Island, and took me to see 'Cathedral Grove', an awesome stand of gigantic Douglas firs; he also supplied many contacts and a comprehensive collection of David Douglas Society newsletters. I am also very grateful to Jack Toovey and his family, who acted as my chauffeurs, and to Betty Stewart, with whom I stayed for one of life's most treasured weeks. Many thanks also to my sister, Elizabeth, who inundated me with American wild-flower books and sought out a mass of fascinating information about Bartram's garden; to Mark Barton, who laboriously transcribed all 120,000 words of Douglas' original diaries; to William Marshall, who primed the computer to make this possible; to Morna Stewart, for tackling the chapter on Hawaii; to Gina Douglas of the Linnean Society, Jennifer Vine at the Royal Horticultural Society in London, and all the librarians at the Royal Botanic Garden, Edinburgh.

I would like to end on a personal note. In 1912, my mother Mary Duncan (then aged nine months), her parents and her grandmother sailed from England for Canada. My grandfather, David Duncan, was a ship's engineer and had been tempted by the offer of an excellent job in the Vancouver shipyards. There was consternation at home shortly before they departed, not because of the distances involved, but because of a shipwreck about a week previously: the sinking of the supposedly unsinkable *Titanic*. Their ship, the *Grampian*, was the first to depart after the tragedy. My grandfather, ever the pragmatist, declared that the *Grampian* would be the safest ship ever to sail, with the crew alert at all times, and so it proved to be.

The family settled on the edge of the forest to the north of Vancouver. Here my grandmother would bang her saucepans together to ward off brown bears intent on demolishing the raspberries. When forest fires raged, the adults had to perch on the roof ridge of their wooden house and spray it to prevent sparks catching hold. On one occasion an enormous Douglas fir fell across their garden and the neighbouring ones, and there are photographs of my grandfather clutching a huge two-man saw used to cut it up – the wood stoked their fires for two years or more.

After several years, the family returned to England, a move they soon regretted. My mother did not return to Vancouver for sixty years. Years later still, eighty-five years after she first set foot in Canada, I made the journey, and visited the family home: an odd reversal of tradition, for Scots generally find themselves returning to Scotland to visit their roots. Writing this book, a task with which one of my sons (also named Duncan) helped enormously, has brought this aspect of life round full circle. In Vancouver, the immense trees I had heard my mother describe and had seen in faded photos came to life and helped me to understand the drama, the isolation and the loneliness that David Douglas must so often have encountered.

Ann Lindsay Mitchell

PREFACE

'It is truthfully said that a congenial companion doubles the
pleasure and halves the discomfort of travel and so it is with
the brotherhood who love plants.'
*Ernest Wilson, the great English plant-hunter,
in the preface to his book* SMOKE THAT THUNDERS, *1927*

The history of hunting for plants, and of their subsequent cultivation
as food and medicine and as ornament of both house and garden, is
an ancient one, and dates back to the earliest moments of human
civilization. Since the seventeenth century, Britons have led the way in
developing a more scientific approach to botany and horticulture, and
Scots in particular have been among the keenest and most enthusiastic explorers and collectors of plants. Alexander Masson of
Aberdeenshire explored in South Africa and the New World in the
seventeenth century; Archibald Menzies of Perthshire served as a
ship's surgeon and botanist with Captain George Vancouver, travelling to the unexplored coast of north-west America in the 1790s; in
the mid-nineteenth century Robert Fortune brought back numerous
plants from the Far East; and in the early years of the twentieth
century George Forrest made many finds in China.

Why were Scots so prominent? Scotland has a tradition of horticultural expertise and excellence, which has always been valued in a
country situated on the extremes. The value attached to education –
much greater than further south – and its universal availability were
major factors. So too was the establishment, as early as 1670, of
Edinburgh's Royal Botanic Garden, which acted as a 'forcing-house'
for gardeners and botanists. In the eighteenth century, a remarkable
number of Scots found employment in great estates throughout
Britain, and many rose to become head gardeners. In the late
eighteenth and nineteenth centuries the voyages of exploration and
the expansion of the British Empire created opportunities further
afield, and it is no surprise that many Scots forsook the limited
horizons of their native country to seek fame and fortune elsewhere.

David Douglas thus forms part of a line of distinguished Scots
plant-collectors. The number and range of his introductions and
their subsequent influence on our gardens and landscape set him
among the greatest. Douglas was fortunate that he was sent to
explore North America, which has a wide range of indigenous plants

and trees. In addition, the latitude and climate are sufficiently similar to that of the British Isles for transplanted trees and flowers to flourish. Douglas was lucky to have travelled at a time of great interest in horticulture, when there were sufficient numbers of wealthy buyers eager to purchase and cultivate the new species he introduced. Together all these factors contributed to Douglas' success. But of course the qualities of the man himself – his single-minded determination to fulfil his plant-hunting remit, his toughness in surviving hostile environments, and not least his skill as a botanist – were fundamental to his success.

The foremost source of information about Douglas is his own journal. The Horticultural Society charged Douglas with writing up his journal for publication after he returned from his first trip to the Pacific North West in 1827. For various reasons, discussed in Chapter 9, the task proved beyond him. Only when a chest of his original papers was discovered in the Society's archives in the early 1900s was the task completed under the editorship of the Reverend W. Wilks, the Society's secretary. This stimulated much interest, which was renewed in 1980 when John Davies, now retired from the Forestry Commission, published an excellent selection of the original edition. The authors' own interest dates from this time.

Unfortunately only the journal from Douglas' first two journeys to North America survives. The journal of his third, including a daily diary, was lost when his canoe capsized on the Fraser River in 1833, along with equipment and many botanical specimens and seeds. Who knows what treasures were lost, the more so since Douglas had travelled in California and had observed such marvels as the giant coast redwood, *Sequoia sempervirens*?

The second important source of information about Douglas is the 'Brief Memoir of the Life of Mr David Douglas, with Extracts from His Letters' published by William Hooker, his great and most loyal friend, in 1836, two years after his death. Douglas was a reasonably prolific and interesting correspondent, and many of his letters to Hooker, the Horticultural Society and other associates survive. These go some way to filling out the events of Douglas' last journey. The 'Memoir' also includes a recollection of Douglas' earliest days by his brother John. In the archives of Kew Gardens and the Royal Horticultural Society are copious letters from, to and about Douglas, all of which help to flesh out the story of this remarkable man. Many others, particularly A.G. Harvey and John Davies, have expertly researched these, but there is still a thrill in reading and handling the originals, with Douglas' scrawled handwriting telling the tale of yet another plant discovery.

The other single most important reference source is Harvey's book *Douglas of the Fir*, published in 1947. This excellent account was exhaustively researched, and we freely acknowledge it as an important assessment of the primary sources for Douglas and as a major mine of information.

David Douglas is a particularly attractive and interesting personality. Although his story has been told before, knowledge of his achievements and adventures remains limited. The bicentenary in 1999 of his birth is a good time to review Douglas' achievements not solely from a historical perspective (and that is interesting enough) but also as a contribution to the gardens and landscapes of Britain. The story of how so many of the large trees that frame and adorn the great estates of the British Isles came to be discovered is the stuff of legend.

A note on plant nomenclature

Botanists use the internationally recognized Linnean classification system by which plants are named in Latin. The genus, or family name, appears first, followed by the species name. Thus the Douglas fir is *Pseudotsuga menziesii*. In naming plants, botanists use a number of distinguishing features, such as the shape of the leaf or the type of seed. Alternatively they may base the scientific name on the name of the person who discovered or introduced the plant, or they may name the plant after a famous person or someone associated with it. Thus Douglas named the big-cone pine *Pinus coulteri* after Dr Coulter, his travelling companion in California.

However, scientific nomenclature is by no means simple. Botanists are forever classifying and re-classifying plants, and the case of the Douglas fir illustrates this perfectly. When Douglas discovered the tree, it became known as *Pinus douglasii*, since at that time all conifers were referred to as pines. The name was subsequently changed to *Abies douglasii*, then to *Pseudotsuga douglasii*, then to *Pseudotsuga taxifolia* and finally to the current name, *Pseudotsuga menziesii*. This ensures that both Menzies and Douglas are recognized, in the Latin and common names respectively.

All this makes research confusing. Many authors have attempted to list the plants Douglas is credited as having found, and we are most grateful to Paul Matthews of Glasgow Botanic Gardens for providing an exhaustive list of the plants discovered, introduced and named by Douglas. This is reproduced on pages 210–22. It is not always clear whether Douglas was responsible for a particular plant. Sometimes this is because his notes were lost, sometimes because of the profusion of seeds he sent back from his travels. These included seeds from entirely new species and also from species that were already known but whose seeds had never been collected.

The situation is even more complex, because Douglas was often uncertain of the correct generic name of many of the plants he found. He often had to identify plants at times of the year when they lacked such distinguishing features as flowers, seeds and cones – every gardener knows this dilemma!

We therefore decided to use Douglas' nomenclature when quoting from his original diaries and letters. Elsewhere we have used current nomenclature and have also tried to supply the common names whenever possible.

Chapter One

THE EARLY YEARS

'He had at all times a very inquisitive disposition, and was not
satisfied with merely seeing a new thing, but must know where it
came from, and how it was procured.'
*John Douglas writing to William Hooker about his
younger brother David*

Though modest by birth, David Douglas hailed from a long line
of illustrious ancestors. Of great power during the Middle Ages,
the Douglas clan is closely associated with Scone, Scotland's
ancient capital, where many Scottish kings were crowned. The 'good'
Sir James, raised in France, dashed off in his early twenties to join the
army of Robert the Bruce. An outstanding military career followed,
and he was knighted on the field after the battle of Bannockburn in
1314. Robert trusted James enough to leave him as his warden in
charge of the Scots while he made forays into Ireland. In 1329 it was
Sir James who promised the dying Bruce that he would carry his
embalmed heart on a crusade to the Holy Land – an adventure during
which he lost his own life. Archibald 'the Grim', his illegitimate son,
proved no less an honoured son of Scotland, removing the only
remaining English garrison by securing the surrender of Lochmaben
Castle in the fourteenth century. A little closer to David Douglas' own
time, his forebear Gavin Douglas (1476–1522) achieved fame by
translating Virgil's *Aeneid* into Scots. Much later, between 1812 and
1815, Thomas Douglas, Earl of Selkirk, transported the Selkirk
Settlers, a group of dispossessed Highlanders, to the Red River area of
Winnipeg, which David Douglas later visited.

The only link between David Douglas' artisan family and the

powerful medieval barons who ruled Scotland may have been their aristocratic name. Nonetheless, some of their fortitude and bravery found its way into the character of David Douglas, who was born on 25 June 1799 to John Douglas, a stonemason who worked on the Scone estate, and his wife, Jean Drummond. David was the second of their six children.

John Douglas was fortunate to be alive at a time and in a place that greatly needed his skills. In the years around 1800, Scone experienced great change and turmoil, principally because of the construction of Scone Palace. To make room for the new building, the Earl of Mansfield razed the higgledy-piggledy village that surrounded the old house and moved its inhabitants lock, stock and barrel to a new hamlet, conveniently situated just out of his sight. Despite this upheaval, mills and bleach-fields opened in the area, bringing prosperity and encouraging young people to marry. Between 1795 and 1811, the population increased by 66 per cent, and young David was part of this baby boom. His father, one of eight stonemasons in the area, earned one shilling and eight pence per day (more than a fisherman or a carpenter, but slightly less than a bricklayer); thus the family was, within the confines of their artisan class, just about prosperous. More important, John Douglas' prospects meant that David was sent to school.

The icon and cornerstone of Scottish society, education, was widely available and hugely valued. If a boy showed promise, he would be encouraged, regardless of his class or background. Douglas would have spent long hours at school, bringing his own lunch to sustain him (almost certainly a 'piece' consisting of a small amount of bread with 'dripping' – clarified fat with perhaps a little cheese or jam made from the berries that grew wild in copious quantities in summer). Although he was not a conscientious scholar, being distracted by the wonders of nature, including his pet owls and rabbits, he was unconsciously developing uncommon powers of observation and preparing for a life devoted to the natural world.

David's older brother, called John after his father, recollected his younger brother's schooldays.

> At about the age of 3 years he was sent to a school in the village kept by a very worthy old lady where he remained 2 or 3 years but being a very spirited boy he literally became [the] master himself and the consequence was his removal to the Parish School of Kinnoul[l] kept by Mr Wilson where he remained a few years longer. He always disliked the restraints of school and when he could form any excuse for absenting himself either in the company of the boys or by himself his time was devoted to

his favourite pursuits of birdwatching or fishing. And poor fellow he was often punished at School for being behind School hours – the want of his labour and for playing truant.

William Hooker, the famous botanist who was to become Douglas' patron and mentor, compiled the story of his protégé's early life from accounts written for him by John Douglas and others. In 1836 Hooker published his 'Brief Memoir of the Life of Mr David Douglas' as a companion volume to *The Botanical Magazine*. He wrote of Douglas' early enthusiasm for wildlife that:

Douglas often found it difficult to maintain some of these favourites [birds], especially hawks and owls. For the sake of feeding a nest of the latter, the poor boy, after exhausting all his skill in catching mice and small birds, used frequently to spend the daily penny with which he should have procured bread for his own lunch, in buying bullock's liver for his owlets, though a walk of six miles to and from school might well have sharpened his youthful appetite.

When he was present in the classroom, Douglas was a thorn in the side of his teachers, endlessly asking awkward questions and questioning authority. Discipline did not come easily. A friend of the family recalled that:

His contempt for the headmaster's thong and his carelessness about those difficulties and hardships which would have weighted hard with other boys, were budding into that strong-minded, self-dependent heroism which enable[d] him afterward to dare and do so much for the advantage of natural history.

But continue to study he did, even embarking on Latin at school, which perhaps testifies to his fundamentally enquiring mind. (He continued to improve his Latin at the classes he attended after leaving school. Little did he know that, less than two decades later and on the other side of the world, he would use the language to communicate with Roman Catholic monks in what is now California.) His brother recalled:

He had at all times a very inquisitive disposition, and was not satisfied with merely seeing a new thing, but must know where it came from, and how it was procured. As an instance of this, I remember one day passing a tobacconist's shop in Perth. He noticed the figure of a black man preparing tobacco, which so aroused his attention that he could not rest satisfied until he had learned its whole history.

Alongside the changes in society during Douglas' youth came great changes in agriculture. The enclosure system was spreading north, and sheep and cattle were no longer allowed to roam over common grazing land. As fields were enclosed by hawthorn hedges, wheat, oats and hay began to flourish, as did new plants and cultivars such as mangel-wurzels, which could be stored for winter feed. As a result, the number of cattle bred increased dramatically.

The new agricultural methods enriched the large landowners, who were now prepared to devote more time to luxuries such as flower gardening. Landscape gardening in Scotland was undergoing a radical, albeit gradual, change. When Douglas left school in 1810 and began work as an apprentice gardener at Scone Palace, he found himself, after crunching his way over the beaten earth and gravel paths of the huge traditional walled kitchen garden, in the midst of a new and fashionable 'natural' landscaping project. In deciding to replant and recreate the parkland and gardens round Scone, the Earl of Mansfield embarked on a project beset with difficulties. Arguments raged from the start. The Earl's first landscape gardener was Thomas White, who worked unhappily at Scone for five years from 1781. The Earl and his landscape expert argued continually about money and also about the clumps of large trees White planted. Summoning a gravitas justified by his years of experience, White explained:

> The system of clumps is necessary ... because the climate in the north of England and Scotland will not allow single trees to get up as I have found by experience, or otherwise I should have planted single trees in many places, wherein I have now planted clumps of trees.

This was a fairly polite way of saying that the northern climate could be so fearsome that carefully planted young trees might easily be decimated by a bad winter and 'burnt' by strong winds. Nonetheless, White's tone no doubt grated on the Earl, for no landowner would happily tolerate returning to his domain in spring after spending the winter in London or Edinburgh to find acres of expensively laid-out woodland standing dead or dying. White had placed himself in an unwinnable situation. If he planted clumps of trees in the hope that least one would survive and, years later, grow into a statuesque parkland specimen, he would be accused of wasting money on lavish planting.

Disagreements about White's fees were finally resolved by arbitration, much to his bitter relief. In his final letter, he closed the relationship with an acid comment: 'I have reason to thank your Lordship that a business that has given me more pain than pleasure is to have an end.'

The next landscape gardener to take up the challenge at Scone was John Loudon, who immediately set about tearing down both White's ideas and his plantings. By the time Loudon reached Scone in 1804, Scottish landscape design was being much influenced by Capability Brown and the cult of the picturesque. Sparse, natural-looking planting was in favour rather than complex and intricate designs. While Loudon was not the most inspired of artists, and his work and that of his sons eventually declined into unimaginative imitations of Capability Brown, nevertheless his criticisms of White were justified. Claiming the advantage of being a Scot, he wrote copious and dogmatic notes in his epic account of what should be planted at Scone, rather unctuously titled *Treatise on Scone*. He was scathing about planting in clumps and shelter belts, criticized lawns for never being cut closely enough, and disliked the gravel paths then prevalent in Scottish gardens. The grandiose plans he put forward included bridging and tunnelling, growing woods of ash, oak, beech and some elm, and replacing birch and larch with poplar. Indeed, between 1803 and 1833 a minimum of 100,000 trees were planted each year.

Loudon's influence, and the disagreements over the theory and specifics of planting, undoubtedly filtered through the ranks of the estate to even the lowliest of garden assistants. But Douglas did not remain in this lowly position for long, for his independent spirit appealed to the head gardener, Willie Beattie. As Douglas served his apprenticeship, he advanced from the forcing beds to the kitchen and flower gardens. Headstrong though Douglas might well have been, Beattie was to remark that he liked 'a devil better than a dolt'. At this time, too, what Douglas later regarded as his real education now began. He studied in the evenings, and in the summer roamed the Highlands collecting plants with the Brown brothers, who ran a nursery in Perth and who spent the summer months searching the nearby hills for new and rare plants to cultivate for sale.

Douglas' family, Presbyterians who took their religion seriously, much influenced their son during his formative years. Young David was 'strictly prohibited' by his father from making excursions on the Sabbath. And on one occasion, when he was searching for more books to read after devouring all that were available, an old family friend, a Mr Scott, put a Bible in his hands, remarking: 'Mr David, I cannot recommend a better or more important book for your perusal.' In later life, the faith that had surrounded him as a child and young man sustained him in the lonely and dangerous path he chose to pursue.

After seven years, Douglas completed his apprenticeship, and was now able to seek a better position. His opportunity arrived in 1818, when he was offered a position as under gardener to Alexander Stewart, the head gardener at Valleyfield, near Dunfermline, another Scottish burgh some 25 miles south of Scone. Valleyfield, the home of Sir Robert Preston, stood in an enviable south-facing position, over-looking the Firth of Forth. In the grounds the soil was so rich that black Italian poplars planted in 1805 had grown to 100 feet just thirty-five years later.

Chapter Two

TOWARDS THE WIDER
WORLD

'His great activity, undaunted courage, singular abstemiousness and
energetic zeal at once pointed him out as an individual eminently
calculated to do himself credit as a scientific traveller.'
*Sir William Hooker, 'Brief Memoir of the Life of Mr David
Douglas', 1836*

Douglas' move to Valleyfield was fortunate, for Sir Robert
Preston was an enthusiast for botany and the natural sciences.
He was an open character, lacking in the arrogance often associated with wealthy landowners, and with an intuitive understanding
of his fellow men. In 1801, Sir Robert had asked Humphrey Repton,
the landscape architect, to draw up and implement improvements to
his estate. Although Repton had never before carried out any work in
Scotland, he succeeded in opening up the vistas and remodelling the
landscape to take full advantage of the natural streams and undula-
tions. The gardens and the classical house in their midst, which
Repton also improved, were much admired in their day.

Sir Robert was a Renaissance man, keenly interested in the world
around him, and it was he who suggested that his bright young
gardener should be allowed to use his extensive library. This was a
generous gesture to one who was a mere employee and a poor one at
that. Douglas would have been hard-pressed to find specialist botanical books on his infrequent days off in Dunfermline, let alone buy
them.

After his time at Valleyfield, Douglas met the man who was to
have the greatest influence on the course of his life. William Jackson
Hooker, the newly appointed Professor of Botany at Glasgow

University, was to become one of the most influential botanists of the nineteenth century. Hooker himself described in his 'Brief Memoir' how Douglas came to Glasgow:

> He [Douglas] remained about two years at Valleyfield, being foreman during the last twelvemonth to Mr Stewart, when he made application and succeeded in gaining admission to the Botanic Garden at Glasgow. In this improving situation it is almost needless to say, that he spent his time most advantageously and with so much industry and application to his professional duties as to have gained the friendship and esteem of all who knew him, and more especially of the able and intelligent curator of that establishment, Mr Stewart Murray, who always evinced the deepest interest in Douglas' success in life. Whilst in this situation he was a diligent attendant at the botanical lectures given by the Professor of Botany [i.e. Hooker himself] in the hall of the garden, and was his favourite companion in some distant excursions to the Highlands and islands of Scotland, where his great activity, undaunted courage, singular abstemiousness, and energetic zeal, at once pointed him out as an individual eminently calculated to do himself credit as a scientific traveller.

Hooker was a self-taught botanist and scientist, a man of extraordinary intellectual gifts allied with a warm and open-hearted nature. He was also a brilliant lecturer. This was a stroke of luck for the university authorities, for Hooker had never delivered a lecture before, nor even attended a lecture course. Hooker's lectures were intended primarily for medical students, and must have included much information on herbs. He attracted students from far and wide – Douglas was not unusual in travelling long distances to crowd into the small and unprepossessing lecture hall.

Out of his many students, Hooker picked Douglas as a young man worthy of encouragement and a character with whom he could empathize. The friendship grew, and gradually Douglas was included in Hooker's family life; Hooker invited him to his home, and also asked him to accompany him on expeditions into the Highlands. As they tramped over hill and moor, often caught out in the rapidly changing weather, and found themselves cooped up in any rough croft willing to shelter them overnight, Hooker came to judge Douglas as a young man of unusually sterling qualities.

It may well have been from Hooker's lectures that Douglas acquired the medical knowledge that proved invaluable later in life.

Hooker's friendship and patronage were also of far greater immediate significance, for they showed Douglas the pathway to higher hopes and aspirations. Most important of all, Hooker recommended Douglas 'to Joseph Sabine Esq., then Honorary Secretary of the Horticultural Society, as a Botanical Collector'. Hooker remained a guiding, fatherly figure for Douglas throughout his life. Douglas had grown apart from his background through knowledge. Now he had found a mentor.

On its formation in 1804, the Horticultural Society had begun the serious business of discussing, writing about and presenting papers on horticulture. Its eight select and influential founding members included John Wedgwood, son of the famous potter Josiah and an enthusiastic botanist and gardener, Sir Joseph Banks, President of the Royal Society and Royal Advisor to the Gardens at Kew, and William Forsyth, gardener to King George III, who gave his name to forsythia. What characterized the founders – apart from their immense knowledge of and enthusiasm for the natural sciences, and botany in particular – were their good connections throughout society. These allowed them to place their explorers, such as David Douglas in years to come, on ships that would take them to far-off lands, and enabled the Society to ride scandal and financial storms, growing in status and ultimately winning royal patronage.

The Society forged ahead in its early years. A library was formed (the archives note that John Loudon, of Scone Palace fame, had retained his books too long, and was not to be lent more). An annual anniversary dinner was held, with dessert, provided by the members, as the high point. (A full complement of members attended in 1822, when pineapple was served.) And a network of foreign correspondents was developed and encouraged (as were members in Britain) to send in plants and fruits for exhibition.

From about 1815, Joseph Sabine – who was to play an influential part in Douglas' life – became the administrative backbone of the Society. A lawyer who had been elected to membership in 1810, he took up the reins when the accounts were found to be in disarray and the Society's financial position was precarious. By the early 1820s, Sabine had the finances well under control, and through prodigious letter-writing had also gained sixty-one foreign correspondents. Plants arrived constantly from home and abroad. Joseph Kirke of Brompton (then a little village west of London) despatched his seventy-two varieties of apple, while from China John Reeves sent chrysanthemums, peonies, azaleas and camellias, and a double-flowering cherry. These, together with various primulas and, perhaps most exquisite of all, Chinese wisteria, have all become garden staples.

To grow these seeds and cuttings, in 1818 the Society acquired a one-and-a-half-acre garden in Kensington. Arrivals from abroad were exempted from customs duty in a deal Sabine did with the Treasury. Donald Munro, another of the army of Scots who became gardeners in London, was appointed to care for the specimens at an annual salary of £105, while William Hooker was asked to draw and paint them; his work forms the basis of the Society's archives today. In 1819, at the age of twenty-three, John Lindley was appointed Assistant Secretary of the Garden, with responsibility for cataloguing. Although very much under Sabine's despotic thumb, he rose to become the first Professor of Botany at the University of London in 1829; twelve years later he founded *Gardener's Chronicle*, and served as its first editor.

The Society's gardeners faced a challenging task in nurturing and preparing for sale plants from all over the world in a young garden and in some of the earliest glass houses. But this was nothing like as testing as collecting tender species in the wild, and then packing them and transporting them on the long and difficult journey home. As well as trying to improve the survival rates of plants on such voyages, the Society now began to consider sending its own botanists on expeditions. They wanted men with an eye to commercial gain, who could recognize plants even when they were not in flower and identify those that would adapt well to the British climate, appeal to British gardeners and so produce substantial revenue for the Society. The need was made more urgent because the collectors sent out from Kew had recently been withdrawn. It was also a propitious time in the Society's own development. Membership was growing (it reached 1500 in 1823), and the Society's many distinguished foreign correspondents included the tsar of Russia and the kings of Denmark, Bavaria and the Netherlands as well as Army and Navy officers, missionaries and other Englishmen working abroad. Such illustrious supporters could open doors the world over.

Accordingly, in 1821, John Potts, a gardener with the Society, embarked for India, courtesy of the East India Company. The total cost of this, the first exploration funded by the Society, was £200; half was Mr Potts' fee, while the remainder paid for his board and other expenses. The expedition was successful, and from Calcutta Potts sent home a consignment of plants, seeds and dried specimens; unfortunately many of the plants did not survive the journey. Potts himself brought back numerous primula seeds, from which many modern varieties are descended. Sadly, Potts became very ill, and reached England in pitiful health. Although the Society endeavoured to find him the best medical care, he died in August 1822, not long after his return.

Eight months earlier, John Forbes, the Society's second plant-collector, had departed on HMS *Leven*, bound for Lisbon, Madeira, Brazil and the Cape of Good Hope. Forbes, who had been recommended by his employers at the Liverpool Botanic Garden, sent home plants, including orchids, from the east African coast. In October 1823, tragedy struck again; Forbes succumbed to an unknown fever and died at Senna on the Zambezi.

The next collector to be despatched was another young man, John Damper Parks, who was sent to China. On his arrival, he met John Reeves, the Society's vigorous correspondent. Parks brought back twenty varieties of chrysanthemum, sixteen of them new. The Society had intended to send David Douglas to China as well, but owing to the unstable political situation there Parks travelled alone, and Douglas was redirected to the east coast of North America.

It was his friendship with William Hooker in Glasgow that brought Douglas into contact with the Society. Hooker and Sabine were friends, and must have discussed at length the merits of whom to send. The Society's invitation arrived soon after Douglas had been promoted to head gardener at Glasgow Botanic Garden at the tender age of twenty-three. Douglas accepted, perhaps relishing the exacting challenge involved and perhaps relieved also to escape the prospect of a tedious, uncertain and poverty-stricken life as a gardener. However distinguished a gardener might become – and Douglas had already won significant promotion at a very young age – he would find it very hard to escape his lowly status. Many of the great contemporary garden designers, John Loudon and Capability Brown among them, were well aware of the hardship gardeners experienced. In 1829, Loudon wrote that 'there is no class of gentleman's servants so badly lodged as gardeners generally are,' and his *Encyclopaedia of Gardening* left readers in no doubt about their appalling living conditions. Wages were also poor – in 1841, a head gardener commanded about one tenth of a cook's pay, and half that of a footman – and job security was non-existent. William Anderson, Curator of the Chelsea Physic Garden, dismissed a number of men for pilfering, fighting or drunkenness; but another lost his job because he was a 'dunce', and yet another a 'blockhead', while a third was discharged for being 'too wise'. And even if a gardener escaped these whims, the weather could play the trump card – during periods of snow, gardeners were simply paid off.

Against this background, the risks in plant-collecting for the Horticultural Society, and the less than generous financial rewards, must have seemed of small significance. So, in the early spring of 1823, Douglas left his native Scotland for London and employment with the Horticultural Society. Here he found that he had much to learn. Well apprenticed in the day-to-day practicalities of gardening, he now studied the new ideas and experimental methods for propagating the many previously unknown species reaching the new garden the Society had leased at Chiswick, west of London, in 1821. Though only a year old, the 33 acres were burgeoning; the orchard contained three thousand fruit trees, there was an arboretum and a shrubbery, an experimental fruit and vegetable garden, and no less than twelve hundred varieties of rose.

The 'job specification' for a Society explorer required extensive knowledge – and the ability to learn even more – of botany and the natural sciences. Other skills such as astronomy, navigation and geography were also useful. On a personal level, great self-discipline and self-motivation were essential – there would be no one to encourage or chide a slacker – together with the ability to live with the awareness, no doubt never made explicit, that survival was not guaranteed. Those who undertook such expeditions risked, if not their lives, at the very least their good health.

Douglas' task in his expedition to the east coast of North America was to investigate the latest developments in fruit-growing and to obtain, if possible as gifts, fruit trees and other interesting species. He was also to acquire samples of new trees, particularly species of oak, and to scour the countryside as far west as Amherstburg on the uncertain Canadian/American border on Lake Erie for promising plants, collecting seeds and samples. The oaks were especially important, as they were intended to replace the many great trees felled to build warships in the long and only recently concluded war against France.

Apples were another of the Society's priorities. American apples, large and juicy, had intrigued Europeans ever since the first reports were received about them in the early seventeenth century. The first orchard in New York, on the Bouwerie farm of Governor Peter Stuyvesant, had been planted in 1647, and most of the rich apple orchards along the Hudson River were descended from these trees.

Douglas might not have thought New York State as exotic as China, but it was a vital area to explore. Nor can it have seemed an easy option; the British still perceived the United States as a narrow strip of country, occupied by a people with whom they had been at war until recently, and on the edge of an uncertain and mainly unexplored interior populated by savages.

The early settlers in America had grown plants to ensure their survival; flower gardens for pleasure were few and far between. As more migrants flowed in, their priority was to cultivate crops guaranteed to succeed and produce the food the young country needed. Few Americans had had the time or inclination to study the native flora at length; Douglas eventually met the few who had. However, several Europeans had already travelled in search of new species. In February 1806, a Frenchman, André Michaux, had been ordered by his government to botanize from Florida north towards Hudson Bay. The Austrian Frederick Pursh (1774–1820) had classified the plants and seeds brought back by Meriwether Lewis and William Clark from their trek across the continent in 1804–05, and published *Flora Americae Septentrionalis* in 1813, which Douglas would have read before his departure. And John Goldie, another pupil of Hooker, had visited the United States in 1817–19.

To this fellowship Douglas grafted himself, and packed for the voyage to New York.

Chapter Three

NEW YORK

'He unites enthusiasm, intelligence and persevering activity . . .
and appears to me to combine the essential qualities required in
trusts of this nature.'
Governor De Witt Clinton writing of Douglas in 1823
after his New York journey

Douglas' anticipation at the start of his first plant-hunting
expedition must have been immense. With his limited experience of botanizing in the Highlands of Scotland he was now
being professionally employed to travel to the New World as a bona
fide plant-collector on behalf of the prestigious Horticultural Society.
As part of his duties, the Society required Douglas to keep a detailed
record of his activities and observations. It is to the survival of his
journal, and the many letters written to Hooker and others, that we
owe much of our knowledge of Douglas and his adventures.

Douglas started his diary with the heightened awareness he had
acquired during his weeks of study. He seemed determined to demonstrate his powers of observation. It was almost as if he needed to be
seen to be taking the task to heart, down to the smallest, most minute
examination – as if he had to demonstrate to the world, or at least to
his superiors in London, that his attention was crystal-clear at every
moment of his journey. He maintained this attitude relentlessly
throughout his diary-keeping years.

June 3rd – London: left Charing Cross by coach for Liverpool.
Morning very pleasant; had rained through the night, country
very fine for seventeen miles from the metropolis; found during

time of changing horses *Coniferva egerops* [Ball] conifer. Beautiful fields at Woburn Abbey tastefully laid out and divided by hedgerows in which are planted Horse-chestnuts at regular distances, all in full flower; had a very imposing appearance. *Menyanthes nymphoides* [Bog Bean or Buckbean – white-flowered bog-loving plant], for the first time I ever saw it in its natural state; Northampton at 2.30 o'clock p.m., rested 25 minutes; reached Lancaster quarter to 10 p.m., took supper, started again half past 10, rain during the night; very cold. Arrived at Liverpool 4 o'clock afternoon. After calling at Monal and Woodward and learning that the *Ann Maria* of New York was to sail the following morning, in which a passage had been taken for me, I arranged my business as to my departure and made for Botanic Garden. Mr Shepherd received me in the most handsome manner; showed me all his treasures (of which not a few are from North America) *Ranunculus aconitifolus* [one of the buttercup family], which I learn is rare; Mr Munro (gardener at the Chiswick garden) says that he never saw it save in the collection of Mr Don of Forfar.

June 5th – Went on board at 6 a.m., when to the great mortification [the captain] could not clear the river. ... I then came on shore again and called at the Botanic Garden a second time. I had thus full scope of seeing it in perfection.

Getting underway at last, *Ann Maria* slowly made its way along the coast of north Wales and out into the ocean.

7th – All day tossing in the channel, made little or nothing; few of the passengers were exempted from sickness. I felt perfectly comfortable, only a headache which was occasioned by a cold when on the way to Liverpool.
10th – This was the first good morning we had; most of passengers still sick. Clouds of sea-fowl continue to surround the vessel; Welsh coast in sight.
13th – Light airs and cloudy; put on allowance of water, two quarts to each individual.
25th and 26th – This being my birthday and the market day of my native place, I could not help thinking over the days that were gone.

As the days drifted on, Douglas passed the time studying his Spanish grammar, which Hooker had suggested might be useful for future trips, and reading the Linnean Society's *Journal*. The Azores came into view, and Douglas was disappointed that a landing was not made. The Captain ordered a couple of his crew to start fishing and the resulting mackerel were much enjoyed. After a heavy shower the dogs on board gratefully licked the decks and the passengers washed their clothes. After six weeks, Douglas noted, everyone had become uneasy – the crew were out of tobacco, and many of the passengers who 'found' for themselves had run out of provisions.

Then, on 2 August, almost two months after leaving Liverpool:

> At 12 o'clock saw light at Sandy Hook [New York]. Considered ourselves at land; 5 o'clock boarded by the Health Officer, who signified that fourteen days of quarantine was requisite in consequence of small-pox; at 6 o'clock went on shore on Staten; returned to the vessel at 7.

On the 5th, Douglas applied to go into the city, but was refused permission to do so with any of his clothes, for fear of spreading infection. He bought new garments, and the following day left *Ann Maria* for the last time.

> August 6th – This morning can never be effaced; Nature's work, which was truly grand – the fine orchards of Long Island on the one side, and the variety of soil and vegetation of Staten on the other. I once more thought myself happy. I went to the city in the afternoon to see what steps I should take as to the progression of my business; I had an interview with Dr Hosack; the cordial manner in which I was received by this gentleman made an impression upon me. I called on Dr Torrey whom I found an intelligent botanist, an agreeable person, and much disposed to aid me. I landed again at Staten Island.

Douglas carried letters of introduction from the Society to American botanists, agriculturalists and gardeners. These were men of considerable means and education, and they must have had a considerable influence on the young Douglas. In the main they were also open and exceedingly generous in their hospitality and gifts of plants. Douglas also found that the Scottish connection, with all its camaraderie, was coming into play. The first such kindred spirit was Dr Hosack, through whom Douglas began to win admission into the ranks of the great and the good, the learned and the influential of New York State.

Dr David Hosack was forty-six years old and a medical doctor. His father hailed from Elgin, on the Moray coast of north-east Scotland, and he himself had studied medicine, botany and mineralogy

LAKE HURON
VERMONT
UPPER CANADA
(PROVINCE OF ONTARIO)
LAKE ONTARIO
Rochester
MICHIGAN
Niagra Falls
Buffalo
NEW YORK
MASS.
Detroit
LAKE ST. CLAIR
Amherstburg
Clermont
CONN.
LAKE ERIE
N
PENNSYLVANIA
DAVID DOUGLAS'
TRAVELS IN
EASTERN UNITED STATES
AND CANADA
New York
Hoboken
Flushing
Philadelphia
ATLANTIC OCEAN
0   Miles   100
VIRGINIA
MARYLAND

in Edinburgh for two years, sailing home in 1794 with a collection of minerals, which he donated to Princeton University in 1821. While Hosack was primarily noted for his medical expertise – on the voyage home he had successfully treated outbreaks of typhus and yellow fever – gardening became his second great interest, to which he devoted all his free time, establishing the Elgin Botanical Garden at his summer home.

Early on Monday 11 August, Douglas went to the vegetable market at Fulton, New York. In any place fruit or vegetables were on sale, Douglas would find his way to the market and there pass a critical and confident eye over the produce. His training in the kitchen gardens at Scone, which supplied the Palace, and his subsequent studies at the Society's garden at Chiswick stood him in good stead.

[The market] had a beautiful appearance, beet of superior variety and fine carrots, raised in this country; I observed a very great deficiency of cauliflower, indeed they were miserably poor; onions were fine, a great supply of pineapples from the West Indies, and cocoanuts. I observed a fine head of *Musa sapientum* [bananas] which weighed 40 lb.

The poor quality and high prices of the produce surprised Douglas.

On 12 and 13 August Douglas crossed the Hudson to examine 'some of the finest fruit-orchards'. On the 14th he visited the New York Botanic Garden, 'which is now, I am sorry to say, in ruins; one of the hot-houses is taken down, one stripped of the glass, and the greenhouse still in a sort of form'.

The journal entry for Friday the 15th demonstrates the earnestness and care with which Douglas collected and recorded information.

> Through the medium of Dr Hosack I learned of a fine plum named 'Washington', a name which every product in the United States that is great or good is called. This gentleman kindly sent me four. Form of a greengage; colour somewhat between cream and sulphur; flavour very delicious, like a greengage; the stone remarkably small, the skin thin. Purchased by a Mrs Miller about thirty years since out of the flower-market. After standing in her garden for five years it was during a thunderstorm cleft nearly to the bottom, which caused its death so far as was rent; next spring it sent up suckers and the great Wm Bolmer, Esq., obtained one of them which he planted in his garden and in a few years produced fruit without any grafting; the fruit has improved every succeeding year, the taste being the best. Soil, pure red sand; the original was removed and three carloads of good soil from a cultivated field taken in and the tree-plant given a little decayed vegetable matter as a manure. He lays the roots totally bare during the winter months. I put the above fruit in spirits.

Sadly, the plums were lost when the ship carrying them to England sank.

On the 19th Douglas left New York on the first of a series of journeys to collect plants and seeds and acquire as much information as he could about the horticulture of the eastern seaboard. His journal demonstrates his growing self-confidence, and soon he becomes a seasoned tourist, mingling with some of the country's most distinguished and wealthy families and being conducted to numerous places of interest.

A steam packet brought Douglas and his new friend Mr Hogg, who had recently left England to follow a career as a florist and nurseryman in America, to New Brunswick. From here they travelled by coach to Burlington, New Jersey, where they called on William Coxe, who had devoted over twenty years to cultivating numerous varieties of hard fruit on his wife's estate, although by now he had retired and was, as Douglas recorded, 'devoting himself to his family, books, the interests of the church and the welfare of those about him'. In their prime, his orchards had contained apple and pear trees of both American and European origin that produced the robust and plump fruits so coveted by the members of the Horticultural Society in London.

Coxe was a modest man. Awarded a medal by the Horticultural Society for introducing the Seckel pear to England, he returned it after a few years as he felt that the honour was out of all proportion to the deed. It was with great difficulty that he was persuaded to put his experiences into print. When it eventually appeared in 1817, his book – fulsomely entitled *A View of the Cultivation of Fruit-Trees, and the Management of Orchards and Cider; with Accurate Descriptions of the Most Fashionable Varieties of Native and Foreign Apples, Pears, Peaches, Plums, and Cherries, Cultivated in the Middle States of America; Illustrated by Cuts of Two Hundreds Kinds of Fruits of the Natural Size* – was an immediate best-seller. Coxe later worked on a second edition, for which his daughters prepared a hundred colour illustrations. Alas, it was never published, and the paintings were lost; when they were found again in the 1930s, they were given to the library of the US Department of Agriculture.

Douglas took his leave from Mr Coxe with a gift of bottles of cider, which later brought the Society's effusive thanks, and embarked on the steamship from Burlington to visit a pocket of Pennsylvania along the banks of the Schuylkill River. Here, conveniently close to Philadelphia, stood, in rolling acres suitable for creating the newly fashionable English landscape garden, a series of the most elegant houses, each owned by a garden enthusiast.

Douglas initially made for the 'garden of the place of the venerable John Bartram'. In the 1730s, Bartram, a staunch Quaker, had created a botanical garden on his farm beside the Schuylkill, and became generally regarded as the father of American botany. He also built up a flourishing trade in plants, seeds and other objects (including maps, drawings, journals, shells, minerals, and turtles' eggs) with Peter Collinson, a London linen draper. Using the profits from his annual shipments of five-guinea boxes of assorted varieties, Bartram explored the Appalachian Mountains and the Shenandoah River and botanized in Florida with his dilettante son William. William took over the farm and botanical garden after his father's death in 1777, and settled to a life of doing exactly as he wished, cultivating his father's garden barefoot and clad in ancient, tattered clothes. William – who was also known as Puc Puggy, an Indian term meaning 'flower-hunter' – died on 22 July 1823, only a few weeks before Douglas arrived at the Bartram home, where there was no one to receive him.

Woodlands, the garden next door to the Bartram's, also proved of great interest: 'the whole place has the appearance of nicety', Douglas wrote when he visited it a few days later. Woodlands had belonged to Andrew Hamilton, who built the house in 1740, and his son James, Governor of Pennsylvania. Andrew Hamilton, wily, secretive and verging on the obsessive, amassed a huge collection of plants, sending large consignments home during a visit to England and procuring seeds from ships freshly arriving from Africa and Asia. He introduced English ivy, planted Lombardy poplars, and was particularly partial to double-flowered plants, such as double 'thorns' (hawthorns) and the double daffodil, rather despised by his neighbour Bartram a few years earlier. Though he embraced the fashionable and lenient High Anglican faith in later life, Hamilton retained something of the solid practicality of his Quaker origins – as well as plants from every continent, he also grew hundreds of humble cabbages.

In Philadelphia, Douglas visited the university garden and, inevitably, the vegetable market:

I found the supply finer than that of New York, and the produce so likewise. The peaches, apples, &c., look superior in every respect; they have not that sickly appearance which is found among the fruit of New York.

On the 27th, Douglas left Philadelphia on the 11 o'clock steamboat and, after some more garden-visiting, took another steamboat on the 28th

at half-past 4 o'clock and passing up past Elizabethtown, Staten Island landed at New York at half-past 10 pm. As soon as possible I had the plants from the office where they had been left, took them to the son of Mr Hogg, and had them planted and secured. I cannot but consider myself happy at meeting Mr Hogg; he carefully attends to the little treasures during my absence.

Now Douglas packed his apples in spirits, praying that the sailors would not sample the alcohol, talked to Mr Prince, a nurseryman, about the plants he required, and attended a specially convened meeting of the New York Horticultural Society at which he was warmly received as the honoured guest. With Mr Prince he was not so impressed; the feeling was mutual, and the reverberations of his encounters with Prince were to follow him home.

A week later, Douglas set off on another expedition, this time up the River Hudson into upper New York State. Once again, the young man from Scone in far-off Scotland found himself mingling with the influential notables – statesmen, military commanders, merchants, naturalists – of the region. Douglas acquitted himself well. He was intelligent, he had prepared for his trip, and, as he himself realized, the favourable impression this created would do him nothing but good.

> Thursday, September 4th – at 5 o'clock this morning I went on board the steamboat James Kent and proceeded up the Hudson River towards Albany. The scenery was particularly fine on the west side: the perpendicular rocks covered with wood gave it an appearance seldom to be met with. About forty miles from New York, in the Highlands, many pleasant villas are seen from the river.

The boat sailed past West Point Military Academy, the United States' prime training school for officers and strategists, situated in a commanding position above the river; the approach, Douglas noted, 'has a beautiful effect'.

On his first day out from New York, Douglas was woken at 5 o'clock by James Thomson, Junior, and taken to see his estate.

> In his woods I found on a point a quarter mile west of his house Gerard lava in great perfection, growing dry gravely soil, partially shadowing another species of *Gerardia*, small and starved. On the outskirts of the wood, *Eupatorium* four or five species, *Inula*, *Solidago*, and *Aster*.

The next day brought a meeting of great significance, with De Witt Clinton, Governor of New York State, to whom Douglas carried a letter of introduction from Joseph Sabine of the Horticultural Society.

> Saturday, September 6th – I embarked in the Richmond steam-boat, on her way to Albany, at 1 o'clock a.m. At 11 o'clock I arrived at Albany. I waited on His Excellency Governor Clinton, who showed me attention. I went to the vegetable market in the afternoon. Here I observed the cabbages and beans were superior to those I had already seen.

It was natural that De Witt Clinton, who had inherited a fortune and owned vast tracts of land, should become embroiled in politics at a young age, for his uncle had been the first Governor of New York State. A giant of a man in many ways, standing well over 6 feet tall,

Clinton served as Mayor of New York almost continuously from 1802 to 1815, and stood unsuccessfully in the 1812 presidential election, when he was defeated by James Madison. Subsequently he served as Governor of New York State.

Clinton's great project was the construction of the Erie Canal scheme, designed to create a shipping route between the Great Lakes and the Hudson River and so link the north and west of the United States with New York. The completion of the canal made New York City the principal gateway to the west and the financial centre of the nation. The project experienced many ups and downs, but by a stroke of good fortune Douglas arrived in Albany just when the first of the canals was being completed and the parties to celebrate this feat of engineering were in full swing. When the final connection was completed in 1825, Clinton famously emptied a couple of barrels of Lake Erie water into the harbour at New York, splashing the dignitaries who had turned out to watch and in so doing signifying his scorn for the many who had doubted his vision.

In the intervals from politics, Clinton studied the natural sciences with his lifelong friend David Hosack, who himself had already befriended Douglas, and became a noted naturalist. He discovered a native American wheat, and a new fish, *Salmo atsego*, and published papers on pigeons, swallows and rice. He was also elected President of the New York Historical Society, was active in the American Academy of Art, and inaugurated the work of translating the State's Dutch archives. His *Memoir of the Antiquities of the Western Parts of the State of New York* was published in 1829, the year after his death.

In the hospitality he offered Douglas, Clinton more than fulfilled Sabine's request that the Society's young envoy should be given 'protection, advice or assistance'. Douglas now pressed on from Albany into Iroquois country, a land that had not long been settled and that contained some of the finest scenery in America.

Sunday, September 7th – This morning I was wakened with tremendous peals of thunder. On looking out of the window the streets were quite inundated; the town standing on a gentle declivity, the water rushed with great rapidity. I waited at 12 on His Excellency the Governor, who said that his opinion for me was to proceed to Canada without delay, the season being far advanced, and particularly as the steamboat *Superior* was to sail from Buffalo on Saturday next. Left Albany at 4 o'clock for Schenectady, (North of Albany) where I arrived at 9 o'clock of the same evening; the rain fell in torrents all the way.

September 8th – At 3 this morning I pursued my journey in the

stage towards Utica. All the farmers here have orchards cultivated: seldom more than ten or twelve varieties of apples; pears
are scarce. They make their own cider. In every village or
cottage I passed stood a cider-mill, casks, and men busily
employed preparing for their cider harvest. At 2 o'clock I came
to Little Falls, 70 miles from Albany. I took the canal boat at
this place. Here is a beautiful, elegant bridge across the
Mohawk, dedicated to De Witt Clinton, etc.
Tuesday, September 9th – At 8 o'clock this morning I left Utica
by canal boat for Rochester; sixty miles from here without a lock.
The boats are fitted up on good principles: accommodation for
twenty-four ladies in one cabin and as many in the men's. I slept
on board, but was much disturbed passing the locks. . . .
Friday, September 12th – Left early in the morning by stage
from Buffalo [travelling along the old Seneca Turnpike].
Breakfasted at Caledonia, a settlement of Scotch people.
Saturday, September 13th – Early in the morning I wrote to Jos.
Sabine, Esq., and then called on Oliver Forward, Esq., a gentle-
man of considerable wealth, and friend of Governor Clinton.
Went on board the steamboat at 9 o'clock a.m., and sailed at
10, and after a pleasant passage of sixty hours landed at
Amherstburg.

As the territory here was still disputed by the United States and
Canada, Douglas could not sail direct from America into Canada, but
had to find his way over the border on foot. Placed ashore on an island
on the Detroit River, he was taken to the nearby village by an Indian
in a small, birch-bark canoe. Here he was met by a Mr Briscoe, an
acquaintance of Sabine's brother Captain Edward Sabine, who had
served as an officer in Canada during the 1812–15 War.

Douglas now set off on his first day of genuine exploration and
botanizing. Until now, he had spent his time visiting gardens and
calling on notables to whom he carried letters of introduction from the
Society. Now at last he was free to roam in the woods and search for
plants. It was a welcome return to the type of botanizing he had done
years before in the Scottish Highlands, and he was much excited at the
prospect of finds. His relief that, at long last, he could explore alone
indicated where his real interests lay: out in the field, searching for
new plant species.

Tuesday, 16th September – This is what I might term my first
day in America. The trees in the woods were of astonishing
magnitude. The soil, in general, over which we were passing was

a very rich black earth, and seemed to be formed of decomposed vegetables. The woods consisted of *Quercus* (oaks, several species, some of immense magnitude). Four miles east of Amherstburg I observed a species of rose of strong growth, the wood resembling *multiflora*, having strong thorns (*Rosa liatris*). All the tender shoots and leaves were eaten off by cattle or sheep, which prevented me from knowing it. I gathered seeds of some species of *Liatris*, which along with *Helianthus*, *Solidago*, *Aster*, *Eupatorium*, and *Veronica* form the majority of which I had an opportunity of seeing in perfection. In a field east of Amherstburg grew spontaneously *Gentiana Saponaria* and *crinita*, and I secured some seeds. Towards mid-afternoon the rain fell in torrents, urging us to leave the woods drenched wet. Wednesday, September 17th – This morning I made a visit to a small island in the River Detroit, opposite Amherstburg. The soil is very rich black loam, covered with trees from 50 to 70 feet high, 40 feet without branches. With my gun I cut some branches, leaves and acorns. They seem to me to be fine and different from any which I have seen before. With a few shots more I secured specimens and paper of seeds. How glad I am to see my rose of yesterday growing in perfection! I lost no time in securing plants and seeds.

I crossed the river and secured plants of *Rosa* and *Lonicera*, and put away my specimens and seeds. In the evening I called on Mr Briscoe for the purpose of soliciting his advice as to the most likely places of affording a harvest. He strongly recommended a visit to the River Thames, as did his friend Rob. Richardson, M.D., physician for the Indian department. (Dr R. knew Captain Sabine when he was at Stamford on the Niagara.) He kindly offered to take me in his car as far as Sandwich, which was fifteen miles from Amherstburg. As there was no time to lose, I proposed to start in the morning. These proposals being agreed to, we parted at 10 o'clock p.m.

Thursday, September 18th – I set out in the morning with Dr Richardson for Sandwich, on the east bank of the River Detroit. Passed a long swamp persecuted by natural ditches in which grew *Nuphar advena*, *N. Kalmianum*, *Eriocaulon* (a small species and much like our British one on Loch Ligachan, Skye). On passing the swamp just mentioned, which is fully four miles long, we came to what is called 'the French Settlement'.

The French Settlement consisted of the first farms settled by French Canadians in Ontario. Douglas was impressed by this area, which was known as the 'Eden of Upper Canada' and stood at the edge of the unclaimed wilderness. The fields were long and narrow, which made for awkward farming but gave some mutual protection against Indian attack. Douglas noted the size and health of the fruit, particularly the pears, a rarity in his travels; he supposed them to have been brought over from France, since they were like the pears he had seen in his childhood days in Scotland, which were of French origin.

The fields were well cultivated and divided by fences; attached to each house is a neat garden laid out and kept with taste. The cultivated apples comprise about eight or ten varieties; they are known as black, red, white, &c. There are a few pears, which are scarcely seen in the western part of the State of New York; probably the emigrants took them from France at the first settling of the country. They have a few peaches, in appearance as in the States. The climate seems to be particularly favourable for them. I am informed they ripen in ordinary seasons; they have not that sickly appearance which they have in the States, occasioned probably by excess of heat.

Douglas was captivated at the fertility and lushness of the landscape: immense oaks and walnut trees, Indian corn stretching into the distance, and tobacco. On the 20th, however, he experienced an incident that reflected the lawlessness of this frontier area.

Saturday, September 20th – Early in the morning got a car and hired a man to conduct me up the country. Came to a morass of about two miles long, succeeded by a passage of sand along Lake St. Clair; rendered the horse so weak that I had to stop for a day. I was glad to do so, as there seemed to be a good field; accordingly towards midday I set off with the man I had taken with me. During my day's labour I had the misfortune to meet with a circumstance which I must record as it concerns not only my business, but also my personal affairs. I got up in the oak for the purpose of procuring seeds and specimens; the day being warm, I was induced to take off my coat and in that state I ascended. I had not been above for five minutes up, when to my surprise the man whom I had hired as guide and assistant took up my coat and made off as fast as he could run with it. I descended almost headlong and followed, but before I could make near him he escaped in the woods. I had in my pockets my notes and some receipt of money, nineteen dollars in paper, a copy of Persoon's *Synopsis Plantarium* with my small vasculum.

I was thus left five miles from where I had left the car, in a miserable condition, and as there was no remedy that could be taken to better myself, I tied my seeds in my neckcloth and made to my lodging. I had to hire a man to take me back to Sandwich as I could not drive; and the horse only understanding the French language, I could not talk to him in his tongue, placed me in an awkward situation. I had to borrow a coat as there was no tailor to make me one. On my getting to Sandwich I remonstrated with the man who recommended my assistant to me, but he said that he never did so to his knowledge, and so on. However I found my guide was a runaway Virginian.

While slavery was to endure for many more years in the United States, it had already been abolished in Canada, and so many fugitive slaves had settled in this area. Douglas was perhaps unaware of these political sensitivities; certainly he was very shaken at being betrayed in this way, and frequently harked back to the incident. Physical challenges he relished, but he was as yet young and he found human frailties awkward. Desperate for money, his guide had undoubtedly found the temptation of a trusting, and perhaps puzzling, tree-climber too much to bear, and had seized his opportunity.

Unnerved by these events, and by the increasingly wet and autumnal weather, Douglas decided to ignore Briscoe's suggestion to journey to Detroit, and turned east once more. To add to his miseries, fearsome winds tore a wheel off the paddle boat he now took to Buffalo. A visit to Niagara Falls rated hardly more than a mention in his journal, although he enjoyed searching for plants, especially tapping the sugar maples close by. The journey on to Albany included a juddering 15-mile stretch along a 'corduroy road' made up of trees laid broadwise. By the time he reached Albany, he was racked with rheumatism in his knees, 'which alarmed me a little'. By this time, however, he had cheered up a little, and soon Governor Clinton's influence opened doors.

> Sunday, October 5th – At 2 o'clock got to Albany. This day is the celebration of the opening of the Western canal. The town was all in an uproar – firing of guns, music, &c. Governor Clinton's situation prevented me from seeing him for the day. I had considerable difficulty in getting lodgings in the inn.
> Thursday, October 9th – *Pterospora andromedea* was to be found near Albany – accordingly I set out visiting every place which was likely for it. After a search of seven hours I had the fortune to find it in a small ravine two miles south of Albany. On

the right hand, going up the channel of a small rivulet for half a mile, where it branched right and left, on the angle, stood a large tree of *Pinus alba*, and under its branches *Pterospora*, 10 feet above the level of the rivulet; soil, light blackish-brown loam and so dry that every other vegetation refused to grow, it looked as if no rain had fallen for the summer. Whether it is annual or perennial I am unable to say. I am of opinion Mr Nuttal's description is very correct, from 14 to 24 inches high. Being late in the season, it was of course out of flower: a rusty stem covered in a glutenous substance; I counted ninety-seven capsules on one stem. How glad Mr Munroe and Mr Lindley would be to see it.

Albany, Friday, October 10th – I waited on Mr Tracy, who Governor Clinton said could and would feel glad to aid me. In the first place he invited me to look at his herbarium, which was extensive and in a good state of preservation, arranged according to the Linnean system. In it he had *Pterospora*. A friend of his who was fond of plants but possessed no knowledge of botany, found it three years since.

Douglas also made another significant call, on Stephen van Rensselaer, whom he described as 'the most wealthy man in the United States'. Stephen van Rensselaer was indeed rumoured to be the wealthiest man in, if not the entire USA, then at least New York State. He was also a successful politician, popular, generous and liberal. His political opponent Martin van Buren described him as 'probably the foremost man in the state in point of wealth and social prominence ... loved for his simple tastes, democratic behaviour and genial manners'.

Van Rensselaer was from a family of wealthy and successful Dutch merchants (mixed with the occasional theologian), and had been brought up by his maternal grandfather, Philip Livingston, after his father died when he was five. Grandfather Livingston had turned his already sizable inheritance into a small fortune through shrewd dealings with the 'devious French' and when in New York lived in an elegant mansion overlooking Brooklyn Heights. He founded a chair of divinity at Yale, and was also one of the signatories of the Declaration of Independence: an ideal influence for a small boy burdened with wealth.

When van Rensselaer grew up, he dealt wisely with his large landholdings, granting his tenants perpetual leases with moderate rents and so bringing as much land as possible under cultivation. He was also keenly interested in canal-building, and became Clinton's partner in the Erie Canal venture.

To Douglas, it was the novelty of his large garden that appealed.

He has a large garden and orchards, and a fine range of hothouses, chiefly filled with vines. The grapes were all cut and hung out on strings in a fruit room. Mr van Rensselaer, being of Dutch extraction, has many friends on the continent of Europe, who furnish him with different kinds of fruit; there were Black Prince, Hamburg, White Sweet Water, Grizzly Frontignan, and Malmsey. No attention is paid to the natives vines of North America. His apples and pears are much the same as at New York and Philadelphia; plums thrive much better. He has a large space of ground occupied as pleasure or flower garden, which is a novelty in America, as little attention is paid to anything but which brings money or luxury for the table. His flower garden is kept in good order, under the direction and management of his daughters, with much taste. Roses from France, herbaceous plants from Germany, grace the plots, with annuals, &c., from London. Mr van Rensselaer is a man of taste. He used me with kindness and invited me to breakfast should I make it convenient.

On Sunday 12 October, Douglas suffered another attack of rheumatism while at church. State Governor General Morgan Lewis, an early graduate of West Point and another member of the close-knit coterie of high-ranking and influential notables in the New York area, cared for him until the worst of the affliction had passed. Five weeks before, on his way up the Hudson, Douglas had called at Lewis' mansion to view his garden, but had found him away.

I can never forget the attention paid to me by General Lewis and family. On Wednesday and Thursday I was able to crawl about a little. I went with Mr Lewis over his estate. He pays great attention to agriculture and has all the newest modes of tillage.

Back in New York, Douglas attended a meeting of the Horticultural Society.

I cannot refrain from mentioning the great exertions which most of the efficient members have made in communicating anything worthy of notice. A great many prominent inhabitants have become members: De Witt Clinton, Dr Hosack, General Lewis, the Mayor of the city, &c. Being the first effort to establish a society in America. The president Martin Hoffman, Esq., is a very worthy respectable gentleman.

Aware that Douglas was soon due to return home, Clinton and Hosack persuaded him to stay a little longer. Entreaties from men of such standing no doubt influenced Douglas' decision, and he must have been confident that the higher echelons of the Society in London would support him.

Douglas used his extra time to rush around the nurseries and seed merchants in New York acquiring plants and seeds and organizing their packing for the sea voyage. On 2 November, he set off for Philadelphia again, where seed-collecting was still possible at this time of year, 'in quest of *Nelumbium* (or *Cyamus*) *luteum*', the American lotus, a magnificent water lily with leaves large enough to support small animals. Douglas had seen it growing there, and wrote that it imparted an 'English appearance' to garden landscapes.

> I made an exertion to procure roots, but I am very sorry to say I could not effect this as the roots run to an immense depth. Hamilton of Woodlands, whose domains lie on the banks of the Schuylkill, took roots and planted them in the mud when the tide ebbed and flowed; this is the only instance which has been successfully tried.
>
> Mr Nuttall informs me that he frequently had a dish of them and thinks them good. I tried for the tubers here, but the immense depth which they run in the mud rendered it impossible.

On the 3rd, Douglas left Philadelphia to revisit some of the gardens along the Schuylkill.

> I set out this morning to the residence of the late Mr Bartram. . . . In front of the house stands a very large cypress, 90 feet high and 23 feet round, planted by the first John Bartram; his son William (the late) held the tree while his father put the earth round. I made an inquiry about *Quercus* (oak) *heterophylla*, as it would be an acquisition, but found it had been cut down by a servant, by mistake. Mr Bartram was not reconciled about it so long as he lived. *Quercus lyrata* from Georgia and *Quercus macrocarpa* from the Allegheny. Some fine specimens of Magnolia – *species auriculata, cordata, macrophylla, tripetala, grandiflora* but quite in miniature to the fine specimens in England. I have not seen any like those in Chelsea Botanical Gardens or at Kew.
>
> Tuesday, November 4th – Went to Mr William Coxe, Esq., whom I found still very ill – but considerably better, since I saw him before. Two specimens of Indian Corn. I obtained all that

was in the house, consisting of about eight or nine varieties and only two or three of each, with two bottles of cider seven years old – one made from Wine-sop, one from Virginian crab-apple: this is a present for Thos. A Knight and Jos. Sabine Esq., from Will. Coxe.

Douglas returned to New York, 'had breakfast as usual at Dr Hosack's', and darted around collecting further plants. He had just received a request for further supplies from Sabine, who no doubt thought that Douglas would pack seeds and specimens more carefully than the American seedsman who regularly sent consignments to Europe. Douglas himself uprooted the trees he wished to take with him, and stowed his seeds carefully. Then there were notes to be completed and friends to bid farewell.

The only sour note arose from his dealing with William Prince of the Linnean Botanic Garden, who was prone to rudeness, charged excessively and presided over a garden that, Douglas maintained, was covered in weeds. So he bought his plants elsewhere whenever possible, despite the Garden's extensive catalogue and its trans-Atlantic reputation. Although Douglas was carrying out his instructions – to obtain plants as gifts if possible, and otherwise at the cheapest possible price – to the letter, Prince was displeased at this snub. Not only did he complain to the Society in London, he also did his best to blacken Douglas' name in and around New York.

The journey home was uneventful, although illness struck down four on the voyage – not human passengers, but Douglas' pigeons, presents from Clinton, who fought each other to death. Douglas wrote ruefully to Clinton that he 'most stupidly had put them in the same cage'. The ducks he was bringing home suffered from sea-sickness, but they rallied and landed safely with Douglas and his treasure trove of plants, plus the bottles of seven-year-old cider made from William Coxe's apples.

Delaying his return had not damaged Douglas' reputation, especially as most of his plants had arrived home safely. Indeed, the Society was effusive in its praise, much to Douglas' relief.

This mission was executed by Mr Douglas with a success beyond expectation: he obtained many plants which were much wanted, and greatly increased our collection of fruit trees by the acquiring of several sorts only known to us by name. It would be unjust here to omit mentioning the uniform kindness and attention with which he was received in every part of the United States that he visited. It is most gratifying to have to add, that the presents of cultivated plants to the Society embraced nearly everything which it was desirous to obtain; and that the liberality with which they were given was only equalled by the hospitality with which the collector was received.

His relentless energy, his self-imposed motivation and his new-found diplomatic skills all combined to make Douglas a success, even though he was described on his return as 'the shyest being'.

To its delight, the Society found that their novelty and rarity meant that the seeds and plants Douglas had so successfully nursed across the Atlantic commanded a good price. He had brought home many small fruit trees of different varieties, cuttings from Governor Stuyvesant's pear, twenty-one varieties of peaches, and also nineteen of the thirty-four varieties of oak described by Pursh. Just as exciting was the safe arrival of *Mahonia acquifolium*, or Oregon grape, carried by Lewis and Clark from the west coast of America and procured and transported across the Atlantic by Douglas. Also in Douglas' many boxes were several varieties of the *Oenothera* family, or evening primrose, pretty orchids and even an interesting form of ice lettuce.

The surviving birds went to the Earl of Liverpool, the deceased to Joshua Brooks, a famous anatomist and dissector.

Following Douglas himself came letters from De Witt Clinton praising his character: 'He unites enthusiasm, intelligence and persevering activity ... and appears to me to combine the essential qualities required in trusts of this nature.' The New York Horticultural Society enrolled Douglas as a corresponding member.

Douglas closeted himself in the offices of the Horticultural Society, carefully putting his collection in order and writing up his travels. By now, however, the plants that were now generating the greatest excitement came not from the east coast of America but from the west. Captain George Vancouver had explored the Pacific North West by sea in the 1790s, bestowing his name on Vancouver Island. Archibald Menzies, a fully trained botanist and doctor from Perthshire, was the surgeon-naturalist on board. He brought back many specimens and descriptions of the plants and trees growing along this remarkable coastline. Then Lewis and Clark had blazed a land trail across the continent in 1804–05. Alexander Mackenzie had become the first man to travel by water across the Continent to the Pacific.

Thus it was to the west of America that the Society, and Douglas in particular, now turned their attention.

Chapter Four

JOURNEY ROUND THE HORN

'Never in my life was I so mortified, touching at a place where
everything, indeed the most trifling particle, becomes of interest
in England, and to have such a miserable collection to show
I have been there.'
Douglas' journal entry on setting sail from the Galapagos Islands

In just a few months, another opportunity for American exploration
arrived.

The stories the early explorers told of the west coast of America,
and the specimens they sent back, had tantalized horticulturalists
and botanists, as well as the general public. But the live plants
remained elusive and unknown. The difficulties of journeying to
this wild and inhospitable land at the right time to collect seeds,
and then of transporting seeds and specimens safely home, seemed
insurmountable.

Now, however, the Horticultural Society saw the possibilities of
glory, and in a leap of faith decided to despatch David Douglas, their
newly proven prodigy. William Hooker probably gave a push behind
the scenes, for he was keen to write the definitive botanical work on
the entire vast continent, and hoped to make use of whatever finds
Douglas brought back. Hooker eventually published *Flora Boreali-
Americana; or the Botany of the Northern Parts of British America* in
twelve parts between 1829 and 1840.

To underwrite an entire expedition – including chartering a ship
and all the associated expenses – would have been well beyond the
Society's means. Fortunately, the Hudson's Bay Company was
persuaded to let Douglas travel on its annual supply ship, which sailed

round the southern tip of South America and then north as far as the mouth of the Columbia River. Once arrived and exploring in the interior, Douglas would find board and lodging in the Company's scattered forts, but elsewhere he would have to fend for himself in the open. The Company reminded the Society dourly that Mr Douglas would 'find the fare of the country rather coarse and be subject to some privations'. Thus, once again, the Society was able to mount an expedition at minimal cost. The cost of the entire three-year trip was just £400, including Douglas' salary and expenses.

Douglas spent the months after his return from New York sorting the plants, specimens and seeds he had collected and editing his field notes. The Society had also put him to work sorting the material sent by earlier travellers to North America. As his departure approached, he studied all the scientific books he could lay his hands on so as to be able to identify the deluge of plants he hoped to find and bring home. He visited gardens around London to view finds from previous expeditions, packed his suit of Royal Stewart tartan, and, following the advice of William Hooker, started to teach himself the rudiments of Spanish, the language of South America and California, which was close to Douglas' destination.

Douglas entitled his diary with all due pomp: *Journal of an Expedition to North-West America; being the Second Journey Undertaken by David Douglas, on behalf of the Horticultural Society.* Few could have been as diligent and precise in their recording when, on Saturday 24 July 1824, setting course for foreign travel, Douglas broke into the pristine manuscript pages with typical Scottish reserve and understatement:

> After several weeks' preparation for a voyage to the Columbia river on the west coast of North America, on the afternoon of Saturday parted with J. Sabine, Esq., and all other friends. In the evening wrote a letter to my father, to Dr Hooker, and Mr Murray of Glasgow.
> July 25th – Left London at half-past eight o'clock in the morning from the Spread Eagle office, Piccadilly, by the Times coach in company with my brother for Gravesend.
>
> The morning was very pleasant, cloudy and calm. Passed some fields of rye, cut down; wheat, oats, and barley nearly ready for the sickle. At Gravesend I met Mr John Scouler of Glasgow, who was going on the same voyage to officiate in the capacity of surgeon. This was to me news of the most welcome kind, being previously acquainted with each other and on the strictest terms of friendship. At twelve o'clock went on board

the Hudson's Bay Company's ship *William and Ann*, Captain Hanwell, bound for the Columbia river, north-west coast of America, and came on shore again at two o'clock. At 4 o'clock in the afternoon saw my brother in the steamboat for London, who was affected at parting with me, and returned to the ship.

Douglas had to fulfil many expectations as he set out on his voyage. There was a commercial motive, in as much as the Society would exploit the plants he found for financial gain and thus earn a return on their investment in sending an envoy to the other side of the globe. But there was a purer, scientific side to his work, for the Society was also interested in botanical, zoological and generally scientific information – whether brand-new discoveries or confirmations of existing knowledge. In addition, Douglas had his own prospects to consider. Not only did he have to track down the exotic plants reported by previous explorers – he also had to send them home in a state fit to be grown successfully. On this his future largely depended. If he failed he would experience a massive loss of status and, more than likely, would be forced into a dispirited retreat to life as a gardener. There were in addition diplomatic and political sides to his mission. Having impressed the eminent men of New York State on his first journey, Douglas now had to use all his skills and charm to strengthen the Society's links with its correspondents on the west coast; the discreet hope was that they would continue to supply plants to the Society, and inform it of the latest finds, in preference to rival private collectors. On top of all this, Douglas was travelling to an area beset by tensions and quarrels over national boundaries. In the traditional manner of the 'diplomatic spy', himself unaware of his role, his reports about the territories of the Hudson's Bay Company – the role of its employees, the potential value of its lands – would be used to assess the value of the area to Britain and whether it was worth fighting for, should its control ever be disputed with the USA.

On board, Douglas occupied himself with practising his skills on the scientific instruments he had brought for the expedition – measuring the precise location, recording air and sea temperatures – and in diligently observing the minutiae of life on board. He recorded that water leaked into the hold, and the relief felt when it transpired that a few inches were safe; the patience needed when the wind failed led to an increasing interest in the strength and direction of the wind and its influence on sailing times.

Monday, 28th – In the morning, employed stowing away all my baggage &c. Went under weigh at four o'clock p.m., having a fine breeze with rain; thermometer 58 degrees. We made only seven miles and then let down the anchor at darkening.

Tuesday, 27th – Cold with thick fog; passed the Nor at daylight; at seven the ship struck on the 'Shivering Sands' and beat about dreadfully for an hour. Fortunately the wind was moderate with little swell at the time, otherwise our situation must have been perilous. On being rescued from our unhappy situation, it afforded the captain and pilot, as well as all on board, much pleasure to learn that the vessel had sustained little or no injury. I confess it gave me pleasure to be enabled to proceed, as delays in such undertakings are by no means agreeable.

The pilot left us off Deal at six o'clock in the evening (thermometer 63 degrees). Did not write as the captain intended to put into Portsmouth, to await the orders of the Company as to his proceeding to sea, not knowing how far he might be justified in his present circumstances: 14 inches of water in the hold.

They passed Dover, then the Isle of Wight and, on the 31st, the Lizard, after which 'in the evening our delightful view of the rocky shores of Cornwall closed'.

The scenery, though but 'sky and water', led Douglas to some flights of poetic fantasy. At night, he wrote on 1 August,

there is a gentle ruffling on the water, the Medusae, Physalae and other zoophytes giving off their phosphoric or illuminating particles over a vast expanse of water produce a very fine effect.

The night was observed as is usual with sailors, succeeded by some songs. The good will shown was more to be admired than the melody.

On Sunday the 8th, when prayers were read by the surgeon at the captain's request, the peaks of Porto Santo were seen, and on the next day the island (one of the Madeira group) was 'perfectly visible, about four leagues distant'. The next day, at seven in the evening, *William and Ann* anchored in the Bay of Funchal.

We were visited by boats from the Customs and Board of Health. The latter made considerable noise as the captain had no bill of health from London. Fair words and a good deal of courtesy had to be used before matters could be adjusted. The number of souls on board, with all the usual formalities, were gone through, and on his taking leave he said that at daylight a white flag must be at the masthead, a sign of quarantine. ... In the meantime the health of all friends was drunk with much pleasure; and with these sensations on my mind which will ever afford satisfaction, I wished my fellow-voyagers 'Good night,' and went to sleep. Thermometer at twelve o'clock, in the shade, 80 degrees. In the water, 76 degrees.

The next day, eager to explore, Douglas went on shore at 8 o'clock, having first written to Joseph Sabine at the Society. As always, Douglas was primarily interested in the local vegetables, which he examined with a practised eye. With a long sea voyage in prospect, he was also assessing whether they would survive at sea.

Without delay my first inquiry was for the vegetable market, which is situated near the south-west side of the town. It is a square of fifty yards, enclosed on the south and west by sheds which are fitted as stalls, on the east by a shed or house serving as the butcher market, on the north by a high iron rail with one gate, which is the only entrance to it. There are four rows of houses or shops, five in each row, equally divided, in the centre of the square, built of wood, ten feet square with pavilion roofs. The whole is neatly paved with round stones kept very clean and has quite a genteel appearance.

There is a daily market, continued throughout the day; officers are in attendance whose duty it is to see that business is conducted with propriety. Their services I valued much; particularly as it was evident, from the movements of merchants, they were not strangers to deception. There appeared to be a scarcity of vegetables.

Douglas commented on cabbages, yams, onions, pumpkins, cucumbers, peppers, tomatoes, and remarked that 'turnips, carrots, parsnips, cauliflowers, celery; not even a single blade of parsley could be seen'. The fruits, he judged, are 'richer and generally of better quality'.

The banana, *Musa sapientum*, is extensively cultivated and perfects its fruit in abundance. It is usually eaten without any preparation, but when fried in a little butter it tastes like a good pancake.

Lemons larger and better than any we are ever accustomed to see; I think them very fine. One variety of apple like Summer Redstreak; which it probably is. It is large, round and redstreaked, dry and mealy, an insipid fruit. Three different pears; one large, in form and colour like Jargonel, but entirely destitute of its flavour, mealy and tasteless; a second of a much smaller size, yellow colour almost approaching to a sulphur-yellow, with a flat compressed head and gradually tapering towards the stalk (like the former a dry fruit, but as all which I saw appeared to be too ripe, probably they may be better in an earlier state); a third resembling what is called in Scotland 'Crawford' pear, both in size, form and flavour; as in all likelihood it is.

Douglas found grapes in abundance, 'four or five varieties', together with two varieties of peach, two of figs and two of plums. The soft fruits, figs, grapes, he noted, 'are carried to market on the head in baskets, like strawberries in England'. Pears, apples, lemons, arrive 'in bags made of hogskin, and some of hemp, on mules, and the poorer class carry them on their backs'.

Having satisfied myself at market, I made a journey north of the town, on the hill where most of the principal vineyards are.

In planting the vines no situation or aspect is studied; they thrive in the valleys and deep ravines, on the little eminences and high grounds, and even on the top of old walls and on the roofs of old thatched cottages. The soil in general is a light brown like burned sand. I could not learn, what (or if any) manure is used. They are planted from 6 to 12 or 14 feet apart, and supported on horizontal rough railing of wood 4 or 5 feet from the ground, inclining sometimes to the north, sometimes to the south, but in all cases following the declination, which on a small space varies much.

In pruning very little old wood is left, leaving spurs of 2 or 4 inches on the principal shoots. From the rivulets, which are numerous, small chinks or channels are dug along the sides of the valleys for the purpose of conveying water to the plantations, which is let off when required – a cheap mode of watering and at the same time adds beauty to the place. A great portion of the clusters were daubed over with mud and some with lime, to prevent the attacks of mealy-bug and also probably to prevent the ravages of wasps and other insects; the undersides of the leaves are almost covered with a species of white mealy-bug similar to that which infests pineapple plants in England. Old women and young girls are employed pinching off the leaves that shade the fruit. This is done by stooping under the trelliswork: a delightful occupation, screened from the influence of a scorching sun.

The observation made to me in the market as to the best fruit being reserved for wine I found correct. On the whole, I confess to be somewhat disappointed about the size and quality – although certainly good, by no means what they are generally represented. Few clusters exceed 2lb or 3lb; the greater part 1lb. I learn the clusters are thinned early in the season when too numerous; thinning berries of course is not practised. In passing along the lanes that lead through the vineyards I was invariably escorted by an elderly matron with her distaff, and a little girl or boy whose suspicious eyes indicated their profession.

The banana has the best and most conspicuous place of the garden assigned it, at the end of houses or in small well-sheltered courts, to prevent its massive leaves being destroyed by the winds. Figs thrive uncommonly well, particularly in low, moist situations on the margins of woods, being partially shaded.

Arum esculentum and Yams are planted in low level beds on the margins of rivulets, so placed that water from the chink is let on the ground when required, in the same manner as for vines. It is studied to keep them almost in a state of saturation. The soil which they thrive best in is a rich, black, alluvial soil carried by the currents from the high grounds. Lemons are to be seen in great luxuriance in moist shady places in northern or eastern aspects. *Eugenia jambos* called 'Jambos', matures its fruit in abundance with little attention. It is considered one of the finest fruits by the Portuguese.

During his travels ashore, Douglas called at the house of Henry Veitch, the British consul in Madeira, but found that he had left a few weeks before 'on a tour to Italy'. Veitch was a fellow Scot, from the border town of Selkirk:

In his garden, which is laid out and kept with considerable taste, there were many fine specimens of trees larger than I have seen anywhere, &c. Banana, *Eugenia Jambos*, lemons, oranges, grapes, peaches, &c., and in a high state of perfection. Groups of flowers of warmer regions. In the centre of the garden a fine specimen of *Artocarpus incisa* (Bread Fruit) in fine health, just coming into flower; requires no protection; fully 20 feet high and 10 inches in diameter.

The following day, Douglas climbed 'the highest peak at four o'clock afternoon temperature 72 degrees. The sun shone in full vigour; the fatigue of descending after a laborious day's work made me enjoy a night's rest.' The same day he and John Scouler purchased 'one sixteenth of a pipe of wine [about eight gallons] for which we paid £7'. Scouler and Douglas were following a well-established tradition – Captain Cook and the young Horatio Nelson had both bought wine here. Although the amount is quite modest, £7 would still have made a large hole in the combined finances of the two men. Madeira was that most elusive of wines, one that improved with travelling – helped by the heat and the brandy added during the maturing process.

Now, the wine stowed safely on board, *William and Ann* got underway 'at six o'clock in the evening of Wednesday [18 August] with a pleasant fanning breeze from the south-east, being, for the short stay I made, much gratified'. By noon the next day, the mountains of Madeira were out of sight and at noon the wind changed to the north-east, 'which carried us speedily on our voyage'. In his journal Douglas continued his relentless record of the temperature, and displayed an increasing interest in sea and bird life. The only break in the monotonous routine came when the vessel crossed the Equator and the sailors paid tribute to Neptune with the time-honoured ritual of a ducking. He must have counted the days until dry land was under his feet again.

Monday, August 23rd – Heavy showers of rain during night, with gusts of wind. Morning still and warm. Sun visible at eight o'clock; cloudy during the remainder of the day, with intervening showers. Evening cool and nearly calm; thermometer in the shade 84 degrees, in the water 78 degrees. Caught two specimens of seaweed: one a variety of *Fucus natans*, attached to it some small shellfish; one probably a species of *Confervae* in close thread tufts of a bright olive colour. Intermingled with the *Confervae* a small species of *Fucus* with circular branches and minute flattened bladders. On the same, two very minute insects of the same species having a beautiful shining azure colour. Sixty miles off Cape Verde Islands. ...

Wednesday, September 1st – Very pleasant and cool in the morning. Thermometer 82 degrees in the shade, on the surface of the water 79 degrees. Warm and close in the afternoon, with light showers. Spoke to the ship *Jane* of Philadelphia, forty-seven days from that port; bound for Valparaiso, we cherished the hope of keeping company with her, but during the night a violent storm came on and we saw no more of her. ...

Saturday, September 11th – Heavy rain during the most of last night, with light wind from the south-east. At ten o'clock this morning Neptune, accompanied with his guard of honour, fulfilled his promise made last night, when all his unqualified sons had an interview with his Majesty. The day was passed with much pleasure.

The voyage then settled into a routine. Morning and evening Douglas meticulously noted the air and water temperatures. He observed the great flocks of birds as they neared the coast of South America and Rio de Janeiro, their next port of call.

Saturday, September 25th – Morning cloudy; loud wind from the north, with heavy showers; the sea running very high. Towards midday it cleared away; the wind became more moderate. At two o'clock noon Cape Frio was seen, about eight leagues distant. Great flock of birds with innumerable swarms of butterflies came to invite us to their coast. Thermometer 75 degrees and 72 degrees in the water. The evening cool but pleasant.

Tuesday September 28th – Entered the mouth of the river at noon and came to anchor at two o'clock. After being visited by officers from the Custom House, Board of Health, Police, &c., I had to go on shore to the Master of Police, which all passengers have to do. Afterwards we were visited by two officers from the British man-of-war enquiring if we had a mail or could spare them any newspapers.

Brazil was dominated by an elite of grand and wealthy landowners, with, beneath them, a teeming mass of African and local slaves, most of whom were subjected to immense cruelty. The country's economy was highly volatile. The West Indies were snatching away the lucrative market for sugar, until now Brazil's principal crop; over-exploitation of the soil and failure to modernize the refineries were putting Brazil at a disadvantage. However, the coffee boom was just beginning, while the development of rubber lay a few years in the future.

Amid this vibrant community were gentlemen gardeners who cultivated a multitude of species with all the largesse of their aristocratic counterparts in Britain. Douglas' first meeting was with John Dickson, a keen botanist who was probably related to the nurserymen of the same name who had set up in business in Edinburgh during the eighteenth century. Douglas was carrying a letter of introduction, and the meeting proved a fortunate one.

Wednesday, September 29th – Went on shore in the evening
with the captain and returned two hours after. Called on John
Dickson, Esq., a friend of Mr Sabine's, and a correspondent of
the Society, who received me with great kindness. In the most
handsome manner he invited me to stay at his house during my
visit and made every preparation to make me comfortable. I
showed him my instructions and informed him of the object of
my voyage, &c. ... Mr Dickson gave me much facility as to my
pursuit by sending his servants and introducing me to the
knowledge of his friends.

My movements were greatly frustrated by rains, and as
the stay of the vessel was uncertain I could not with propriety
make long journeys. The approach to Rio is particularly
grand. The entrance to the bay to the harbour is about half a
mile broad, at the mouth of which are four or five small
islands all covered with wood. ... The ground is mountainous,
but not rugged, and covered with wood to the summit; and
what appears singular, the palm grows more luxuriantly in
such a place than in lower situations. On the left is a conspicuous conical hill, known by the name of Sugar-loaf Mountain,
of primitive rock, not unlike the Aberdeen granite with which
the London streets are paved. A small fort is built at its base,
on which are a few guns; on the opposite side stands one of
larger dimensions. In general the houses are regularly built,
but of coarse workmanship, of freestone; the rooms are lofty,
with large doors and windows. Many of the windows are not
glazed but have a sort of shutter of lattice-work, with hinges
at the top. The only buildings worthy of notice are the
churches, among which is the Emperor's Private chapel and
one adjoining it in the Palace Square, both of Gothic, neat and
reflecting great credit on the architect.

Rather boldly, Douglas recorded that he had attended Midnight Mass,
Brazil being a Roman Catholic country. Years later, after living in far-
flung parts of the globe, he vigorously defended his friendship with
people of different religious beliefs in the face of criticism back in
Britain.

The vividness of Brazilian life, the sharp contrasts with life at
home, had an impact on his diary, for his observations became less
succinct and increasingly effusive. The visit to Midnight Mass had
clearly moved him: 'the gorgeous tapestry hung round the saints, the

brilliancy of the lamps and candles, with the general neatness of the edifice, impress on the mind of a stranger a pleasing sensation'.

On the same day, Douglas also met another gardener and botanist. This was

> William Harrison, Esq., of Liverpool (a brother of Arnold Harrison, Esq., of Aighburgh, who is a Fellow of the Society), who is fond of plants and birds and has introduced many interesting plants to the Botanic Garden of Liverpool; he has a fine garden five miles from town and a collection of African, European and indigenous plants. The number of his live birds in cages amounts to seventy, mostly Brazilian, many of them very beautiful. This gentleman showed me many civilities and he informed me that most of his relations were Fellows of the Society.

Douglas collected two boxes of plants to send off to the Society in London. However, 'this afterwards I thought as useless work, for they would arrive in England in the winter. ... Mr Harrison kindly undertook to see they would be sent with one of the vessels employed by himself.' On 9 October, the day before Douglas expected to sail, John Dickson

> invited some of his friends in town, Mr Louden, the Admiral's Secretary, and Dr Scott, his physician, to dinner to meet me. The good feeling and harmony that were shown by every guest at table among themselves and good wishes towards my welfare at parting was, I must confess, gratifying to me. I left their agreeable society at eight in the evening. Just as I stepped in the boat it began to rain heavily, with thunder and lightning. I had to take off my coat and vest to keep my specimens dry. I had among the numerous vessels lying in harbour some difficulty in finding the right one, she having hauled out to a more commodious place for sailing since I was last on board.

Douglas' pessimism about the chances of the plants he had collected for the Society surviving the long voyage back to England proved unfounded. In due course, the Society recorded that they had received 'fine orchids from Mr Douglas', including *Brassavola nodosa* and *Oncidium pubes*. These appealing and highly scented flowers were heaven-sent for the glass houses now being built in grand country mansions.

Eventually, after several days' delay while they waited for

favourable weather, *William and Ann* set sail once more. Douglas' regrets at not having achieved all he wished, and collected as many plants as he would have liked, were soon put aside. Bird-watching proved excellent sport, as the great shadow of the white wandering albatross, with its black-tipped wings, soared high above the boat. Despite the traditional belief that albatross should not be harmed, Douglas seemed to have no qualms about capturing specimens to be sent home. For this he used a hook and line baited with fat or pork.

Given the size of *William and Ann*, going 'round the Horn' must have been a terrifying prospect, for this most stormy and volatile of ocean passages was the graveyard of many ships. However, Douglas' account displays little apprehension and remains that of a detached observer more interested in practising his technique of methodical description.

> The weather was stormy with generally a fine clear sky. The motion of the vessel was great, the waves frequently breaking over it, and no sleep until completely worn out with fatigue. When the wind blows from the south or south-west the cold is insupportable, and yet the thermometer never was lower than 39 [degrees] 45 the greatest; there is a piercing rawness in the atmosphere (laying aside being so lately in the tropics and of course more susceptible of cold) quite unknown in the northern hemisphere in similar latitudes. Daylight sixteen hours, sky generally clear azure and beautifully tinted in the evenings just as the sun leaves the horizon.
>
> November 16th – We were considered round, and gladly we bad adieu to such inhospitable regions. The weather moderated gradually and soon found ourselves navigating more pacific water.
>
> As we passed the Straits of Magellan the weather contin-ued variable, was boisterous with a rough sea, rain, and thick fogs.

The days of tedium set in again as they set course northwards once more. Douglas noted laconically that 'this time to the 14th of December nothing worthy to be noticed'. On that day, they approached the Juan Fernandez Islands, the islands of Daniel Defoe's *Robinson Crusoe*. The Islands, which lie some 400 miles off the Chilean coast, are emergent peaks from a submarine mountain range, and are now a national park because of their unique flora and fauna.

Towards noon the Island of Mas-a-Fuera was seen, distant bout
seven leagues and appears like a conical black rock. As we drew
near it became more like an island. At four in the afternoon of
the same day passed within two miles of it; the surge on the
beach prevented the commander from landing. On the whole its
appearance is barren, although in the valleys there is herbage
and some trees on the hills; goats were seen in abundance. Our
course was then directed towards the island of Juan Fernandez,
about eighty miles distant to the north-east. It afforded me
much gratification to see Juan Fernandez on the morning word
of the second day. . . .

The whole island is very mountainous, volcanic, and
beautifully covered with wood to the summit of the hills, tops of
which are rarely seen, being enveloped in the clouds. On Friday
and Saturday I went on shore and was much gratified . . . . As we
approached the shore we were surprised to see a small vessel at
anchor, and on the beach a hut with smoke rising from it.

Now Douglas experienced a curious meeting that brought the adventures of Robinson Crusoe to mind.

As we were about to step out of the boat, a man sprang out of
the thicket to our astonishment and directed us into a sheltered
creek. He gave me the following account of his adventures. His
name, William Clark; a sailor; native of Whitechapel, London;
came to the coast of Chile five years ago in a Liverpool ship
called Lolland, and was there discharged. He is now in the
employment of the Spaniards, who visit the island for the
purpose of killing seals and wild bullocks, which are both
numerous.

Five of his Companions were on the opposite side, in their
pursuit, and came to see him once a week; he was left to take
care of the little bark and other property. When he saw the boat
first he abandoned his hut and fled to the wood, thinking us to
be pirates.

On hearing us speak English he sprang from his place of
retreat, and no language can convey the pleasure he seemed to
feel. He had been there five weeks and intended to stay five
more; he came from Coquimbo, in Chile. His clothing was one
pair of blue woollen trousers, a flannel and a cotton shirt, and
a hat, but he chose to go bareheaded; he had no coat. The
surgeon and I gave him as much as could be spared from our
small stock, for which he expressed many thanks. His little hut

was made of turf and stones thatched with the Straw of a wild oat. In one corner lay a bunch of straw and his blanket; a log of wood to sit on was all the furniture; the only cooking utensil was a common cast-iron pot with a wooden bottom, which he had sunk a few inches in the floor – and placed the fire round the sides! He longed to taste roast beef (having had none for seven years) and one day tried to indulge with a little baked, as he termed it; but in the baking the bottom gave way, as might reasonably be expected; so poor Clark could not effect the new mode of cooking. I told him under his circumstances roasting beef was an easier task than boiling. He is a man of some information; his library amounted to seventeen volumes – Bible and Book of Common Prayer, which he had to keep a secret place when his Spanish friends were there; an odd volume of *Tales of My Landlord* and *Old Mortality*, some of voyages and Cowper's poems. He had the one by heart addressed to Alexander Selkirk; but what is still more worthy to be noticed, a fine bound copy of Crusoe's adventures, who himself was the latest and most complete edition.

Defoe's famous novel *Robinson Crusoe* had been published in 1720, over a century before Douglas visited Juan Fernandez. The story was based on the life of Alexander Selkirk, son of a shoemaker from the fishing village of Largo in Fife, on the east coast of Scotland (and thus another product of a homespun Scottish background). Selkirk ran away to sea, and was put ashore at his own request on the island of Juan Fernandez, where he lived alone for four years and four months before rescue arrived. Selkirk's account of his adventures inspired Defoe to elaborate the story and produce a novel of outstanding popularity and influence. The book became an instant best-seller, which both Douglas and Scouler would certainly have read as boys. After the encounter with their 'real-life Robinson Crusoe', Scouler wrote in his diary that he, William Clark and *William and Ann*'s crew decided that the real cave occupied by the real Robinson Crusoe was in Cruz Bay.

Douglas explored the islands and found the now abandoned gardens created by previous Spanish colonists of the islands.

In the old gardens were abundance of three or four different peaches in a half ripe state, very luxuriant; one apple, a quince, and two pears; a quantity of the last three we took for puddings. Abundance of figs in vigorous state of bearing, and vines, one of which thrives luxuriantly; it is just in blossom. The only ripe fruit was a sort of strawberry with large fruit of a pale whitish-red, not unpleasant; leaves, stern, and calyx very downy; dried a paper of seeds of this species lest it may prove indigenous to the island or the coast of Chile. The only culinary vegetable was radish, which grows to a large size.

I sowed a small portion of vine, pear, and some other fruit seeds which I had of Mr Atkinson and some culinary vegetables, and gave some to Clark to sow on various parts of the island. Saturday afternoon was set apart for fishing; a sort of rock codfish and a smaller fish unknown to me were caught in abundance, both good eating, and after such a length of time on salted food were considered a luxury.

Douglas also advised Clark to use the eggs of a 'small species of blue pigeon'. As they came to leave the island, they exchanged gifts.

Clark, like all other English sailors he had no aversion to rum; I gave him a single dram, which, not being accustomed to before for a great length of time, made him forget his exile. He was like the heroes of Troy: 'fought his battle over again and slew the slain three times'. . . .

On our quitting the shore Clark presented us with a fine female goat, but not one of Robinson Crusoe's, for it was young. We left him standing on a large stone on the shore on the evening of Saturday, intending to visit him again in the morning. Scarcely had we reached the ship when a strong south-easterly wind set in, which obliged me reluctantly to leave such an interesting speck of the globe and my new acquaintance Clark. The weather continued unfavourable for making the land again: for three days we were so much driven by its violence that the captain considered it a sacrifice to return.

Our course directed towards the Islands of Galapagos under the Equator in Long. 80 degrees W. On the morning of Thursday the wind became moderate and we got the south-east trade wind, which we were fortunate enough [to have] with us within 1 degrees of the Equator.

The goat taken on board just a week previously became a welcome Christmas dinner, and Douglas wrote that they were 'comfortable and happy'. In the evening, perhaps with the help of a bottle or so of the Madeira wine, they drank the health of 'our friends in England'.

1825. Saturday, January 1st – In Lat. 19 degrees S. Weather continued good and nothing occurred deserving to be mentioned. As we approached the Line the heat sensibly increased, but by no means so oppressive as in the Atlantic. Although the difference of the mercury is trifling, there is always a cooling atmosphere which renders it more supportable and agreeable.

Now *William and Ann* reached the Galapagos Islands, soon to become famous through their association with Charles Darwin and his theory of evolution. Darwin visited the Galapagos some ten years after Douglas as part of a more thorough scientific expedition. The variety of different species of animals, particularly birds, helped Darwin to collect his thoughts on how species evolved and how different ecological niches might be filled in different ways through the process of natural selection. The sheer variety of animal and plant life on and between the islands helped Darwin to explain the mechanism of species development that is now broadly recognized and accepted as the key to understanding the natural world.

At noon on Sunday, 9th, Chatham Island [Isla San Cristobal] was seen; we passed along the east side at 4 P.M. of the same day, fifteen miles from the shore. It is not mountainous and apparently but little herbage on it. On the morning of 10th (Monday) I went on shore on James Island [Isla San Salvador], thirty-seven miles to the west of Chatham Island. It is volcanic, mountainous, and very rugged, with some fine vestiges of volcano craters and vitrified lava; the hills are not high, the highest being about 2000 feet above the level of the sea. The verdure is scanty in comparison with most tropical climates, arising, no doubt, from the scarcity of fresh water, although at the same time some of the trees in the valleys are large, but very little variety; few of them were known to me. My stay was three days, two hours on shore each time. Few of its plants were known to me. The birds are very numerous, and some of them pretty, so little acquainted with man's devices that they were readily killed with a stick; a gun was not necessary except to bring them from the rocks or from the tops of the trees.

Many of the smaller ones perched on my hat, and when I carried my gun on my shoulder would sit on the muzzle. During my stay I killed forty-five, of nineteen genera, all of which I skinned carefully, and had the mortification to lose them all except one species of Sula by the almost constant rain of twelve days after leaving the island I could not expose them on deck and no room for them below.

Among them were two species of pelican, four of Sula, four of hawk (one particularly fine, nearly orange colour), one very curious small pigeon. I was nearly as unfortunate with plants, my collection amounting to 175 specimens, many of them, no doubt, interesting. I was able only to save forty. Never in my life was I so mortified, touching at a place where everything, indeed the most trifling particle, becomes of interest in England, and to have such a miserable collection to show I have been there.

Plant-collecting was a struggle. Heartbreaking losses frequently occurred, and it was to his credit that Douglas often recorded these in a matter-of-fact way. At times, however, he seems to be writing through clenched teeth as yet more finds died. Dry weather was essential to preserve samples of both plants and animals. Without it, dampness would encourage the organisms of decay – insects, fungi and mould – to break down any dead material or rot any seeds collected. If the specimens were properly dried, however, the lack of water would discourage such a breakdown and help to preserve the material. The same technique was used to preserve meat and biscuits on long sea voyages.

Douglas' excitement and interest were evident. So too was his frustration. He had been granted a few hours to explore a landscape with animals and vegetation that he recognized as unique – 'a species of tortoise, some of them very large, one weighing 400 lb; a lizard, 3 feet long, of a bright orange-yellow' – and he was unable even to preserve an adequate amount: 'A fine skin of the lizard I lost, and regret it exceedingly, not being described.'

On the shore are abundance of turtle of good quality, probably the green turtle of the West Indies.

No fresh water was found except a small spring flowing from the crevices of one of the craters. The last day on shore it ceased to rain for about an hour; the sun broke through and raised a steam from the ground almost suffocating. My thermometer stood at 96 degrees, not a breath of wind.

Setting sail again, they encountered a great thunderstorm.

On Sunday, 16th, we had a tremendous thunderstorm, vivid lightning lasting from 4 A.M. to 2 P.M.; I never saw anything equal to it. Five tons of water was had from the sails this was a great relief, for our allowance was more and we had our clothes washed.

During the storm, the second mate fell on the deck and fractured his right thigh. Perhaps predicting his future interest in medical care, Douglas wrote that 'the excruciating pain which this poor man suffered until the termination of our voyage can hardly be expressed'.

After almost four weeks, they approached the treacherous mouth of the Columbia River on 12 February. 'The weather was so boisterous and frightful that it forbade everything like approaching the coast as useless.' For six long, storm-tossed weeks the ship drifted up and down the coast, attempting every few days to enter the river. The captain's caution was justifiable – there were innumerable wrecks, and indeed, four years later, *William and Ann* herself foundered, with the loss of everyone on board. The long wait proved frustrating in the extreme. Douglas recorded in his journal:

> Here we experienced the furious hurricanes of North-west America in the fullest extent a thousand times worse than Cape Horn. In this latitude where is an abundance of a small species of *Physalae* of an azure transparent colour, which were frequently washed on the mainyard by the spray breaking over the vessel. Prevailing winds from the south-west and north-west. Many efforts were made during this time to reach our destined port in the short intervals of favourable weather. ...
>
> Sunday, April 3rd – Calm in the morning and cold; a keen easterly breeze carried us within four miles of the River, when another violent storm from the west obliged us again to put to sea. ...
>
> April 7th – At daylight on Thursday our course was again directed to the coast, being only 40 miles distant, every person breathing a wish we might be more fortunate than on Sunday. The weather seemingly more steady with a keen north-east wind, such an opportunity was not lost, all sail was set, joy and expectation was on every countenance, all glad to make themselves useful.
>
> The Doctor and I kept the soundings. At one o'clock noon we entered the river and passed the sand bank in safety (which is considered dangerous and on which, I learn, many vessels have been injured and some wrecked). At four we came to anchor in Baker's Bay, on the north side of the river.
>
> Several shots of the cannon were immediately fired to announce our arrival to the establishment 7 miles up the river, but were not answered.
>
> Thus my long and tedious voyage of 8 months 14 days from England terminated. The joy of viewing land, the hope of

in a few days ranging through the long wished-for spot and the pleasure of again resuming my wonted employment may be readily calculated. We spent the evening with great mirth and at an early hour went to sleep, to sleep without noise and motion, the disagreeable attendants of a sea voyage. With truth I may count this one of the happy moments of my life. As might naturally be supposed to enjoy the sight of land, free from the excessive motion and noise of the ship – from all deprived nearly nine months – was to me truly a luxury.

The euphoria of the release from *William and Ann* was to last for several weeks.

Chapter Five

EXPLORING THE
COLUMBIA RIVER

'The luxury of a night's sleep on a bed of pine branches can only be
appreciated by those who have experienced a route over a barren
plain scorched by the sun, or fatigued by groping their way through
a thick forest, crossing gullies, dead wood, lakes, stones, &c. Indeed
so much worn out was I three times by fatigue and hunger that twice
I crawled, for I could hardly walk, to a small abandoned hut.'
Douglas' journal, 20 June 1825

For Douglas, the relief at having arrived safely was clearly heart-
felt. On 9 April, he and John Scouler 'went on shore on Cape
Disappointment', the name given to the mouth of the Columbia
River, 'as the ship could not proceed up the river in consequence of
heavy rains and thick fog'.

Little did Douglas realize that among the first trees that he saw –
his first impression of the natural world of the Pacific North West
after eight tedious months at sea – was the Douglas fir, the tree by
which foresters forever recall him and commemorate his pioneering
work. Although he collected hundreds of plants, many of which came
to grace front gardens from cottages to stately homes and were naturalized in riverbank and woodland, the irony was that he could have
stepped ashore, collected some seed, returned to Britain and still be
remembered for an outstanding find. But that would have been to miss
a lifetime's adventure and the excitement of travel in a little-known
wilderness, not to mention the achievement of collecting hundreds of
specimens and flowers.

The Douglas fir was not unknown in Britain. It had already been
described by Archibald Menzies, the Scottish surgeon-naturalist who

had joined George Vancouver's voyage of exploration along the Pacific North West coast in 1792. Menzies hailed from near Aberfeldy in Perthshire, where nowadays stand some of the tallest Douglas firs in Britain, barely 20 miles from Scone, where Douglas had learned his craft as an apprentice gardener. The botanist Aylmer Bourke Lambert had used Menzies' specimens to describe the tree in his *Description of the Genus Pinus* (1803), calling it *Pinus taxifolia*, which was the scientific name Douglas used. However, it was Douglas who succeeded in sending home cone specimens and seeds, from which the first tree was grown in England. Nowadays, the name given to the Douglas fir commemorates the two Scotsmen associated with its earliest discovery by Europeans. Its English name recognizes David Douglas, while its Latin name, *Pseudotsuga menziesii*, is a reminder of Archibald Menzies, who first described it and collected specimens of its foliage.

In his matter-of-fact and diligent way, Douglas described how he discovered the tree that was to be forever associated with his name.

> The ground on the south side of the river is low, covered thickly with wood, chiefly *Pinus canadensis P. balsamea*, and a species which may prove to be *P. taxifolia*. The north (Cape Disappointment) is a remarkable promontory, elevation about 700 feet above the sea, covered with wood of the same kinds as on the other side.

From the first, Douglas proved a determined collector and observer. It is not difficult to imagine his excitement when he set foot on shore and found himself surrounded by the plants he had anticipated from his studies and from Menzies' work.

> On stepping on the shore *Gaultheria Shallon* was the first plant I took in my hands. So pleased was I that I could scarcely see anything but it. Mr Menzies correctly observes that it grows under thick pine-forests in great luxuriance and would make a valuable addition to our gardens. It grows most luxuriantly on the margins of woods, particularly near the ocean. ...
>
> On our return to the ship [on Sunday the 10th] we found a canoe with one Canadian and several Indians ... who brought some potatos, milk, and fresh butter. The potatos were so much relished that we had some in the evening for tea.
>
> The natives viewed us with curiosity and put to us many questions. Some of them have a few words of English and by the assistance of signing make themselves very well understood.

The practice of compressing the forehead, of perforating the septum of the nose amid ears with shells, bits of copper, beads, or in fact any hardware, gives a stranger a curious idea of their singular habits. They brought dry salmon, fresh sturgeon, game, and some prepared roots with dry berries for sale and soon showed themselves to be a dextrous people at bargaining.

Fifty or so of the visiting natives, clad in arrow-proof elk skins and war paint, danced, rattling and shaking the shells sewn on to their clothes in time to yells and chants. Scouler wrote later that in his opinion their clothing was 'alike useless for the purpose of decency or of comfort'; the more modest petticoats of the women were dismissed with equal disapproval.

On Monday, the 11th, we went up the river to the [Hudson Bay] Company's establishment [Fort Astoria], distant from the entrance about seven or eight miles. We learned they had nearly abandoned their fort there and had made one seventy miles up the river on the opposite side, to which all persons in their employ were to repair in a few days. I went on shore on Tuesday (12th April, 1825) and was very civilly received by a Mr McKenzie, the other person in authority; he informed me they were about to abandon the present place for a more commodious situation ninety miles up the river on the north side, also that the chief factor, John McLoughlin, Esq., was up the river at the new establishment, but would be down as soon as he received the news of the ship's arrival.

Delighted to be able to start on his mission at last, and accompanied by Scouler, who was very much a kindred spirit, Douglas started to explore the countryside. He observed new species and the differences in growing characteristics of plants in varying soils and conditions, noting carefully where to return to collect seed.

I did not leave the ship until Saturday, but was daily on shore. With respect to the appearance of the country and its fertility my expectations were fully realised. It is very varied, diversified by hills and extensive plains, very good soil. The greater part of the whole country as far as eye can reach is closely covered with pine of several species. In trees there is no variety or comparison to the Atlantic side, no *Fagus*, *Gleditschia*, *Mangolia*, *Juglans*, one *Quercus*, one *Fraxinus*. The country to the northward near the ocean is hilly, Point Round or Point Adams of Lewis and Clarke on the south side of the river is low and many places swampy. For the distance of 40 miles as far as Cape Lookout there is a ridge of hills that run in a south-west direction and is so named by Vancouver. Mr McKenzie made me as comfortable as his circumstances would admit, until he could see the chief factor. My paper being all in the hold, except a very small quantity, and the ship not yet taking out the cargo, I could do but little in the way of collecting.

Douglas did start to record his observations. The pretty plant *Gaultheria shallon* and its charming rustic effect on the forest floor enthralled him, and he carefully recorded that the natives called it *salal*, not *shallon*. At this early stage, he was unlikely to have detected the plant's grave disadvantage: its robust growth smothered the forest floor, and would later infuriate foresters as they struggled through its jungle-like tentacles to arrive at the base of a tree for felling.

I have since seen it [*Gaultheria shallon*] as far as 40 miles above the Grand Rapids of the Columbia, but as it leaves the coast it becomes less vigorous; was in flower when I arrived and continued so till August and in fruit. Bears abundantly, fruit good, indeed by far the best in the country. Should the seeds now sent home rise, as I hope they may, I have little doubt but it will ere long find a place in the fruit garden as well as in the ornamental. In my walks I have frequently seen the young plants on the stumps of trees 4 to 10 feet from the ground and on dead wood growing luxuriantly. ... It flowers the whole summer through and the fruit is ripe in July and continues bearing until checked by the frost; thick woods and banks of rivers.

Douglas was also excited at finding the flowering currant, *Ribes sanguineum*, that was to become a popular staple of the Victorian garden.

Flowers pink or rose colour, inside of the petals white, anthers white in long racemes; a most beautiful shrub in open, dry places; 7 to 10 feet high. This exceedingly handsome plant is abundant on the rocky shores of the Columbia and its branches, and in such places produces a great profusion of flowers but little fruit. In the shady woods the flowers are less numerous and beautiful but produce more fruit. I am happy to send a good portion of its seed; flowers in April; fruit ripe in August.

Sent back to the Society in London, the currant quickly became popular. Only a few years later, in 1833, the garden designer John Loudon, who had produced such memorable designs for landscapes at Scone when Douglas was a youngster, described a visit to Reading Gaol in *Gardener's Magazine*:

> The Governor has a taste not only for gardening, but for natural history. He has a lawn or grass plot, a beautiful piece of rock-work, composed of flints and fragments or mural antiquities. He has also a variety of plants of the choicest kinds, such as *Wisteria*, double furze, *Ribes* several species, *Petunia phoenicia* and numerous pelargoniums, the whole mixed with fruit trees.

Douglas was now fully engaged in the business of plant-collecting and recording his observations. Apart from *Gaultheria*, *Ribes sanguineum* and Douglas fir, he also recorded at this early stage of his explorations various other plants, including (among many others) several different types of *Ribes*, *Rubus spectabilis* (salmonberry), *Camash*, the bulbs of which were a staple of the local native diet, *Mahonia* (the Oregon grape now beloved of landscape gardeners), *Acer macrophyllum*, *Acer circinnatum* (the vine-leaved maple) and lupins.

On 16 April, Dr John McLoughlin, the chief factor for the Hudson's Bay Company, travelled downriver and received Douglas 'with much kindness', assuring him that 'everything in his power would be done to promote the views of the [Horticultural] Society'. Now Douglas began to learn the ways of the Company, which was established in 1670 as the 'Company of Adventurers' and has passed into folklore as one of the main institutions involved in opening up and developing Canada. Its main purpose was to supply Europe with furs acquired from native Americans. Based in London, it had close connections with the British government, and following the colonial wars with France in the eighteenth century was granted trading rights in, and virtual control over, vast parts of British North America. In the early 1820s, it was emerging from a ruthless and violent trade war with the rival North West Company, based in Montreal. The North West Company had been more adventurous in moving into the Pacific North West to exploit the beaver and otter populations to feed the voracious European fur market. Following in the footsteps of such distinguished men as Sir Alexander Mackenzie, the first European to cross the Rockies to the Pacific Ocean, the North West Company had opened a series of forts and trading posts. The Hudson's Bay Company followed suit, and a bitter trade war ensued. However, the competition proved too much, and in 1821 the two companies merged, though in practice the merger was more of a takeover by the Hudson's Bay Company.

McLoughlin was an impressive individual. Tall, with a shock of white hair, he was a 'North Wester' but had retained his position after the takeover. Virtually the only source of law and authority in the area, he carried out his responsibilities in a serious yet humane manner. Subsequently, he fell out with the Hudson's Bay Company on account of the help he gave prospective American settlers. Eventually he became a US citizen, and was honoured as the 'Father of Oregon'.

McLoughlin's help and support were critical to Douglas' venture. Without them, Douglas could have accomplished very little. He sailed upriver with McLoughlin on 19 April to Fort Vancouver (near present-day Portland) at the confluence of the Willamette River (known at that time as the Multnomah River) and the Columbia. From here the view of the snow-covered Cascade Mountains was spectacular. Due east was Mount Hood, to the north was Mount St Helens, with Mount Jefferson prominent to the south. Douglas estimated all these to be between 10,000 and 12,000 feet (3000 to 3600 metres) high.

As the Fort was not yet complete, Douglas slept in a tent, setting a pattern that characterized his botanizing adventures. He wrote in his journal that:

> I have only been three nights in a house since my arrival, the three first on shore. On my journeys I have a tent where it can be carried, which rarely can be done; sometimes I sleep in one, sometimes under a canoe turned upside down, but most commonly under the shade of a pine tree without anything.

Soon after arriving at Fort Vancouver, Douglas resumed botanizing. Apart from a short return trip to sea in company with Scouler, he did not travel far from the Fort until 20 June:

> Sunday May 1st – Early in the morning left the fort for the purpose of visiting an extensive plain seven miles below on the same side of the river. Passed several Indian steaming huts or vapour baths; a hole is dug about 1 foot deep, in which hot stones are placed and water thrown on them so as to produce steam; the bather then goes in naked and remains until well steamed; he immediately plunges into some pool or river, which is chosen so as not to be far distant. They are formed of sticks, mud, and turfs, with a small hole for means of entering. They

are most used when the natives come from their hunting parties, after the fatigues of war, and also before they go on any expedition which requires bodily exertion. My curiosity was not so strong as to regale myself with a visit.

Starting in June, Douglas made several expeditions along the Columbia and Multnomah to explore and collect plants.

June 20th – Towards midday left my residence for a journey up the river in company with the canoes going to the different posts in the interior, a few miles above the Great Falls, about two hundred miles from the ocean. I was at a loss to decide whether my time would be better employed there or here and the ocean. In the latter, from what I have already seen, I should reap a rich harvest, and leave it probably for a less fertile one; although, on the other hand, I might obtain some interesting objects to the plains and mountains of the interior, as John McLoughlin, (the chief factor), from whom I have experienced every attention and assistance as to the furthering of my pursuit and comfort which he has in his power to show, assures me there will he no obstacle to my crossing the continent, and that he will use every means to make my stay beneficial to the Society and agreeable to myself.

Before the vessel left the river for Nootka [further up the coast] and thereabouts, I had some thought of there. But as he informed me, that my opportunities of collecting, from the turbulent disposition of the natives, would be so limited – persons being under the necessity of meeting them armed and in a large party – in unison with his opinion I thought my time would be devoted to the best advantage by remaining on the Columbia, and to make journeys in various directions as opportunities would occur.

The water ran with such rapidity that when the wind blows from a contrary direction it produces a swell like an inland sea; frequently we had to take shelter in the creeks, although our canoes were considered good, yet we could not see each other except at a short distance, so great was the swell.

Douglas was following in the famous footsteps of Meriwether Lewis and William Clark (which Douglas always misspelt Clarke), whom Thomas Jefferson, the wily President of the United States, had despatched in 1804 to blaze a land trail across the great land mass to the Pacific Ocean. On their travels, and when they arrived, they were to gather scientific data, discover whether a transcontinental water route was feasible, and strengthen the United States' claim to the area around the Columbia River. The two men fulfilled their commission beyond expectations. By the time Douglas arrived, their names were spoken of with reverence, even by the hard-bitten men of the Hudson's Bay Company.

Douglas was now travelling upriver towards the Great Falls, near the point where the Deschutes River joins the Columbia, and was approaching the Grand Rapids, some 60 miles below the Great Falls.

The Grand Rapids, as they are termed by Lewis and Clarke, are formed by the river passing and through a narrow channel about 270 yards broad in a south-west direction, very rocky, the fall of water about 147 feet above which stand three small islands; one of them is the burial-place of the natives who inhabit the southern banks of the river. The extreme length of the Rapids may be about two miles, but for only a short space (about 600 yards where the river makes a turn S.W.) the water passes with great agitation. At this season they are seen to a disadvantage, the river being 9 feet higher water than in May (from May 24 to July 16 the river rose 12 feet 8 inches); I am informed it is lower this season than generally. The banks are high, steep, and in many places rugged; limestone, sandstone, on blue and grey granite. Many large trees in a petrified state are to be seen lying in a horizontal position between the layers of rock, the ends touching the water in many places. ...

At the Rapids an almost incredible number of salmon are caught. They are taken in the following manner: before the water rises on the approach of summer, small channels are made among the stones and rocks, two feet broad and running out into various branches, over which is placed a platform for the person to stand. Several channels are made, some higher some lower, so as to suit the water as it falls or rises. A scoop net fastened round a hoop at the end of a long pole, 12 to 15 feet, is all that is used; the person stands on the extremity of the stage or platform and places his net at the top of the channel, which is always made to it exactly, and it is carried down with the current.

The poor salmon, coming up his smooth and agreeable road as he conceives it to be, finds himself in the net and is immediately thrown on the stage; the handle or pole of the net is tied to the platform by a rope lest the pressure of water or strength of the fish should snatch it out of the hands of the fisherman. The hoop is made of *Acer circinnatum* ... , which is very tough and not unlike *A. rubrum*. The pole is balsam pine, which after drying is very light. The net is made from the bark of a species of *Apocynum*, which is very durable.

The fish are of good quality, much about the same size as those caught in the rivers of Europe, 15 to 25 lb. generally, some more. I measured two, the one 3 feet 5 inches from the snout to the extremity of the tail, 10 inches broad at the thickest part, weighing about 35 lb, another 3 feet, and 9 inches broad, a little lighter. Both were purchased for 2 inches of tobacco ($^1/_2$ oz.) value two pence, or one penny each.

How little the value from that in England, where the same quantity would cost £3 or £4, and not crisped salmon as it is termed by those acquainted with refinement of dishes, as I have it, cooked under the shade of a lordly pine or rocky dell far removed from the abodes of civilised life.

Douglas was fascinated by the methods of catching and preserving fish, and must already have realized how important fish would be in his diet. He also observed that the native people ate hardly any fruit and vegetables.

Douglas' admiration for the 'voyageurs' of the Hudson's Bay Company was not surprising. These rugged individuals, generally a mixture of French and native blood, have become one of the great legends in Canadian history and folklore. Before trains and roads, the best way of travelling was by water across the great rivers and lakes. In their birch-bark canoes, the voyageurs would travel for twelve or fourteen hours or more a day transporting furs and goods from one end of the Company's empire to the other, singing their songs to maintain the rhythm of the paddle strokes. The ideal voyageur was said to be about 5 feet tall with arms down to his knees, a thick, strong body and very short legs. In exploring the Columbia, Douglas travelled with these tough characters as they moved from trading post to trading post, relying on their expertise with all forms of canoes. He frequently mentioned the sheer bravery of his crews in handling their craft and quickly gained a healthy (though at times grudging) respect for their river skills. As he became accustomed to the remote and lonely life, he also became less apprehensive of the dangers of attack.

It is very wonderful the comfort, at least the pleasant idea of being comfortable in such a place surrounded by multitudes of individuals who perhaps had never seen a white person before, and were we to judge by their appearance are very hostile, viewing us narrowly with surprise.

The luxury of a night's sleep on a bed of pine branches can only be appreciated by those who have experienced a route over a barren plain scorched by the sun, or fatigued by groping their way through a thick forest, crossing gullies, dead wood, lakes, stones, &c. Indeed so much worn out was I three times by fatigue and hunger that twice I crawled, for I could hardly walk, to a small abandoned hut. I had in my knapsack one biscuit; the third and last time I was not so bad with hunger, but very weak. I killed two partridges an hour before I camped, which I placed in my little kettle to boil for supper.

The Canadian and the two Indians had eaten their dry salmon and were asleep. Before my birds were cooked Morpheus seized me also; I awoke at daybreak and beheld my supper burned to ashes and three holes in the bottom of my kettle. Before leaving my resting place I had to make a little tea, which is the monarch of all food after fatiguing journeys. This I did by scouring out the lid of my tinder-box and boiling the water in it! I have oftentimes heard that 'Necessity has many inventions,' which I now know and partly believe.

The natives are inquisitive in the extreme, treacherous, and will pillage or murder when they can do it with impunity. Most of the tribes on the coast (the Chenooks, Cladsaps, Clikiats, and Killimucks) from the association they have had with Europeans are anxious to imitate them and are on the whole not unfriendly. Some of them are by no means deficient of ability. Some will converse in English tolerably well, make after the European models, &c. They are much prejudiced in favour of their own way of living, although at the same time will not fail to eat a most inordinate quantity if offered to them.

My canoe-men and guides were much surprised to see me make an effervescent draught and drink it boiling, as they thought it. They think there are good and bad spirits, and that I belong to the latter class, in consequence of drinking water, lighting my tobacco pipe with my lens and the sun, and they call me 'Olla-piska', which in the Chenook tongue signifies fire.

The native American peoples of the Pacific North West coast around the mouth of the Columbia River were of the Chinook and coastal Salish tribes. Further inland in the plateau and high plains between the Cascades and the Rockies were the Shuswap, Okanagan, Kalispel, Nez Perce, Klikitat, Wallawalla, Umatilla and Yakima, among others.

The coastal tribes enjoyed a relatively prosperous lifestyle, living off the plentiful salmon in the numerous rivers, wildfowl from the coast and deer from the forests. Such affluence, unrivalled elsewhere in North America, eliminated the need to develop any form of agricultural system, and allowed them to develop a sophisticated society in terms of hierarchy, rank and rituals. The abundant timber was used to carve totem poles (a relatively recent phenomenon made possible by the iron tools acquired from Europeans); these expressed the myths, legends and family stories that occupied much of their time. They lived in huge houses made of cedarwood and considered a tapered skull and sloping brow a sign of beauty, a trait that encouraged the practice of deliberately deforming infant skulls by shaping them between padded boards.

The plateau tribes were less fortunate in terms of food supply, although salmon were still plentiful in the big rivers that cross the plains. Plants were also very important, as Douglas noted. *Camas* or *Camash* (*Quamasia*), a type of wild hyacinth, was the staple. The roots were eaten in a variety of forms, including raw, boiled and roasted.

By and large, the native tribes Douglas met were relatively peaceful. There were no major wars until the 1840s, when large-scale European immigration to Oregon caused inevitable conflict with the plateau tribes. However, the native peoples often engaged with neighbouring tribes or even with villages from the same tribe but different family groups. Slaves were commonly kept as a prize from a raid or conflict, which could often be precipitated by no more than a supposed insult. The coastal tribes were active traders, which made them suitably receptive to offers from the Hudson's Bay Company.

The journey was now taking Douglas through the dramatic scenery of the Cascade Mountains into the dry, barren plains in their rainshadow. Here it was much hotter. Although he still used the river, Douglas also made several journeys on foot across the plains.

Nothing but extensive plains and barren hills, with the greater part of the herbage scorched and dead [in] the intense heat. I had to cross a plain nineteen miles without a drop of water, of pure white sand, thermometer in the shade 97 degrees. Suffered much from the heat and reflection of the sun's rays; and scarcely can I describe the state of my feet in the evening from the heat in the dry sand; all the upper part of them were in one blister.

Six miles below the [Great] Falls the water rushes through several narrow channels, formed by high, barren, and extremely rugged rocks about two miles long. It is called by the voyageurs

The Dalles. On both sides of the river very singular rocks of a great height are to be seen, having all the appearance of being water-worn; not unlikely they have been the boundaries of the river at some former period. The present bed of the river is more than 6000 feet lower.

The Dalles were given their name by French Canadian travellers. *Les dalles* is French for flagstones, which the giant basaltic rocks resemble.

The Falls stretch across the whole breadth of the river in an oblique direction, which may be about 400 yards, about 10 or 12 feet of a perpendicular pitch. At present its effect is somewhat hid, the water being high, but I am told it is fine when the river is low.

Douglas continued to collect plants apace. He recorded in detail what he saw and collected, including seeds and specimens of more lupins, *Helianthus* (sunflower), phlox, penstemons, *Erigeron* (fleabane), the wild hyacinth *Broadiaea grandiflora*, *Oenothera* (evening primrose), *Mimulus* (monkey-flower) and *Spiraea*, all of which he intended to send back to the Society in England. It was an incredible harvest, and formed the basis of Douglas' fame on his return home.

On 19 July, Douglas moved downriver towards the ocean.

July 19th – Early in the morning I left my residence in a small canoe, with one Canadian and two Indians, for a journey to the shores of the ocean, principally for the purpose of searching for and inquiring after the tuberous-rooted *Cyperus* mentioned by Pursh in his preface, the root of which is said to afford the natives food something like potatos when boiled. After a laborious route of twelve days along the shore north of Cape Disappointment, I was obliged reluctantly to return without being fortunate enough to meet with it. I observed several dead roots, washed on the shore by the surge and agreeing exactly with the description given by Lewis and Clarke, which I conjecture to be it.

My guide, who is tolerably conversant with many of the tongues spoken by the inhabitants of the coast, learned that it is very abundant along the shore from Point Adams, the southern entrance of the river, at no great distance. I am for the present prevented from prosecuting my journey in that direction, several of the tribes being at war with each other. I laboured under very great disadvantage by the almost continual rain. Many of my specimens I lost, and although I had several oilcloths, I was unable to keep my plants and blanket dry or to preserve a single bird. Saw Pelicans of one species, but could not obtain any. (I believe it to be the same as one I killed in the Galapagos.) ...

On my return I visited Cockqua, the principal chief of the Chenooks and Chochalii tribes, who is exceedingly fond of all the chiefs that come from King George.

It was during his stay with Cockqua and the Chinook (or 'Chenook', as Douglas refers to them) that Douglas performed one of his 'party tricks' to impress his native audience. He describes the episode in his journal.

He [Cockqua] was at war with the Cladsap tribe, inhabitants of the opposite bank of the river, and that night expected an attack (which was not made). He pressed me hard to sleep in his lodge lest anything should befall me: this offer I would have most gladly accepted, but as fear should never be known I slept in my tent fifty yards from the village. In the evening about 300 men danced the war dance and sang several death songs. ... In the morning he said I was a great chief, for I was not afraid of the Cladsaps. One of his men, with not a little self-consequence, showed me his skill with the bow and arrow, and then with the gun. He passed arrows through a small hoop of grass 6 inches in diameter, thrown in the air a considerable height by another person; with his rifle he placed a ball within an inch of the mark at a distance of 110 yards. He said no chief from King George could shoot like him, neither could they sing the death song nor dance the war dance. Of shooting on the wing they have no idea. A large species of eagle, *Falco leococephela*, was perched on a dead stump close to the village; I charged my gun with swan shot, walked up to within 45 yards of the bird, threw a stone to raise him, and when flying brought him down. This had the desired effect: many of them placed their right hands on their mouths – the token for astonishment or dread. This fellow still had a little confidence in his abilities and offered me a shot at his hat; he threw it up and I carried the whole of the crown away leaving only the brim. Great value was then laid on my gun and high offers made. My fame sounded through the camp. Cockqua said 'Cladsap cannot shoot like you.' I find it to be of the utmost value to bring down a bird when going near lodges, at the same time taking care to make it appear as a little thing and as if you were not observed.

Throughout the rest of the summer, Douglas carried on collecting, making occasional trips, including travelling up the Multnomah, and organizing his collections for eventual transport back to England. He noted the scarcity of beaver. This was probably the outcome of the Hudson's Bay Company's policy of eliminating beaver in order to discourage American hunters from moving into the territory. During this time he came across the

> seeds of a remarkable large pine which they [the natives] eat as nuts, and from whom I learned it existed in the mountains to the south. No time was lost in ascertaining the existence of this truly grand tree, which I named *Pinus Lambertiana*, but no perfect seeds could I find.

The sugar pine fascinated him at this first encounter. Its discovery was to become almost an obsession.

Occasional incidents reveal a lighter side to the serious business of plant-collecting. Coming across a small plantation of native tobacco, Douglas helped himself to seeds and specimens without hesitating. Assailed by the owner, who took exception to the unauthorized removal of his property, the intrepid plant-hunter had to part with two finger-lengths of tobacco to assuage the outraged native. A further finger-length elicited a detailed description of how to cultivate it.

Returning from the Multnomah at the end of August, Douglas set out to return up the Columbia.

> Thursday, September 1st – Employed drying, arranging, putting up seeds, and making up my notes. Early on Thursday went on a journey to the Grand Rapids to collect seeds of several plants seen in flower in June and July. Went up in a canoe accompanied by one Canadian and a chief (called Chumtalia) of the tribe inhabiting the north banks of the river at the Rapids. I arrived on the evening of the second day and pitched my tent a short distance from the village.
>
> I caused my Canadian to drench the ground well with water to prevent me from being annoyed with fleas, although I was not altogether exempt from them, yet it had a good effect. I found my Indian friend during my stay very attentive and I received no harm or insult. He accompanied me on some of my journeys. (They were only a few years since very hostile. The Company's boats were frequently pillaged by them and some of their people killed.) My visit was the first ever made without a

guard. On Saturday morning went on a journey to the summit of the mountain near the Rapids on the north of the river, with the chief's brother as my guide, leaving the Canadian to take care of the tent and property. This took three days, and was one the most laborious undertakings I ever experienced, the way was so much over dead wood, detached rocks, rivulets, &c., that very little personal effects could be carried. Indeed I was obliged to leave my blanket at my first encampment.

My provision was 3 oz. tea, 1 lb. sugar, and four small biscuits. The next day I caught no fish, and at such a great altitude the only birds to be seen were hawks, eagles, vultures, &c. I was fortunate enough to kill one young white-headed eagle, which (then) I found very good eating. I roasted it, having only a small pan for making tea. On the summit of the hill I slept one night. I made a small fire of grass and twigs and dried my clothes which were wet with perspiration and then laid myself down on the grass with my feet to the fire. I found it very cold and had to rise four times and walk to keep myself warm, fortunately it was dry and a keen north wind prevented dew.

On Monday evening at dusk I reached my tent at the village much fatigued and weak and found all things going on smoothly. Made a trip to the opposite side two days after, also to the summit of the hills, which I found of easier ascent, the only steep part near the top. My food during my stay was fresh salmon, without salt, pepper, or any other spice, with a very little biscuit and tea, which is a great luxury after a day's march. ...

Last night my Indian friend Cockqua arrived here from his tribe on the coast and brought me three of the hats made in the English fashion, which I ordered when there in July; the fourth, which will have some initials wrought in it, is not finished, but will be sent by the other ship. I think them a good specimen of the ingenuity of the natives and particularly also being made by the little girl, twelve years old, spoken of when at the village. I paid one blanket (value 7s.) for them, the fourth included.

We smoked; I gave him a dram and a few needles, heads, pins, and rings as a present for the little girl. Faithful to his proposition he brought me a large paper of seeds of *Vaccinium ovatum* [evergreen huckleberry] in a perfect state, which I showed him when there, then in an unripe state. I have circulated notices among my Indian acquaintances to obtain it for me.

It was during this trip that Douglas first came across two of the remarkable conifers he subsequently introduced to Europe. He was climbing in the mountains to the north side of the river from Fort Vancouver when he 'had the good fortune to find two new species of pines, *Pinus Nobilis* [noble fir] and *P. Amabilis* [lovely fir], two of the noblest species of the tribe'. On 13 September, he returned to Fort Vancouver, where he met his friend Scouler again. It was now important to ensure that his collections of seeds and specimens were properly transported back to England.

> The remainder of this month was devoted to packing up my gleanings of dried plants, consisting of sixteen large bundles of American [specimens] and eight from other places, a large chest of seeds, one of birds and quadrupeds, and one of various articles of dress &c. A portion of each of the varieties of seeds was reserved for the purpose of sending across the continent in the ensuing spring.

Such meticulous attention to detail in looking after his collections contributed in no small measure to Douglas' plant-collecting success. Sending materials home halfway round the world was not easy. Douglas hedged his bets. Not only did he send back seed on the Hudson's Bay Company ships, he also used ships going on other trade routes, via Hawaii for instance. In addition, he kept some material with him to care for personally. His intention on this occasion was to load his collections on *William and Ann*, which was lying at Fort George (present-day Astoria) for the return voyage to England and the Society. He also had letters he wished to go on board, keeping his various contacts informed of his activities. The recipients included Joseph Sabine, Dr Hooker, Mr Murray at the Botanic Gardens in Glasgow, Archibald Menzies, no doubt eager to hear of his old stomping-ground, and his brother John.

During this packing, Douglas injured his knee quite badly by falling on a rusty nail. For the next three weeks, until 22 October, he was unable to travel with his collection, which went on without him, with instructions to the ship's captain about its treatment. Douglas was eager to reach the ship before it sailed. On recovering, he rushed down the river, only to find that it had departed an hour earlier.

As he was at the mouth of the Columbia, Douglas now journeyed along the coast in his normal pursuit of plants and specimens. For this purpose he had the services of local native guides from the Chinook tribe. His notes for 24 October continue:

In the evening I returned to the lodge of Madsue or Thunder, one of the Chenook chiefs, where I found his brother Tha-a-muxi, or the Bear, a chief from Whitbey Harbour. As he was then going to his home he offered to accompany me, to which I agreed. On Tuesday the 25th Coni Comly or Madsue ferried us across the Bay. Our canoe being small, and as I found his so much more commodious, I negotiated with him to lend it to me, which he did in Baker's Bay at the entrance of Knight's River.

In the evening I gave the two chiefs a dram of well-watered rum, which pernicious liquor they will make any sacrifice to obtain. I found an exception in my guide Tha-a-muxi; he would not taste any. I inquired the reason, when he informed me with much merriment that some years since he got drunk and became very quarrelsome in his village; so much so that the young men had to bind his hands and feet which he looked on as a great affront. He has not tasted any since.

Douglas was able to observe at close range the appalling impact alcohol had on native society in the remote regions of North America. Rum became the major trading currency, and vast quantities were bartered for furs. While Douglas was exploring, the Hudson's Bay Company rolled some fifty thousand gallons of strong rum and brandy overland – a staggering quantity, which, when diluted, made up at least a quarter of a million gallons for a native population of some one hundred and twenty thousand. This pernicious trade led to mass addiction and the destruction of families, communities and the indigenous way of life. Many employees of the Hudson's Bay Company in North America pleaded with their high command in London to cease trading in rum, but went unheard. In his book, *The Owners of Eden*, the historian Robert MacDonald observed that the native American

had never before tasted alcohol. He had no customs of social or convivial drinking. But he did have beliefs and rituals which required hallucinogenic experiences, such as visions. Here, suddenly, was a surprising and powerful intoxicant. Never was it represented to him as something to be used just in moderation.

Later, firearms were also used as barter, and these proved quite as destructive as alcohol. Douglas was travelling at a time when guns were just reaching the North West, and found that his shooting skills – as demonstrated to the Chinook Chief Cockqua – earned him instant respect and status.

Douglas proceeded up the coast north from the mouth of the Columbia. He remained in the area until 15 November, although the constant rain and foul weather meant that his stay was not particularly happy. Although he saw and collected new plants, he 'experienced more fatigue and misery, and gleaned less than in any trip I have had in the country'. His own account outlines the misery in a matter-of-fact way:

> The following day we made a short portage over the bite or neck of Cape Disappointment. ... The rain fell in torrents without intermission all day. ... The wind about midnight increased to a hurricane with sleet and hail, and twice we were obliged to shift our camp, the sea rising so unusually high. ... Long ere daylight we were ready to leave Cape Foulweather, which name it truly deserves, and we walked along a sandy beach to Whitbey Harbour, where we found the village deserted. ... We remained here several days ... and from continual exposure to the wind and cold and want of proper sustenance I became greatly reduced.

Douglas returned to the Fort on 15 November, having travelled up to Gray's Harbour on the coast and then inland on the Chehalis and Cowlitz Rivers back to the Columbia. On the 18th, Douglas saw the eagerly anticipated 'Hudson's Bay Express' arrive at Fort Vancouver. This was the Fort's main overland communication with the Company's headquarters. For those isolated to the west of the Rockies, the arrival of the Express was an important occasion, for it brought provisions, trading goods, letters and news. The Express travelled mainly by water along the rivers and lakes, interrupted by the constant 'portages', or foot journeys to bypass rapids, negotiate mountain passes and overcome other gaps in the navigable waterways. Such portages required prodigious feats of strength on the part of the voyageurs, who carried huge bundles on their backs in addition to the vital canoes. In spring 1827, Douglas himself travelled home with the Express.

Mr McLeod, who was in charge of the Express, told Douglas that he had met Captain John Franklin at Cumberland Bay on Hudson Bay. Franklin's expedition was heading north for the Arctic Circle. One of its number was Thomas Drummond, another enterprising Scottish explorer and botanist, who eventually struck out on his own, as Franklin's far-north travels offered little opportunity for botanizing. Drummond, who had run a plant business in Forfar, had spent his first winter in Canada alone and a year later had travelled overland to

Carlton House in central Canada, one of the stops on the Express'
route.

The period between mid-November and Christmas was one of
recuperation and consolidation. The season for botanizing was past,
much to Douglas' regret, though he continued to hunt for bird and
animal specimens. The end of the year encouraged a contemplative if
melancholy mood, perhaps not surprising given the tasks confronting
him. On New Year's Day 1826, he wrote in his journal:

> Commencing a year in such a far removed corner of the earth,
> where I am nearly destitute of civilised society, there is some
> scope for reflection. In 1824 I was on the Atlantic on my way to
> England; 1825, between the island[s] of Juan Fernandez and the
> Galapagos in the Pacific; I am now here, and God only knows
> where I may be the next. In all probability, if a change does not
> take place, I will shortly be consigned to the tomb. I can die
> satisfied with myself. I have never given cause for remonstrance
> or pain to an individual on earth. I am in my twenty-seventh
> year.

Chapter Six

BOTANIZING IN THE
BLUE MOUNTAINS

'As McLeod was putting his hand on one of their shoulders to push
him back, a fellow immediately pulled from his quiver a bow and a
handful of arrows, and presented it at Mr McLeod. As I was
standing outside of the crowd I perceived it, and, as no time was to
be lost, I instantly slipped the cover off my gun, which at the time
was charged with buckshot, and presented it at him, and invited him
to fire his arrow, and then I should certainly shoot him.'
Douglas' journal, 24 March 1826

Douglas started 1826 in melancholy mood. The period from the
beginning of January until March was spent mainly in collecting bird and animal specimens and in preparing for the coming
season's expeditions. In addition, he still needed to recover from his
plant-collecting exertions after his arrival on the Columbia.

Douglas' robust constitution and general good health had
declined. As well as being laid low the previous autumn, when he had
fallen on a rusty nail and punctured his knee, he was generally
exhausted by his endeavours. His knees remained painful – no doubt
the damp, cold conditions in which he habitually botanized were
contributing to the onset of either arthritis or rheumatism. The brilliant sun and the blindingly white snow of the Columbia basin were
also causing his eyesight to deteriorate. This was a serious matter.
Accurate shooting was an essential skill for a plant-collector, and
sometimes a matter of survival in a wild environment – his life might
depend on his prowess with a gun when threatened by aggressive bears
or native Americans. He used his gun to shoot animals for food or
scientific investigation, and also to dislodge cones from trees that were

too high for him to climb. He was inordinately proud of his accuracy, and noted in his diary the occasion when he shot five ducks with a single bullet.

The companionship Douglas had enjoyed with John Scouler had also come to an end, for Scouler had sailed home in October on *William and Ann*; Douglas had just missed bidding him farewell. He was thousands of miles from home, had few kindred spirits, and also faced the added uncertainty of his employer's reaction should he decide to delay his return.

And it was raining. His little bark hut had flooded, and only the kindness of John McLoughlin, the Hudson's Bay Company's chief factor, appears to have given him comfort.

Apart from hunters and traders, Douglas was the first guest at Fort Vancouver. He must have been out of sympathy with the Company's employees, who in the main were rough and solitary trappers, given to wild excesses of heavy drinking whenever they returned to a fort. Most of the Company's forts, which were positioned close to the main trading routes all over Canada, were little more than small, rough log houses with a palisade for protection. They were built to provide a collection-point for the trappers, and abandoned once they became obsolete. Unlike the forts erected further south in the United States, which accommodated large companies of soldiers to protect travellers on routes such as the Oregon Trail, most Hudson's Bay forts housed only a factor and his assistant. By the 1820s, however, Fort Vancouver was becoming more established and life there was rather more civilized.

Douglas had arrived in the Pacific North West in the very month when Fort Vancouver was sufficiently complete for the Company to move its headquarters upriver from Fort Astoria, which was close to the mouth of the Columbia. Fort Vancouver was an oasis of civilization in a rugged country. It was run on hierarchical, almost military, lines, but the way of life was well ordered and comfortable. Thousands of miles from its nearest comparable neighbour, the Fort housed in various wooden dwellings many of the trappings of self-sufficiency. Carpenters, gardeners, cooks, coopers and all the important shops were in separate buildings, with the factor's residence in a commanding position in the centre of the compound. In this big house, occupied by Mr McLoughlin, dinner was served to men freshly arrived from months of hard living in the hinterland who were expected to transform themselves from leather-clad ruffians with months of unkempt hair into the smart, well-dressed representatives of a trading company with high expectations. The candlelit conversation was of a high order, for many of the Company's employees were highly educated men. Reminders of far-off Britain were much in evidence. The painting of a cricket match at Lord's ground in London that hung in the dining-room at Fort Langley, built in 1827 on the Fraser River, must have puzzled those who had neither observed the game nor travelled across the Atlantic, even though all the gentlemen players wore beaver-skin hats.

The Hudson's Bay Company had been founded to exploit the beaver trade in Canada. Its policy was not to encourage settlers but to leave the land clear and undisturbed – a vast and empty commercial empire based on the fur trade. Thus Douglas was a rarity, since he did not wish to exploit the land – after all, no one would miss a few seeds. The local natives named him the 'Grass Man'. Puzzled at first by his interest in such mundane things as plants and trees, they came to look on him as a harmless, if strange, visitor.

Following a miserable Christmas – Douglas' injured knee forced him to miss horse-riding – the weather improved. He gathered and studied mosses, and sorted out his collection of preserved animal skins and his samples of wood and seeds. After six consecutive nights of patient watching and waiting, he shot an owl. He saw hawks and small eagles, ducks and geese and a buzzard, and observed ground rats, rabbits, hares, elk and deer. On one red-letter day, he caught and killed a lynx with the aid of a small bull-terrier dog.

On 20 February, Douglas' fascination with the sugar pine was revived.

Jean Baptist McKay, one of the hunters, returned to the establishment from his hunting excursion on the Multnomah; he brought me one cone of a species of *Pinus* which I requested of him last August when there. – The first thing that gave me any knowledge of it, was the very large seeds and scales of the cones which I saw in an Indian's shot-pouch; after treating him to a smoke, which must be done before any questions are put, I enquired and found it grew a little to the south on the mountains. As McKay was going in that direction I asked him to bring me twelve cones, a few twigs, and a small bag of seeds and some of the gum. He informed me that the seed was all gone before he went in the autumn, and he only brought one cone to show me. The cone measures 16 inches long and 10 inches round at the thickest part. The pine is found on the mountains two degrees south of the Columbia in the country occupied by the Umptqua tribe of Indians. He is in a few days to start for the same quarter and as he has left orders with some of the Indians to collect seed cones and twigs, I am certain of obtaining it. ... The trees, 20 to 50 feet in circumference and 170 to 220 feet high, are almost destitute of branches till within a short distance of the top which, forms a perfect umbel. ...

As I have offered McKay a reasonable compensation to bring it to me, lest it may be impossible for me to visit that quarter myself, I am pretty certain of gaining more information of this very desirable tree.

By this time, Douglas was facing yet another dilemma. He had to decide between returning to England or prolonging his explorations. The instructions the Society had given him before he left England had been explicit. He was to return home in 1826, either on board the Hudson's Bay Company boat or by joining the annual Hudson's Bay Express, the overland expedition to York Factory on Hudson Bay. This was due to leave Fort Vancouver in March, and would take four months to travel the two thousand or so miles across the continent. There was no way he could consult his employers – indeed, any letter informing the Society of his decision would be unlikely to reach London much before he was due home.

In the end, Douglas decided to stay. He felt that he still had much to do, and was eager to collect more species. He required no more than a few paragraphs of his journal to convince himself and, he hoped, his masters at the Horticultural Society.

From what I have seen in the country, and what I have been enabled to do, there is still much to be done; after a careful consideration as to the propriety of remaining for a season longer than instructed to do, I resolved not to leave for another year to come.

From what I have seen myself of the upper country towards the head-waters of this river and the boundless track contiguous to the Rocky Mountains, I cannot in justice to the Society's interest do otherwise. However, I am uncertain how far I may be justified in so doing. If the motive which induces me to make this arrangement should not be approved of, I beg at least be pardoned. In doing so, two considerations presented themselves: first, as I am incurring very little expense; second, being laid up an invalid last autumn during my seed harvest, I lost doubtless many interesting things which I would have otherwise had.

Lest the former should be made any objection to, most cheerfully will I labour for this year without any remuneration,

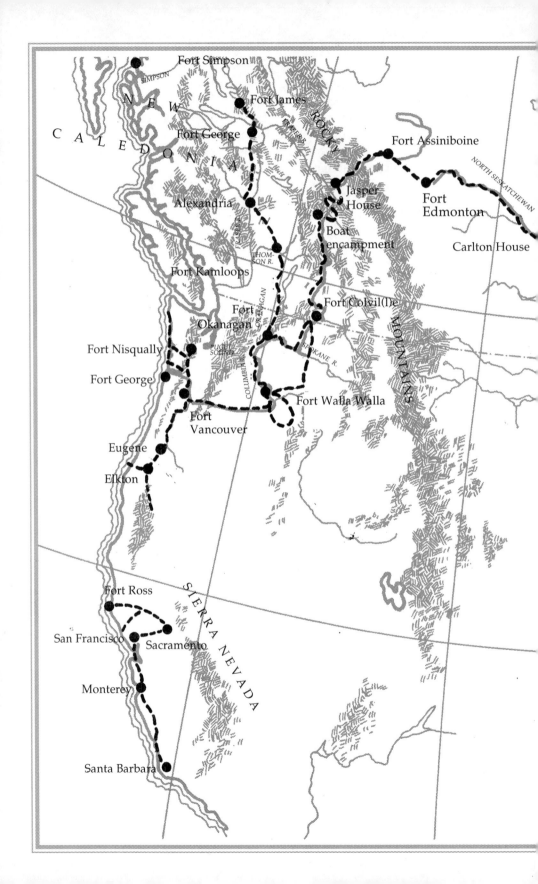

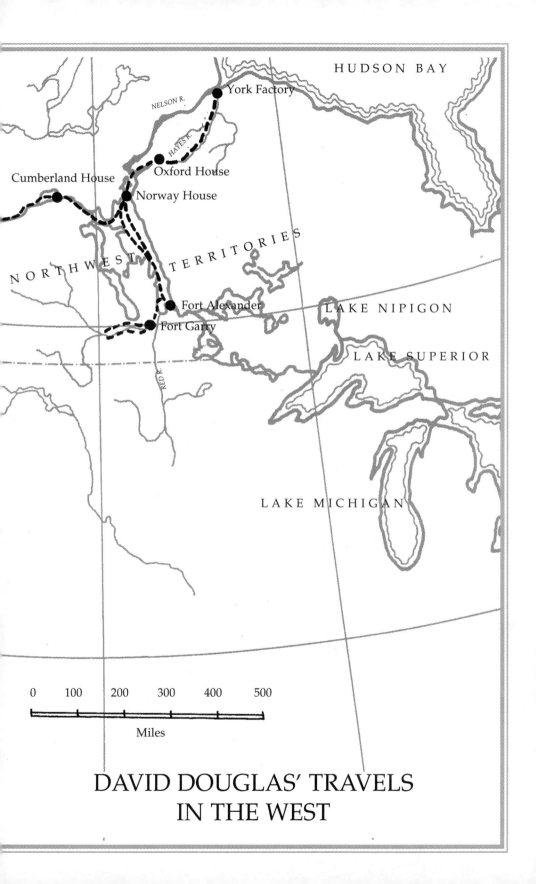

HUDSON BAY

NELSON R.

York Factory

HAYES R.

Oxford House

Cumberland House

Norway House

N O R T H W E S T   T E R R I T O R I E S

LAKE NIPIGON

Fort Alexander

Fort Garry

LAKE SUPERIOR

RED R.

LAKE MICHIGAN

| 0 | 100 | 200 | 300 | 400 | 500 |

Miles

DAVID DOUGLAS' TRAVELS
IN THE WEST

if I get only wherewith to purchase a little clothing. I could have crossed the continent this season to Montreal, and most gladly would I have availed myself of such an opportunity but could never for a moment forget myself so far as to pass over unnoticed a country deserving the strictest research. Lest it should be impossible for me to cross in the spring of 1827, I shall without loss of time embrace the first opportunity of reaching London by sea after that period.

That, however, I should be sorry to do, as so much time is lost, and as George Simpson, Esq., the Governor of the Western District, will be on the Columbia early in September, most likely I shall not lie under the disagreeable necessity of undertaking such a long voyage.

My headquarters will be either at Wallawallah the lowest, Spokane the middle, or Kettle Falls the highest, establishment on the Columbia, and its branches as may appear most interesting; I shall make such stays at each of the establishments as shall appear necessary, and as the extreme distance does not exceed more than 800 miles, frequent journeys can be made to and from each in the course of the season – I shall probably reach the Rocky Mountains in August.

In all probability a vessel will soon arrive in the river, in which it is expected I will return, but as I shall not be on the coast till November, if then, I will pack the whole of my collection up to this time, to be transmitted in her to England; also send my package of seeds which I intended to carry across myself to Hudson's Bay to the care of J.G. McTavish, and make extracts of my Journal, although at this season it can be of but little interest to the Society.

Having set out his reasons, Douglas made ready. Meanwhile he packed 197 different seed samples in a tin box for the next vessel to make the long sea voyage home. For safety's sake, he also put together a duplicate set to travel overland to Hudson Bay and thence home by sea. Now he gathered the essential items for his first major expedition of the year up the Columbia, a trip that he had long planned. He decided, as 'an enormous indulgence', to carry thirty quires of paper weighing 102 pounds for preserving specimens and seeds, but economized on his clothing, restricting himself to 'two shirts, two handkerchiefs, blanket and cloak and one pair of shoes but no stockings'.

Douglas' plan was to remain in the Columbia region but to accompany the Express as it travelled upriver from Fort Vancouver, leaving it when he reached his next plant-hunting destination.

On the afternoon of Monday, the 20th, (March) at four o'clock, I left Fort Vancouver in company with John McLeod, Esq., a gentleman going across to Hudson's Bay, and Mr Francis Ermatinger, for the interior, with two boats and fourteen men.

Also on board the two boats were supplies for the new Fort Colville at Kettle Falls and three calves and three pigs, the first livestock ever to be imported into the interior. At The Dalles portage, 70 miles upriver, where the party had to walk heavily loaded overland, they found themselves in a threatening situation. Douglas, forcing himself to stay awake and watchful during the night, described what happened in his journal and also in a letter to Hooker.

Friday, 24th – After a tedious night, daybreak was to me particularly gratifying, as might be well guessed, being surrounded by at least 460 savages who, judging from appearances, were everything but amicable. As no one in the brigade could converse with them better than myself, little could be done by persuasion. However, finding two of the principal men who understood the Chenook tongue, with which I am partially acquainted, the little I had I found on this occasion very useful. Took a little breakfast on the rocks at The Dalles, four miles below. The day was very pleasant, with a clear sky. – At five in the evening we made the portage over the Falls where we found the Indians very troublesome. I learned from Mr McLeod they had collected for the purpose of pillaging the boats, which we soon found to be the case.

After they had the usual presents of tobacco, they became desirous of our camping there for the night, no doubt expecting to effect their purpose. The first thing that was observed was their cunningly throwing water on the gun locks, and then on the boats being ordered to be put in the water they refused to allow them.

As McLeod was putting his hand on one of their shoulders to push him back, a fellow immediately pulled from his quiver a bow and a handful of arrows, and presented it at Mr McLeod. As I was standing on the outside of the crowd I perceived it, and, as no time was to be lost, I instantly slipped the cover off my gun, which at the time was charged with buckshot, and presented it at him, and invited him to fire his arrow, and then I should certainly shoot him.

Just at this time a chief of the Kyeuuse and three of his young men, who are the terror of all other tribes west of the mountains and great friends of the white people, stepped in and settled the matter in a few words without any further trouble.

This very friendly Indian, who is the finest figure of a man that I have seen, standing nearly 6 feet 6 inches high, accompanied us a few miles up the river, where we camped for the night, after being remunerated by Mr McLeod for his friendship – I being King George's Chief or the Grass Man, as I am called. I bored a hole in the only shilling I had, one which has been in my pocket since I left London, and, the septum of his nose being perforated, I suspended it to it with a brass wire. This was to him the great seal of friendship. – After smoking, he returned to the Indian village and promised that he would not allow us to be molested. – Of course no sleep was had this night, and to keep myself awake I wrote a letter to Dr Hooker. Heavy rain during the night.

The following day, at daylight we resumed our route; sleet and rain, with a keen north wind. – Being almost benumbed with cold, I preferred walking along the banks of the river, my path in many places was very rugged.

While the boats were paddled upstream or 'lined' (pulled by ropes from the shore), Douglas remained on the bank, struggling through the undergrowth in his search for plants. When he found *Artemesia*, a wild sagebrush, he quartered the ground and discovered no fewer than sixteen varieties. All were recorded in his journal, together with other herbs, animals, rocks and birds – Douglas had long since moved on from his original interest in plants and had become an all-round naturalist and observer. The party rested for a few days at Fort Okanagan, but this was not a productive time for Douglas, as the snow, even in early April, was too deep for botanizing. Then, on 10 April, in warm and pleasant weather:

Arrived at the junction of the Spokane River with the Columbia at sunset, where we found John Warren Dease, Esq., commandant in the interior, and a party of fourteen men, on their way to the Kettle Falls, ninety miles further up the Columbia. This gentleman received me with extreme kindness and had every attention that could add to my comfort. This is a brother of the gentleman now accompanying Captain Franklin on his two journeys to the Polar Sea. Mr Dease, to whom I was made known through general notice sent by that agreeable gentleman Mr McLoughlin, at Fort Vancouver, gave me greater hopes than ever of making a rich harvest.

Now the main contingent left on the long overland journey to Hudson Bay, carrying with them the essential letters from the forts that they had visited as well as Douglas' seeds. That particular expedition, led by McLeod, suffered much hardship because of the ferociously hard winter – at up to 30 feet, the snow was much deeper than usual – and McLeod was forced to slice up his leather trousers to make replacement shoes. But they kept the seeds safe, which when they reached London were unpacked to universal acclaim and interest.

Douglas found the landscape 'by far the most beautiful that I have seen'. Dease, the Company's chief trader at Fort Colville, which covered much of the interior, invited him to join his party to Kettle Falls and Fort Colville, 90 miles upstream. Douglas accepted with alacrity. On the way they crossed immense rapids. Although well known to trappers, they had not as yet been named – so in a grand gesture Douglas named them on the spot after David Thompson, an intrepid explorer who was the first European to descend the river from its source to the ocean.

Douglas was concerned about the condition of his precious gun, which the previous year had been exposed to torrents, lashing rain and baking heat. On learning that an able craftsman and gunsmith, a French Canadian called Jacques Rafael Finlay, lived only 100 miles to the south-east, he decided to go in search of him. Finlay had lived in the area longer than any of the trappers, so Douglas also hoped to tap him for any useful local information, presumably about opportunities for plant-collecting. Dease lent Douglas three horses, and also arranged for two local guides to accompany him.

Few journeys into the interior were dull, and this was no exception.

Wednesday, [May] 10th – Rose at daylight and had my horses saddled, and being desirous of making the most of my time I took no breakfast further than a little dried meat and a drink of water, and proceeded on my journey at five o'clock. At twelve noon reached a small rapid river called Barriere River by my guides, which took up an hour in crossing.

As there were no Indians near the place, we had to choose either making a raft or to swim. As the latter was the easier method, and all of us good water-men, we unsaddled the horses and drove them in. They all went over well except the last, which entangled itself by the hind legs among some brushwood and struggled much for a considerable time; fortunately the wood gave way and I reached the shore much better than I had any reason to expect. I made two trips on my back, one with my paper and pen, the other with my blanket and clothes – holding my property above water in my hands. My guides made three trips each with saddles and provisions. ...

Thursday, 11th – Reached the old establishment at Spokane at eleven o'clock, where I was very kindly received by Mr Finlay. He regretted exceedingly that he had not a single morsel of food to offer me.

He and his family were living for the last six weeks on the roots of *Phalangiumn Quamash* (called by the natives all over the country *Camass*) and a species of black lichen which grows on the pines. ...

By the kindness of Mr Dease, I had ample provisions for fourteen days, with a good stock of game in the saddle-bags which I killed on my way, and this enabled me to share the half of my stock with him; such fare as I had, although very palatable, cannot be considered fine living, but was to him the best meal he had enjoyed for some time. As the principal object of my journey was to get my firelock arranged by him, being the only person within the space of eight hundred miles who could do it, and being an item of the utmost consequence to have done soon, I lost no time in informing him of my request.

Unfortunately he did not speak the English language, and my very partial knowledge of French prevented me from obtaining information which I wished to acquire. – I returned at dusk, when I found he had obligingly put my gun in good order, for which I presented him with a pound of tobacco, being the only thing I had to give.

As I thought of bending my steps again towards the Columbia, Mr Finlay offered that one of his sons should escort me, which I accepted. Before parting with him I made inquiry about a sort of sheep found in this neighbourhood, about the same size as that described by Lewis and Clarke, but instead of wool it has short thick coarse hair of a brownish-grey, from which it gets the name of *Mouton Gris* of the voyagers.

Close to the old establishment an Indian burying-ground is to be seen, certainly one of the most curious spectacles I have seen in the country. All the property of the dead, consisting of war implements, garments, gambling articles, in fact everything. Even the favourite horse of the departed is shot with his bow and arrow, and his skin with the hoofs and skull hung over the remains of deceased owner. On trees around the ground small bundles are to be seen tied up in the same manner as they tie provisions when travelling. I could not learn if this was as food or as a sacrifice to some of their deities.

The body is placed in the grave in a sitting position, with the knees touching the chin and the arms folded across the chest. It is very difficult to get any information on this point, for nothing seems to hurt their feelings more than even mentioning the name of a departed friend.

Douglas had travelled a considerable distance up the Columbia. From Fort Vancouver he had voyaged to the Dalles, then on to the Great Falls and from there to the junction with Spokane River, a total of 532 miles along the course of the river as it turns north, sneaking towards its source in the Rockies. Kettle Falls lay a further 90 miles upriver.

Having been soaked to the skin several times, Douglas was struck down by a fever on returning to Fort Colville. He dosed himself with Dover powder, a compound of opium and potassium sulphate, and Epsom salts, a popular remedy at the time, and slept the fever off in a couple of days. While waiting to descend the Columbia to Fort Walla Walla, where he intended to stay for six or eight weeks, Douglas collected another large selection of specimens and seeds. One of his new finds he named *Penstemon scouleri*, after his friend John Scouler. A few days after the party left on 5 June, an Indian messenger carrying mail from a ship newly arrived from England caught up with them. Douglas was desperate for a letter from the Society, or at least from Hooker, and was very downcast when he found that McLoughlin had thought it too risky to entrust letters from London to a native messenger.

Having had little sleep for the last five nights, I felt somewhat fatigued. I went to bed earlier than usual, and shortly after dusk an Indian arrived from Fort Vancouver with news of the arrival of a ship in the river, and brought me letters and a small parcel of newspapers. ...

Never in my life did I feel in such a state; an uneasy, melancholy, but pleasing sensation stole on my mind, with an inordinate longing for the remaining part, and although I did not hear directly from my friends, I now for once in my life enjoy and relish the luxury of hearing from England. I had letters from all my kind friends on the coast, full of expressive hopes that my labours might be amply rewarded. It is a circumstance worthy of notice that I should write to England in the

morning and receive letters on the same day, for in this un-
inhabited distant land the post calls but seldom. The express for
the Coast with my letters had only left me six hours when the
Indian arrived.

He eventually received his letters when he reached Fort Walla
Walla on 8 June, where he spent a sleepless night reading and re-
reading them. There he met Francis Ermatinger once again and also
his namesake, James Douglas. Ermatinger, who later became
Treasurer of the Provisional Government of Oregon, had been his
companion on the journey up the Columbia a few months previously.
James Douglas was an altogether more colourful character, and
shared David Douglas' Scottish roots. His Glaswegian father owned a
sugar plantation in Demerara; his mother was the daughter of a freed
slave. James was educated in Scotland and later in England; perhaps
his isolated adolescence in a strange country, where his skin colour
clearly identified his mixed-race parentage, gave him his formidable
strength of character. At any rate, at the age of seventeen he was out
in the west of Canada, where he married the half-native daughter of a
Hudson's Bay Company factor. Ultimately he became Governor of
Vancouver Island and British Columbia, winning a reputation for
forging excellent relationships with native tribes. David Douglas too
was about to learn much about the delicate and time-consuming art of
dealing with the native inhabitants.

Douglas was now impatient to set off for the Blue Mountains, an
evocatively named ridge south and east of Walla Walla. Until his
eventual return to Fort Vancouver at the end of August, Douglas
carried out a considerable amount of botanizing. From 20 June until
the end of the month, he travelled across the Blue Mountains, then
returning to the junction of the Snake River and the Columbia,
where he remained until 8 July. The essential negotiations with a guide
delayed his departure.

> Saturday, June 17th – My guide did not arrive from the camp
> until 8 A.M. and as I was uncertain if he would come that day,
> the horses were not brought in from the meadow, nor my provi-
> sions put up. Considerable time was taken up explaining to him
> the nature of my journey, which was done in the following way:
> I told Mr Black [Chief Trader at Fort Walla Walla] in English
> my intended route, who translated it to his Canadian inter-
> preter, and this person communicated it to the Indian in the
> Kyuuse language, to which tribe he belongs.
>   As a proof of the fickle disposition and keenness of bargain

making in these people, he made without delay strict inquiry what he should get for his trouble. This being soon settled, then came the smaller list of present wants, beginning, as his family had been starving for the last two months, and he going just at the commencement of the salmon season, by asking Mr Black to allow them something to eat should they call, which was promised.

Afterwards a pair of shoes, and, as his leggings were much worn, leather to make new ones was necessary; a scalping knife, a small piece of tobacco, and a strip of red coarse cloth to make an ornamental cap. This occupied two hours and was sealed by volumes of smoke from a large stone pipe. Mr B kindly offered to send a boy twelve years of age, the son of the interpreter, who speaks the language fluently, with me, which I gladly accepted. As he spoke a little French, I would be the better able to make known my wants to my guide. I had provided for me three excellent horses for carrying my paper, blanket, and provisions, which was equally divided, and as I choose to walk except on bad places of the road or crossing the creeks, I placed a little more on my horse.

For food, Douglas took a supply of pemmican, a little biscuit, sugar and, most important of all, tea. Tobacco he might use for exchange and barter, game he might shoot and give away, items of clothing he would gladly exchange for a guide or much sought-after seeds, but tea he never traded.

Pemmican was the essential all-purpose food for everyone, from the lowliest trapper, canoeman and traveller to the factor himself. Resembling dried animal food, it was concocted from dried buffalo meat, pounded and pulverized, melted tallow or animal fat, and dried berries from one of the many varieties of the *Vaccinum* family – tart and prolific little berries packed with vitamin C. The proportions were simple: one buffalo to 16 pounds of berries. The method was equally simple. The hide of the buffalo was sewn into a sack that would contain about 90 pounds. The hide was half-filled with pounded meat, and topped up with dried berries; the boiling fat was tipped in, the contents were stirred, and then the sack was sewn up and left to set. This basic food, carried across thousands of miles, and eaten raw, sliced up and fried, or made into thick soup, was said to last for ever, and certainly for two to three years. Some remembered it with affection, others were less sure.

By the third day of the journey, Douglas' guide had started to become awkward, while the weather had also changed for the worse.

Lacking adequate snowshoes, he found it difficult to climb in the deep snow.

> The further I went the more difficult I found my undertaking. At midday I made a short stop, where I passed the first snow and collected several plants. – Immediately after eating a little dried salmon and a mouthful of water from a chilly crystal spring, I continued my route until 4 P.M. –, where the horses were stopped by deep wreaths of eternal snow, about 1500 feet below the extreme height of the range. As my object was, if possible, to reach the low alluvial grounds on the opposite side, where I had great expectations, my disappointment may be imagined. In the meantime I selected my camp under a projecting rock, saw the horses hobbled, and as it appeared to me my guide seemed somewhat alarmed, I thought it prudent to give him a little time to cool or change his opinion. – Therefore I set out on foot with my gun and a small quantity of paper under my arm to gain the summit, leaving them to take care of the horses and camp.
>
> In the lower parts I found it exceedingly fatiguing walking on the soft snow, having no snowshoes, but on reaching within a few hundred feet of the top, where there was a hard crust of frost, I without the least difficulty placed my foot on the highest peak of those regions where never European was before me. The height must be great – 7000 to 7500 feet from the platform of the mountain, and on least calculation 9000 above the level of the sea. (Thermometer at 5 P.M., 26F Fahr.)

Despite Douglas' triumph at becoming the first white man to reach the summit – though of precisely which mountain remains unclear – it cannot have been much more than over 6200 feet (1900 metres), for this is the maximum height of the Blue Mountains.

> The view of the surrounding country is extensive and grand. I had not been there above three-quarters of an hour when the upper part of the mountain was suddenly enveloped in dense black cloud; then commenced a most dreadful storm of thunder, lightning, hail, and wind. I never beheld anything that could equal the lightning. Sometimes it would appear in massive sheets, as if the heavens were in a blaze; at others, in vivid zigzag flashes at short intervals with the thunder resounding through the valleys below, and before the echo of the former peal died away the succeeding was begun, so that it was impressed on my mind as if only one.

The wind was whistling through the low stunted dead pines accompanied by the merciless cutting hail. As my situation was not a desirable one for spending the night, and it was creeping on me, I hastily bent my steps to my camp below, which I providentially reached at eight o'clock, just in the twilight, the storm raging still without the least appearance of abating. The horses were so alarmed that I found it necessary to tie them to some trees close to the camp.

As no fire could be kept in, my supper was of the same quality as my breakfast; and as all my clothes were wet, and having nothing to change, I stripped and rolled myself in my blanket and went soundly to sleep shortly afterwards. Precisely at twelve I was so benumbed with cold that on endeavoring to get up I found my knees refused to do their office. I scoured them well with a rough towel, and as the storm was over made a cheering fire.

I could not resist the temptation of making a little tea, which I found restored me greatly (thermometer 26 degrees F). If I have any zeal, for once and the first time it began to cool.

Hung my clothes up to dry and lay down and slept until three o'clock.

Douglas found his native companions less than enthusiastic, and eventually discovered that 'the young rascally boy' had told the Indian the 'reverse of what I wished him to do'. Douglas contented himself with 'gleaning' for plants and specimens until he had found 'all that appeared peculiar to that district of the hills'.

Returning to the Fort, he immediately planned 'as soon as the plants are dry that are collected, to start for another eight days in a different direction'. The journey had not been a wasted one, for he had discovered a large yellow lupin, which reminded him of the 'bonnie broom' in his native Perthshire, as well as the first peony ever found in America, *Paeonia brownii*, which he named for Robert Brown, reputedly the greatest botanist of his day and the first Keeper of the Botanical Department of the British Museum. He also discovered the reputation he had won with the natives.

I learned that the Young Wasp, the interpreter's son, who accompanied me, had told [the native guide] I was a great medicine-man, which is always good as a newcomer, or being possessed of or conversant with evil, and had the power of doing great wonders; and should he go with me, and not do as I wanted, though very likely I did not kill him, he might die and

I would turn him into a grisly bear to run and live in the mountains, he should never see his wife again, which of course acted powerfully on him.

At the end of this expedition, Douglas was growing tired 'of this barren country which scarcely afforded food'. His health was also suffering; he was 'much worn down and suffering great pain from violent inflammation of the eyes. To read and write I cannot.' He now descended the river to the Great Falls, meeting one of the Hudson's Bay Company's boats travelling to the interior and carrying 'letters for me from England'. These were from Sabine and his brother, among others. Inevitably such correspondence was eagerly received:

There is a sensation felt on receiving news after such a long silence, and in such a remote corner of the globe more easily felt than described. I am not ashamed to say I rose from my mat four different times during the night to read my letters; in fact before morning I might say I had them by heart – my eyes never closed.

On 9 July, Douglas wrote to Mr Sabine of the Horticultural Society to give an account of his travels.

DEAR SIR, – This day last month I wrote you from this place, and at that time I stated how my time would be taken up during the summer. I have a few days ago arrived from a fatiguing journey on the Blue Mountains, spoken of in my last letter, and have been very successful. I have found on those alpine snowy regions a most beautiful species of *Paeonia, Lupinaster macrocephalus*, a splendid species of *Trifolium* equally fine, *Lupinus argenteus* of Pursh, and another species by far the finest of the tribe, not even excepting *L. nootkatensis*; has a spike a foot to 20 inches of full blossom of a deep golden-yellow; ... the plant 4 to 6 feet high.
    One species of *Pentstemon* different from any spoken of with an assemblage of smaller plants. I have been continually on my feet, scarcely three nights in one encampment.
    As I have accidentally met with a Mr McDonald on his return from a hunting excursion in the south and the same person I accompanied on a few days' march last August on the Multnomah River, he has kindly offered to take the result of my labours for the last month, which I willingly accept. The collection consists of ninety-seven distinct species, and one curious rat, which I hope you will receive safely.

A week later, Douglas departed for Blue Mountain country and Kettle Falls again, accompanying a party of Hudson's Bay men who were travelling up the Snake River to buy horses. The temperatures were so high that by noon the canoeists had to rest in the shade. Douglas compared the conditions with Arabia, although fresh water was available. Bathing, which they did at every stop, provided the only respite. Salmon and even pemmican were in short supply, and horse flesh was the staple diet. The journey took Douglas into new territory, and while the men argued with the horse-sellers for the best deals, a process that took days, Douglas went off with a French Canadian guide, 'Cock de Lard'. As they reached a mountain peak (most likely Craig Mountain, near Lewiston and just inside the present-day state of Idaho), even the adventure-jaded Douglas was stirred by an amazing sight. At the end of July he noted in his journal:

> Reached the highest peak ... on the top of which is a very remarkable spring, a circle of 11 feet in diameter, the water rising from 9 inches to 3 and a half feet above the surface, lowering and rising at intervals in sudden gushes, the stream that flows from it is 15 feet broad ... running with great force it disappears at the foot of a hill into a small marsh.

As the spring had no name, he christened it Munro's Fountain, after his old friend Donald Munro, a gardener at the Horticultural Society in far-distant London.

Rejoining the Hudson's Bay men, who had successfully bought 114 horses, they pressed on overland for 200 miles to Fort Colville on the Upper Columbia. Here Douglas discovered that a ship was due to leave from the Columbia River on 1 September. This was an ideal opportunity to send his seed and plant collection back to England, so he decided to make his way downriver with a guide as quickly as possible, especially since McLoughlin had suggested that this could be the last ship to sail to England for 'some years'. Douglas was therefore anxious to ensure that his collections, both those he had recently made and those he had left downriver, were safely despatched to his employers. His latest collections were extensive, for the area where he had botanized was a rich one, particularly in attractive flowering plants found in the alpine meadows and the drier, more open grasslands of the interior. Before leaving, however, he carefully packed up a duplicate set of material. This was to be transported from Fort Colville to Fort Edmonton, where Douglas planned to collect it when he joined the overland expedition to Hudson Bay in spring the next year.

John Dease had arranged for Little Wolf, chief of the Okanagan tribe, to act as Douglas' guide. A guide was essential for, as the river was dangerously swollen following exceptionally heavy rain, the first 200 miles were to be overland, and they would have to start the journey on horseback. But events delayed their departure.

17th August – A party of Cootanie Indians arrived, with whom and the Little Woolf's people an old grievance existed, when war was instantly declared by the Wolf. An old quarrel of nine years' standing existing between them and the tribes on the Columbia lakes [Little Wolf's people], sixty miles above this place, who are here at present at the salmon fishing at the Falls, gave Mr Dease and every other person much uneasiness. The parties met stark naked in our camp, painted, some red, black, white, and yellow, with their bows strung, and such as had muskets and ammunition were charged.

Warcaps of calumet-eagle feathers were the only particle of dress they had on. As one was in the act of letting the arrow from his bow, aiming at a chief of the other party, Mr Dease fortunately brought him a blow on the nose which stunned him. The arrow grazed the skin and passed along the rib opposite the heart without doing much injury. The whole day was spent in clamour and haranguing, and as we were not too sure what might be the result, we were prepared for the worst. Mr D proposed that they should make peace to-morrow, and that it would he much better they should go to each other's lands as friends than butchering each other like dogs. His advice they said they should follow; that they would come early in the morning. The Wolf, being the principals on one side, told me he cannot go to-morrow, as the peace is to be made, which could not be well done without his presence.

Following this dramatic confrontation, there was more uproar the following morning. Then, towards evening, peace was signed and sealed by an exchange of presents, and Douglas looked forward to starting his journey.

As there is to be a great feast for the occasion, the Wolf is un-certain when he can be spared from his office. As my time is very short, Mr D spoke to an Indian who is in the habit of attaching himself to the establishment and going on journeys with his people, to go with me – to which he agreed at once. So I will start tomorrow early.

Mr Dease gave me a pair of leather trousers made of deerskin and a few pairs of shoes, which in my present state were very acceptable. He provided me with three of his best horses, one for my guide, one for carrying my little articles, and one for myself.

The only thing in the way of clothing except what was on my back, was one shirt and one blanket, and in this shape I set out for Okanagan, distant 250 miles north-west of this place. It was my intention to have gone by water, but was dissuaded by Mr D, that part of the river at this season being high and from numerous cascades and rapids perhaps dangerous. Proceeded along the south banks of the Columbia, intending to cut the angle between the Columbia and Spokane Rivers. My path very mountainous and rugged, in many places covered with timber of the same sorts as are commonly seen abundantly over all the country. ...

August, Sunday 20th – Shortly after two o'clock I had my horses saddled, and, the ground being very uneven and stony, drove them before me; and the moon shining delightfully clear, I found it by far more pleasant travelling during the night than the day. Arrived on the Spokane River nine miles from the Columbia, where there was a large number of Indian lodges, being a fishing ground. After making a short stay and presenting them with a little tobacco, four of them accompanied me two miles further down the river, where they assisted me in crossing the horses and carried myself and all my property across in their canoe. At ten o'clock left the woody country and began my course through a trackless barren plain, not a vestige of green herbage to be seen, soil gravel and sand. About one o'clock I halted, to rest the horses and take some breakfast, opposite the Grand Rapids – having already made nearly fifty miles – and made a pan of tea, which I let stand till it cooled and settled, and then sucked water of the leaves. In the interval I gleaned a few seeds, bathed in the rapid, which recruited me greatly, and again in the cool of the evening resumed my route, course west. Towards dusk came to a small pool of stagnant water, very bad, and having nothing to qualify it I was urged to continue till eleven o'clock, when I came to a small spring, but without a single twig for fuel. I made an effort to boil my little pan with dry grass, a large species of *Triticum*, but was unable to succeed. Being near an abandoned encampment I fortunately found some horse-droppings, by the aid of which and the grass mentioned I managed to make some tea, when shortly afterwards I laid myself down to sleep on the grass.

I have a tent, but generally am so much fatigued that the labour of pitching it is too great. Here it could not be done for want of wood, and tent-poles cannot be carried.

Monday, 21st – To-day I overslept myself; started at four o'clock. The country same as yesterday; at eight passed what is called by the voyageurs the Grand Coulee, a most singular channel and at one time must have been the channel of the Columbia. Some places from eight to nine miles broad; parts perfectly level and places with all the appearances of falls of very extraordinary height and cascades. The perpendicular rocks in the middle, which bear evident vestiges of islands, and those on the sides in many places are 1500 to 1800 feet high. The rock is volcanic and in some places small fragments of vitri-fied lava are to be seen. Can carry only pieces the size of nuts. The whole chain of this wonderful specimen of Nature is about 200 miles. ...

Coming to a low gravelly point where there were some small pools of water with its surfaces covered with duck weed, and shaded by long grass, one of the horses, eager to obtain water, fell in head foremost.

My guide and myself made every effort to extricate it but were too weak. As I was just putting some powder in the pan of my pistol to put an end to the poor animal's misery, the Indian, having had some skin pulled off his right hand by the cord, through a fit of ill-nature struck the poor creature on the nose a tremendous blow with his foot, on which the horse reared up to defend himself and placed his fore-feet on the bank, which was steep, when the Indian immediately caught him by the bridle and I pricked him in the flank with my pen-knife, and not being accustomed to such treatment with much exertion he wrestled himself from his supposed grave. The water was so bad that it was impossible for me to use it, and as I was more thirsty than hungry I passed the night without any water.

22nd – Last night being very warm, with the whole firmament in a blaze of sheet lightning, and parched to a cinder, I passed a few miserable hours of rest but no sleep, and as usual set out before day; and, my road being less mountainous, with little exertion I found myself on the Columbia at midday opposite the establishment. Seeing an old man spearing salmon I had the horses watered and hobbled, and crossed in a small canoe with my guide. Here I found my old friends Messrs McDonald and Ermatinger who received me with every kindness. After washing and having a clean shirt handed me, I sat down to a comfortable dinner. I was glad to find the small box, which I thought might have been overlooked in one of the portages, brought to this place by the former gentleman and left until I should pass. As my time was of great consequence I communicated to them my wish, and immediately they purchased a small canoe for me, and hired for me two Indians to go with me to the junction of Lewis and Clarke's River [the Snake River]. In the meantime I wrote to Mr Dease by my old guide, who behaved himself in every way worthy of trust and is to make a stay of two or three days to rest, and I then put up a few and changed some plants collected on the journey.

Douglas was now moving down the river rapidly, travelling from Fort Okanagan towards the junction of the Columbia and the Snake River, close to Fort Walla Walla.

In passing a long rapid ... about ten miles below the house, I took the precaution to take out my paper, seeds, and blanket, and was walking along the shore by them while the Indians ran the canoe down. When in the middle of the rapid a heavy surge broke over them and swept every article out of it except the dry meat, which being weighty by chance was wedged in the canoe, it being very narrow.

The loss of the tea and sugar with the pot was a great one in my present situation, but I considered myself happy, having saved my papers and seeds. ...

Thursday, 24th – By eight o'clock gained the Stony Islands, an extremely dangerous part of the river where the channels are very narrow, not more than 20 to 30 feet broad. As my guides were little acquainted with this part of the river, I hired an Indian of the place to pilot my canoe and after landing her safe below, I paid with a few crumbs of tobacco a smoke from my own pipe. As I had nothing to cook I ate some crumbs of dried meat and salmon, and when I wanted to smoke kindled my pipe with my lens, so I was not under the necessity of making a stay to kindle a fire. Reached the top of the Priest Rapids at six o'clock, and although late I undertook to run the canoe down, making my old guide carry my little parcels, he being tired. Night stole in on me too soon, and I was obliged to camp on the north side of the river.

Friday, 25th – I could not leave my encampment before daylight having still four and a half miles of very bad water. I had left by land an hour before the canoe, and, after waiting nearly an hour at the foot of the rapid, as my guides did not make their appearance I became alarmed for their safety and returned, when I discovered them about a mile and a half above where I halted, comfortably seated in a small cove treating some of their friends to a smoke with some tobacco I had given them the preceding evening. As I had now a fine sheet of water without any rapids, but a very powerful current, I went rapidly on, like the day before scarcely out of my canoe, and arrived at Wallawallah, the establishment near Lewis and Clarke's River, at sundown. I felt so much reduced that I was too weak to eat, and after informing Mr Black of my going to the sea and asking him to procure me two guides to carry me to the Great Falls in the morning, I laid myself down to rest on a heap of firewood, to be free from mosquitoes.

Saturday, 26th – Wrote to Mr McDonald by the old guide and gave him ten charges of ammunition and a little tobacco to buy his food on the way home, and after obtaining a larger canoe from Mr Black in lieu of my present one, and two guides, I took my leave for the sea at six o'clock. At the foot of a rapid twenty-five miles below I purchased a fresh salmon, the half of which I roasted on a stick for breakfast and reserved the other half for next day, lest I should not get anything. As I knew all the bad places of the river, I went on all night drifting before the stream, taking the steering in turn, and as I had to pass a camp of Indians who are noted pillagers, made me anxious to pass during the night, which I accomplished.

Sunday, 27th – Precisely at noon I reached the Great Falls, and finding my canoe too heavy to carry over the rocks I left it and hired one to carry me to The Dalles six miles below. Here I purchased a pair of horns of a male grey sheep of the voyageurs, for which I paid three balls and powder to fire them. The Indian had the skin dressed, forming a sort of shirt, but refused it me unless I should give him mine in return, which at present I cannot spare. On The Dalles were at least from five hundred to seven hundred persons. I learned that the chief Pawquanawaka, who would have been my last guide to the sea, was not at home; but as I am now in my own province again, and understand the language tolerably well, I had no difficulty in procuring two, and was glad to find one who was well known to me. While he and his companion brought the canoe down The Dalles, after being refreshed with a few nuts and whortleberries I proceeded over a point of land fifteen miles, taking an Indian to assist me in carrying my things. The canoe did not appear till after dark.

In the evening a large party of seventy-three men came to smoke with me, and all seemed to behave decently till I discovered that my tobacco-box was off. I had hung up my jacket and to dry, being drenched in the canoe descending The Dalles. As soon as I discovered this I perched myself on a rock, and in their own tongue I gave them a furious reprimand, calling them all the low names used to each other among themselves. I told them they saw me only one man but I was more than that, I was the grass man, and was not afraid. I could not recover it. After all the quarrel, I slept here unmolested.

Monday, 28th – Detained by a strong west wind till eight o'clock, when it became more moderate and I proceeded. Made but little progress. Camped fifteen miles above the Grand Rapids.

Tuesday, 29th – As the wind increased with the day, I could not venture out in the stream, and even near the shore the waves were so high that I had all my property on my back along the high shelving rocks, leaving Indians to bring down the canoe. Arrived at the village on the Grand Rapids at three and repaired to the house of Chumtalia, the chief, and my guide last year, where I had some salmon and whortleberries laid before on a mat. I made a hearty meal and then spoke of procuring a large canoe and Indians to take me to the sea.

He offered to go himself, but as he was busily employed curing salmon I was loath to accept his services, and took in preference his brother and nephew, with a fine large canoe, and proceeded down the lower end of the rapid in the evening. Camped on a low bank of sand in the channel where was no herbage, so of course was as not annoyed with insects. Long before daylight I was under way I should be detained with wind, which for the last three days rose with sun. Passed Point Vancouver at sunrise.

I had the gratification of arriving safe at Fort Vancouver at midday, after traversing nearly eight hundred miles of the Columbia Valley in twelve days and unattended by a single person, my Indian guides excepted. My old friends here gave every attention a wayworn wanderer is entitled to. On their discovering me plodding up the low plain from the river to the house alone, unpleasant thoughts struck them.

As the river was river seen higher than it has been this year, and of course caution is requisite in descending, they apprehended I was the only survivor. I confess astonishment came over me to meet people from whom I had had more kindness a thousand times more than I could ever have expected, look so strange on me; but as soon as I dispelled the cloud of melancholy that sat on every brow I had that unaffected welcome so characteristic among people so far from home. I had a shirt, a pair of leather trousers, an old straw hat, neither shoe nor stocking nor handkerchief of any description, and perhaps from my careworn visage had some appearance of escaping from the gates of death.

Douglas had travelled 600 miles from Fort Colville in just twelve days, accompanied only by Indian guides. Just in time, for *Dryad* was due to depart for England in two days' time; he wrote as many letters as he could accomplish and packed up 120 species of seeds. Many of these, when they reached the Society in London months later, caused a sensation. Notable among them were *Gaultheria shallon* (salal), the red flowering currant *Ribes sanguineum*, the broad-leafed maple *Acer macrophyllum*, the vine maple *Acer circinatum* and the tall Oregon grape *Mahonia aquifolium*, and, of course, the Douglas fir.

Chapter Seven

IN SEARCH OF THE
SUGAR PINE

'I rejoice to tell you of a new species of *Pinus*, the most princely of
the genus, perhaps even the grandest specimen of vegetation.'
*Douglas writing to Hooker in 1826 about his
discovery of the sugar pine*

D
ouglas returned to Fort Vancouver with his confidence
boosted by his success in undertaking a journey at which even
the most robust trappers and Hudson's Bay Company men
would have baulked. Now he was determined to venture into the
little-known mountainous territory south of the Fort. Here he hoped
to find the sugar pines whose giant cones had come to fascinate him.
Natives whom he had seen eating pine nuts had indicated that the tree
grew in this area, and the previous February an explorer and trapper
called Jean Baptiste Desportes McKay had presented Douglas with a
single cone. All this had fired his determination to discover the tree for
himself. He wrote enthusiastically to Hooker about the sugar pine and
its glutinous resin:

> I am almost afraid to say that it is sugar. ... It is found abun-
> dantly in the Country of the Umpqua, who collect its seeds in
> autumn and pound them into a kind of cake, which they
> consider as a kind of luxury, using also the saccharine substance
> ... in the same way as civilised nations do sugar.

McKay (whose name Douglas generally misspelt as Baptist Mackay)
had made his way overland from the east coast in 1809 to establish
Fort Astoria on behalf of John Jacob Astor, who built his family's

considerable fortune on the profits of the fur trade.

Before setting off again, Douglas allowed himself the luxury of a few weeks' recovery in the now almost comfortable surroundings of the Fort. The party he was to accompany was planning to search for fresh rivers and waterways where beaver could be trapped, and as usual he made careful preparations for his new adventure.

Saturday 16 to Tuesday 19 September – Employed making preparations for my march. As my gun has entirely failed me, I am under the necessity of purchasing a new one, which costs £2. Being a new country and no knowledge whatever south of the Umpqua, each has to confine himself to as little encumbrance as possible; and as nearly the whole must be land carriage, this increases the difficulty. Packed six quires of paper and other little articles for my business, and provided myself with a small copper kettle and a few trifles, with a little tobacco for presents and to pay my way on my return.

The 'little encumbrance' of which Douglas wrote was truly sparse. Apart from the clothes he was wearing, he took 'one linen and one flannel shirt' and, 'as heavy rains may be expected near the coast', he indulged himself with 'two blankets and my tent'.

Searching the stores for items for the journey, Douglas drew on his small allowance from the Society for buying goods to offer as presents and exchanges. Tobacco was always popular, but when supplies ran low – as they often did, because of the limited amounts he was able to carry – he resorted to shooting game and presenting his kills as an offering. The native people were unfamiliar and unskilled with guns, and even those who possessed a weapon had not yet learned to shoot moving objects. Douglas made much of being able to shoot five birds with a single bullet – no doubt such feats elevated his reputation among the natives to God-like proportions.

On Wednesday 20 September, Douglas left Fort Vancouver in the company of 'Manson, one of the persons in authority, and a party of twelve men in one boat, with their hunting implements'. (Douglas omits from his count the native men whose job it was to carry the baggage, pitch camp and act as translators.) Mr McLoughlin had sent 'one of his finest and most powerful horses for carrying my baggage and for riding ... which is of great service': a sign of the respect in which Douglas was now held.

Ten days into the journey, the party encountered tracts of burnt vegetation.

> Saturday, 30th – Most parts of the country burned; only on little patches in the valleys and on the flats near the low hills that verdure is to be seen. Some of the natives tell me it is done for the purpose of urging the deer to frequent certain parts, to feed, which they leave unburned, and, of course they are easily killed. Others say that it is done in order that they might the better find wild honey and grasshoppers, which both serve as articles of winter food.

The trek was tedious. The burnt land proved unproductive for botanizing, and Douglas found the overland journey painfully slow in comparison with his recent headlong dash down the Columbia River. The dense vegetation, especially the massive brambles, made walking a constant struggle, while the sheer ascents and descents damaged the horses' hoofs. The horses wandered off overnight, and had to be recovered the next morning, and the pursuit of game to feed the thirty-strong party took up yet more valuable time. To frustration was added a sense of unease, for little was known of this land – few Hudson's Bay men had penetrated it and no one knew whether the local tribes were friendly.

> Sunday, October 1st – Passed at noon some Indians digging the roots of *Phalangium quamash* in one of the low plains. Bulbs

much larger than any I have seen, except those on Lewis and Clarke's River. Camped at four on the banks of a small stream which falls into the Multnomah three miles to the east. In the like journeys Sunday is known only by the people changing their linen, and such of them as can read in the evenings peruse religious tracts, &c., whose tenets are agreeable to the Church of Rome. In the dusk I walked out with my gun. I had not gone more than half a mile from the camp when I observed a very large wasp-nest, which had been attached to a tree, lying on the plain where the ground was perfectly bare and the herbage burned, taken there by the bears.

Saturday 7th – Bargained with Baptist Mackay for a skin of a very large female grizzly bear which he had killed seven days before. I gave him an old, small blanket and a little tobacco. This was to make myself an under-robe to lie on, as I found it cold, from the dew, lying on the grass. Mackay is to endeavour to kill me male and female, so that I might have it in my power to measure them if not to skin them.

John Kennedy had this morning gone out hunting two hours before day, and about ten o'clock was attacked by a large male grizzly bear. He was within a few yards of him before he was discovered, and as he saw that it was impossible to outrun him he fired his rifle without effect and instantly sprang up a small oak tree which happened to be near him. The bear caught with one paw under the right arm and the left on his back. Very fortunately his clothing was not strong, or he must have perished. His blanket, coat, and trousers were almost torn to pieces. This species of bear cannot climb trees. A party went out in search of him but could not fall in with him.

Monday, 9th – Hunters out and fell in with a small herd of elk; but being in the close and almost impenetrable thickets, only one could be secured, which fell after receiving eleven shots. At this season the males are very lean and tough eating: weighed about 500 lb. Horns very large, 33 inches between the tips, with five prongs on each, all inclining forward, the two largest, 11 inches long, running parallel with the nose and reaching nearly to the nostrils, body of a uniform brown, with a black mane 4 inches long. I am pretty certain this is the same sort of animal which I have seen at the Duke of Devonshire's, and unquestionably a very distinct species from the European stag.

Friday, 13th – ... Mackay made us some fine steaks, and roasted a shoulder of doe for breakfast, with an infusion of

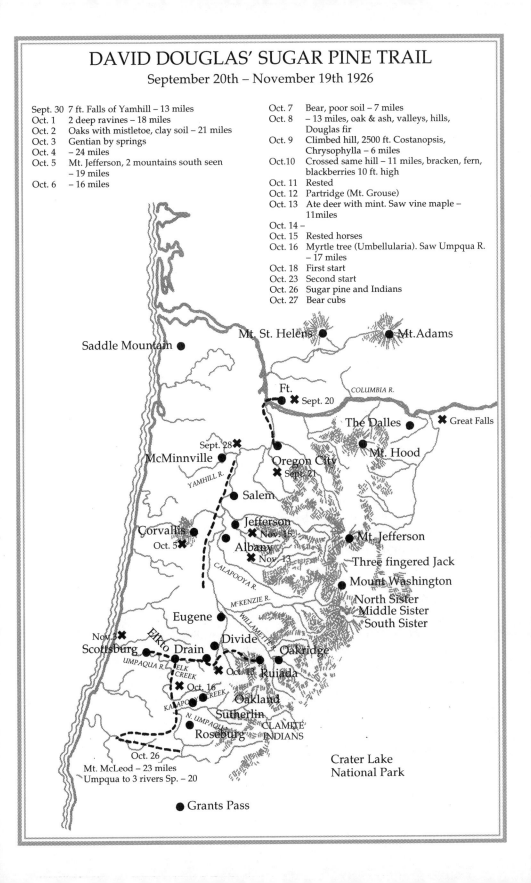

DAVID DOUGLAS' SUGAR PINE TRAIL

September 20th – November 19th 1926

Sept. 30 7 ft. Falls of Yamhill – 13 miles
Oct. 1 2 deep ravines – 18 miles
Oct. 2 Oaks with mistletoe, clay soil – 21 miles
Oct. 3 Gentian by springs
Oct. 4 – 24 miles
Oct. 5 Mt. Jefferson, 2 mountains south seen – 19 miles
Oct. 6 – 16 miles

Oct. 7 Bear, poor soil – 7 miles
Oct. 8 – 13 miles, oak & ash, valleys, hills, Douglas fir
Oct. 9 Climbed hill, 2500 ft. Costanopsis, Chrysophylla – 6 miles
Oct.10 Crossed same hill – 11 miles, bracken, fern, blackberries 10 ft. high
Oct. 11 Rested
Oct. 12 Partridge (Mt. Grouse)
Oct. 13 Ate deer with mint. Saw vine maple – 11miles
Oct. 14 –
Oct. 15 Rested horses
Oct. 16 Myrtle tree (Umbellularia). Saw Umpqua R. – 17 miles
Oct. 18 First start
Oct. 23 Second start
Oct. 26 Sugar pine and Indians
Oct. 27 Bear cubs

Saddle Mountain ●

Mt. St. Helens ● ✖ Mt.Adams

Ft. ✖ Sept. 20

COLUMBIA R.

The Dalles ● ✖ Great Falls

Sept. 28 ✖
McMinnville ●

Oregon City
✖ Sept. 21

Mt. Hood

YAMHILL R.

● Salem

Jefferson
✖ Nov. 15

Mt. Jefferson

Corvallis ●
Oct. 5 ✖

● Albany
✖ Nov. 13

Three fingered Jack

CALAPOOYA R.

Mount Washington

McKENZIE R.

North Sister
Middle Sister
South Sister

Eugene ●

WILLAMETTE

Nov. 3 ✖
Scottsburg ●

Elk to Drain ●

Divide ●

● Oakridge

UMPAQUA R.   ELK CREEK

✖ Oct. 18 Ruiada

KALAPO CREEK   ✖ Oct. 16

Oakland

N. UMPQUA

Sutherlin

CLAMITE INDIANS

Roseburg

Crater Lake
National Park

Oct. 26

Mt. McLeod – 23 miles
Umpqua to 3 rivers Sp. – 20

● Grants Pass

Mentha borealis sweetened with a small portion of sugar. The meal laid on the clean mossy foliage of *Gaultheria shallon* in lieu of a plate and our tea in a large wooden dish hewn out of the solid, and supping it with spoons made from the horns of the mountain sheep or *Mouton gris* of the voyageurs. A stranger can hardly imagine the hospitality and kindness shown among these people, if they have a hut, or failing that, if the day is wet, one of brushwood is made for you, and whatever they have in the way of food you are ceremoniously and seemingly with much good will invited to partake.

Now, having reached the Umpqua Valley about 150 miles south of Fort Vancouver, Douglas was determined to set off into the territory where he thought the elusive sugar pine might grow. Most of the Hudson's Bay Company men had little or no interest in botany and natural history, and were in any case intent on the Company's business. So Douglas had little option but to travel alone, in the knowledge that his best allies in searching for new species would be the local people.

Tuesday, 17th – Baptist Mackay has given me one of his Indian hunters, a young man about eighteen years old, as a guide; of what nation he belongs to he does not know, but tells me he was brought from the south by a war party when a child and kept as a slave until Mackay took him: he is very fond of this sort of life and has no wish of returning to his Indian relations. He speaks a few words of the Umpqua tongue and understands the Chenook, so I will have no difficulty in conversing with this, my only companion.

Like all his contemporaries, Douglas wrote of the native tribes and individuals whom he met with undisguised paternalism. Initially he thought himself superior, and behaved as such, and always seems to have preferred a 'white' man as a travelling companion. Gradually, however, his attitude changed. Grudging respect came to replace initial scepticism, and he learned several of the languages spoken by the peoples he encountered. But though they softened a little, his personal attitudes remained aloof – his European contemporaries would have regarded him with suspicion had he treated the local people with anything other than mild arrogance. At best, he doled out parsimonious amounts of praise.

Douglas struggled with the native languages. Some he managed to understand relatively easily; others continued to baffle him. In his diaries, he frequently complains of not being able to understand one Indian soon after conversing successfully with another. Many of the native languages had not a syllable in common, even those spoken by tribes living relatively close to each other but isolated by geography. For all his difficulties, Douglas probably had a greater command of native languages than his contemporaries in the Hudson's Bay Company. He would have found it essential to communicate with local people when travelling off the beaten track and alone, and his success in finding botanical specimens depended at least partly on his ability to communicate. In addition, at this stage in his life he had made himself a highly educated, highly disciplined man, and would have applied himself to learning native languages with great diligence. Even in present-day Canada no less than fifty-three distinct native languages survive, split between eleven different language families. (It is also worth noting that 'Umpqua' is only one of many spellings. It was many years before Indian languages were written down, and visitors spelt words as they heard them.)

Douglas' diaries on this trip continue to be full of businesslike accounts of where he went and what he saw, together with clinical descriptions of his botanical finds. One constant thread is the quite understandable preoccupation with locating and cooking food. Although he frequently shot goats and birds, on the coast and near rivers his diet consisted chiefly of fish. The tribes of the Lower Umpqua, the rain-soaked coastal area south of the Straits of Juan de Fuca, which separate Vancouver Island and what is now Washington State, travelled by sea and river, and were skilled navigators. Fish – chiefly huge quantities of salmon, which they stunned in the water by casting in crushed camphor weed – were their staple. The dense trees and undergrowth of their land made both travel and cultivation very difficult, and the plant foods eaten further inland were not available here.

In the Umpqua Valley, by contrast, food was abundant, with plentiful game and fish and also wild plants from which food was obtained. (Douglas reported that, in the eloquent sign language of one elderly tribesman, the name Umpqua meant 'good life' or 'full tummy', which he signified by rubbing his stomach.) The women collected acorns which they ground into flour and treated with hot water to mask the bitter tannic acid. The Yoncalla women dug the bulbs of the camas lily from the meadows alongside creeks and baked them in rock-lined ovens gouged out of the earth. They also gathered the seeds of wild sunflower and tarweed. Salmon were caught, chiefly with spears, and elk and deer were hunted for their meat. 'The snare is used in taking the elk and Long (white) and black tailed Deer, and in point of strength will hold the strongest bullock and is not thicker than the little finger.'

On 18 October, Douglas reached an Umpqua settlement consisting of two lodges and twenty-five people. His journal provides the first-ever description of their way of life.

> Heavy dew during the night, morning dull and heavy. Before I could get all ready for my march it was eleven o'clock: took my course due south through a broken varied country and crossed the river five miles from our encampment, where there were two lodges and about twenty-five souls, the greater part women and wives of Centrenose (an Indian word), the chief of the tribe inhabiting the upper part of the river, and who is at present forty-five miles higher up the river. They very courteously brought one very large canoe, in which I embarked and swam the horses at the stern, holding the bridles in my hand. I made a stay of a few minutes, and, as I found my young guide to be less conversant in their tongue than I expected, my visit was to me the less interesting. Had some nuts of *Corylus*, roots of *Phalangium quamash*, and a preparation of meal made from the seeds of a *Syngenesia* already in my possession, with the nuts of my smelling-tree, which are roasted in the embers previous to use. . . . The dress of the men is skins of the small deer undressed, formed into shirts and trousers and those of the richer sort striped and ornamented with shell, principally marine which proves our distance from the ocean to be short. The women, a petticoat like that worn by Chenook females, and a sort of gown of dressed leather, in form differing from the men's only by the sleeves being more open. . . . I had gathered for me a quantity of nuts of my smelling-tree, for which I presented them with a few beads, brass rings, and a pipe of tobacco. . . . The children on seeing me ran with indescribable fear, and on the first interview only one man and one woman could be seen. The others I conceive came on being made acquainted with my friendly disposition.

Centrenose was a chief well known to, and much respected by, visiting Europeans. He was favourably disposed to the Hudson's Bay men, even though, nine years earlier, a pair of fur trappers, who wanted to trade in exchange for native women, had fired on the locals, killing fourteen people before they turned round and fled. Douglas noted that most of the women were tattooed, 'principally the whole of the lower jaw from the ear, some in lines from the ear to the mouth, some across, some spotted and some completely blue; it is done by a sharp piece of bone and cinder from the fire'. The women also decorated their faces with red and green paints.

Douglas' 'smelling-tree' was a Californian laurel (*Umbellularia californica*). As he crushed the leaves in his hands, a powerful, pungent smell, like that of camphor and far from 'sweet-smelling', was released, causing him to sneeze. Although he was pleased with the find, he did not risk drinking the tea the local people brewed from the bark. Douglas recognized the laurel as one Menzies had previously identified.

Douglas' visit was timely. In the early 1830s, many Indians succumbed to an epidemic of fever – probably imported from Europe – that spread through the Willamette Valley and the Lower Columbia River and into the Umpqua Valley. In 1840, the Reverend Gustavus Hines, an enthusiastic diarist and traveller, reported that the population had fallen to 'less than 75 souls'. There was a recovery, however, for in 1856, the US government removed more than 300 people to the Grand Ronde Reservation.

After he had hacked his way through often dense undergrowth, Douglas' hands became blistered and sore. He does not mention wearing gloves or mittens at night, when temperatures frequently plunged, and so must have suffered from chilblains, as well as the arthritis with which he was already afflicted. He would rise several times in the night to stoke up the fire, not only so as to ward off bears but also to keep warm.

Thursday, 19th – Although the thermometer stood not lower than 41°, it was so chilly and raw, with a very heavy dew, that I was under the necessity of rising three times to make up the fire, having only one blanket over me and a small piece of buffalo-skin under which during the day serves in lieu of a horse-rug. My hands being so bad that I could not use the hatchet, and being only nine miles from Mr McLeod, I addressed a note to him informing him of my case and sent it by my Indian guide. In the meantime, I took my gun and went out on the chase. Got only one mile from my camp when I wounded a very large buck through the shoulder, and as he was limping away from me I was in hopes of overtaking him, when unfortunately I fell into a deep gully among a quantity of dead wood, in which position I know not (it was at least five hours). I was on my belly and my face covered with mud when I recovered. I find now, 5 P.M., a severe pain in the chest.

Typically, Douglas made light of his situation. He was fortunate to be found, and even more fortunate to be cared for so generously.

Six Indians of the Calapooie tribe assisted me to my camp, and as it would be very imprudent to undertake any journey as I am, I resolved to return to the camp and asked them to saddle my horse and place the things on it, which they readily did.

It gave me more pleasure than I can well describe to think I had wherewith for them to eat, and after expressing my gratitude in the best way I could, one came to lead the horse while I crept along by the help of a stick and my gun. On arriving at the Indian lodges I passed yesterday, I found John Kennedy, who had instantly been despatched by Mr McLeod to make me a raft, and who on learning my case turned and gave me his horse to ride. I had a little tea made me and bled myself in the left foot, and since I feel somewhat relieved. I find eight small deer and two very large bucks have been killed today. Evening cool.
Monday, 23rd – Proceeded on the opposite side and camped a short distance from the lodge. I could not utter a single sylla- ble [to two natives] but by signs they kindled my fire, brought me water, nuts, roots of *Phalangium quamash*, and the sort of meal made of the *Syngenesious* plant spoken of before and some salmon-trout. Finding them not only hospitable but kind in the extreme, I gave them all the flesh of the deer except one shoulder, some presents of beads, rings, and tobacco.

Douglas did not often accept hospitality in Indian lodges, preferring (even in his present sickly state) instead to stay outdoors. One reason was to avoid the fleas that often infested these homes, as well as the lack of privacy and the noise – each dwelling housed several families huddling together through the dark, damp months of winter. The alien culture – the lack of 'European decorum', as one visitor archly wrote – may also have contributed to his decision. Perhaps the marital prac- tices of his guide's father offended his Scottish puritan sensibilities: 'among the riches of his father's home were fifteen wives, one of whom he was at pains to make me understand was his mother'.

The lodges themselves were constructed from massive planks of western red cedar, *Thuja plicata*. Huge cedar posts, roof beams and rafters formed a framework that was covered with split cedar plants. The roof planks projected over the ends of the gables, making effec- tive eaves that gave protection from the rain and snow. The cooking area, generally in the centre, consisted of a large collection of stones, with an open place in the roof above to allow the smoke to escape. Aromatic cedar was an ideal construction material as it was light, easily pliable and straight-grained; the bark was scraped and woven into clothing and mats.

Douglas' decision to remain outside in deteriorating weather meant that he experienced the full force of a storm.

Wednesday, 25th – Last night was one of the most dreadful I ever witnessed. The rain, driven by the violence of the wind, rendered it impossible for me to keep any fire, and to add misery to my affliction my tent was blown down at midnight, when I lay among *Pteris* [bracken]. I rolled in my wet blanket and tent till morning. Sleep of course was not to be had, every ten or fifteen minutes immense trees falling producing a crash as if the earth was cleaving asunder, which with the thunder peal on peal before the echo of the former died away, and the lightning in zigzag and forked flashes. I had on my mind a sensation more than I can ever give vent to and more so, when I think of the place and my circumstances.

My poor horses were unable to endure the violence of the storm without craving of my protection, which they did by hanging their heads over me and neighing.

Towards day it moderated and before sunrise clear, but very cold. I could not stir before making a fire and drying part of my clothing, everything being completely drenched, and indulging myself with a fume of tobacco being the only thing I could afford. Started at ten o'clock, still shivering with cold, although I rubbed myself with my handkerchief before the fire until I was no longer able to endure the pain.

Shortly after I was seized with a severe headache and pain in the stomach, with giddiness and dimness of sight; having no medicine except a few grains of calomel [a compound of mercury and chlorine] all others being alone, I could not think of taking that and therefore threw myself into a violent perspiration and in the evening felt a little relieved.

Went through an open hilly country some thirteen miles, where I crossed the river to the south side near three lodges of Indians, who gave me some salmon such as is caught in the Columbia and at this season scarcely eatable, but I was thankful to obtain it. Made a short stay and took my course southerly towards a ridge of mountains, where I hope to find my pine. The night being dry I camped early in the afternoon, in order to dry the remaining part of my clothing. Travelled eighteen miles.

Thursday, 26th – Weather dull and cloudy. When my people in England are made acquainted with my travels, they may perhaps think I have told them nothing but my miseries. That may be very correct, but I now know that such objects as I am in quest of are not obtained without a share of labour, anxiety of mind, and sometimes risk of personal safety. I left my camp this morning at daylight on an excursion, leaving my guide to take care of the camp and horses until my return in the evening, when I found everything as I wished; in the interval he had dried my wet paper as I desired him.

Douglas was now closing in on his objective: the sugar pine. In all probability he was in an area west of present-day Roseburg in Oregon, now known as Sugar Pine Mountain.

About an hour's walk from my camp I was met by an Indian, who on discovering me strung his bow and placed on his left arm a sleeve of raccoon-skin and stood ready on the defence. As I was well convinced this was prompted through fear, he never before having seen such a being I laid my gun at my feet on the ground and waved my hand for him to come to me, which he did with great caution. I made him place his bow and quiver beside my gun although struck a light and gave him to smoke and a few beads.

With my pencil I made a rough sketch of the cone and pine I wanted and showed him it. When he instantly pointed to the hills about fifteen or twenty miles to the south. As I wanted to go in that direction, he seemingly with much goodwill went with me. At midday I reached my long-wished *Pinus* (called by the Umpqua tribe *Natele*), and lost no time in examining and endeavouring to collect the seeds. New or strange things seldom fail to make great impression, and often at-first are liable to over-rate them and lest I should never see my friends to tell them verbally of this most beautiful and immensely large tree, I now state the dimensions of the largest one I could find that was blown down by the wind: [at] three feet from the ground, [the trunk measured] 57 feet 9 inches in circumference, [at] 134 feet from the ground [it was] 17 feet 5 inches [in circumference], extreme [width] 215 feet.

The trees are remarkably straight, bark uncommonly smooth for such large timber, of a whitish or light brown colour and yields a great quantity of gum of a bright amber colour. The large trees are destitute of branches, generally for two-thirds the length of the tree branches pendulous, and the cones hanging from their points like small sugar loaves in a grocer's shop. It being only on the very largest trees that cones are seen, and the putting myself in possession of three cones (all I could) nearly brought my life to an end. Being unable to climb or hew down any, I took my gun and was busy clipping them from the branches with ball when eight Indians came at the report of my gun. They were all painted with red earth, armed with bows, arrows, spears of bone, and flint knives, and seemed to me anything but friendly. I endeavoured to explain to them what I wanted and they seemed satisfied and sat down to smoke, but had no sooner gone so than I perceived one string his bow and another sharpen his flint knife with a pair of wooden pincers and hang it on the wrist of the right hand, which gave me ample testimony of their inclination.

To save myself I could not do by flight, and without any hesitation I went backwards six paces and cocked my gun, and then pulled from my belt one of my pistols, which I held in my left hand.

I was determined to fight for life. As I as much as possible endeavoured to preserve my coolness and perhaps did so, I stood eight or ten minutes looking at them and they at me without a word passing, till one at last, who seemed to be the leader, made a sign for tobacco, which I said they should get on condition of going and fetching me some cones.

They went and as soon as out of sight I picked up my three cones and a few twigs, and made a quick retreat to my camp, which I gained at dusk. The Indian who undertook to be my last guide I sent oft, lest he should betray me.

Wood of the pine fine, and very heavy; leaves short, in five, with a very short sheath, bright green cones, one 14 inches long, one 14, and one 13, and all containing fine seed. A little before this the cones are gathered by the Indians, roasted on the embers, quartered, and the seeds shaken out, which are then dried before the fire and I pounded into a sort of flour, and sometimes eaten round.

How irksome a night is to such a one as in under such circumstances. Cannot speak a word to my guide, not a book to read, constantly in expectation of an attack, and the position I am now in is lying on the grass with my gun beside me, writing by the light of my Columbian candle – namely, a piece of wood containing rosin.

How frustrated Douglas must have been. At long last he had discovered the tree that he had been seeking for so long – that had assumed almost mythic proportions in his thoughts – yet there was no one to share the excitement with. Nor, for fear of attack, could he even rest. To make matters worse, late at night his guide returned to camp having been chased by a large grizzly bear.

> Friday, 27th – My last guide went at midnight in quest of trout with a flare and brought one small one in the morning, which I roasted for breakfast. He came two hours before in great terror and hurry, and uttered a shriek.
>
> I sprang to my feet, thinking the Indians I saw yesterday had found me out, but by gesture I learned that he had been attacked by a large grizzly bear. I signed to him to wait for daylight and perhaps I would go and kill it. A little before day Bruin had the boldness to pay me a visit, accompanied by two whelps, one last year's and one of this. As I could not consistently with my safety receive them so early in the morning, I waited for daylight and accordingly did so.
>
> I had all my articles in the saddle-bags and the horse a mile from the camp. When I mounted my own, which stands fire admirably, and rode back and found the three feeding under the shade of the oak, I allowed the horse to walk slowly up to within twenty yards, when they all stood up and growled at little.
>
> I levelled my gun at the heart of the mother, but as she was protecting one of the young, keeping them right before her and one standing before her, my ball entered the palate of the young one and came out at the back part of the head. It dropped instantly, and as the mother stood up a second time I lodged a ball in her chest, which on receiving she abandoned the remaining live young and fled to an adjoining hummock of wood. The wound was mortal, as they never leave their young until ready to sink. With the carcass of the young one I paid my last guide, who seemed to lay great store by it. I abandoned the chase and thought it prudent from what happened yesterday to turn my steps back again without delay. So I returned and crossed the river two miles further down, and camped for the night in a low point of wood near a small stream.

After these tumultuous events, Douglas finished his account with a laconic report on the weather: 'heavy rain throughout the day'.

The discovery of the sugar pine, *Pinus lambertina*, is one of the most momentous stories of Douglas' eventful life. Certainly he himself regarded it as one of the greatest achievements of his first trip to the

Pacific North West. We will never know how far he embellished the story in order to demonstrate to the Horticultural Society how much danger he had faced. Yet there is much evidence from the accounts of others that Douglas did indeed confront danger, so perhaps his account is not too far removed from the truth. The great irony, given the importance Douglas attached to finding the tree, is that, despite his predictions, it does not grow well in Britain, unlike the Douglas fir, and generally succumbs to fungus before it can fulfil its true potential. Hence none of the trees grown from the seeds sent back by Douglas have survived.

Douglas now made his way slowly back to his original travelling companions. There was a dramatic incident when his horse lost its footing and fell headlong towards the river. Only a couple of trees 'lying across the hill' prevented him tumbling into the water and drowning, and Douglas managed to cut the animal free. 'I felt over this occasion much, for I got him from Mr McLoughlin and it was his favourite horse.' Eventually, they reached the camp, where they rejoined Mr McLeod. The rainy season was now setting in, and Douglas decided to accompany two of McLeod's men who were returning to Fort Vancouver.

Saturday, 4th November – Mr McLeod tells me that two of his men are going to Fort Vancouver with a despatch on Monday morning and as the season is far spent and the rainy season set in, and at the same time doubtful if he will have any more communication before I should start on March 1st for the other side of the continent, I have made up my mind to return with them and shall retain a grateful recollection of his kindness and assistance I have uniformly had from this gentleman. (Recollect on your arrival in London to get him a good rifle as a present.)

The return trek was not easy. The weather was deteriorating, and the trail was more testing than on the outward journey. Game was scarce, and they were constantly hungry; Douglas longed for a little tea, 'the greatest and best of comforts after a hard labour', but there was none. Tempers were fraying, and there were arguments about the exact location of the trail.

The men proposed to have a sort of soup for supper made of pounded *Camass*, or the roots of *Phalangium quamash* by its correct botanical name of Pursh, to which I agreed, they observing it was very fine. I had not more than two spoonfuls when, with its sweet sickening taste together with the exertion I had made during the day, I became very sick and did not sleep during the whole night. Saw several deer, but could not get a shot at them. ... The fact [is] plainly this; all hungry and no means of cooking a little of our stock; travelled thirty three miles, drenched and bleached with rain or sleet, chilled with a piercing north wind; and then to finish the day experienced the cooling, comfortless consolation for lying down wet without supper or fire. On such occasions I am very liable to become fretful.

The horses were exhausted, and they began to fear that they would either have to abandon them or at least kill one and eat it. Douglas, whose iron constitution was holding up, grew impatient. On one occasion, he almost lost himself again, having wandered off without telling his companions in which direction he was going. Fortunately, he eventually reappeared with game he had killed, and was warmly welcomed, all differences now buried and forgotten.

By six o'clock I had three geese and one duck, and on my way home, I observed a large duck a little to the left of my path. I laid down my hunt, gun-slip and hat to approach them, and after securing one returned in search of my articles, but was unsuccessful in finding them, although I devoted two hours to it.

Reluctantly I gave it up and proceeded to the camp, and as the night was exceedingly dark I would have had some difficulty in finding it had they not made signals with their guns to guide me. Close to the camp fired among a cloud of ducks that were flying over my head and killed one. I was hailed to the camp with 'Be seated at the fire, Sir,' and then laughed at for losing myself in the morning, my game and other property in the evening. There is a curious feeling among voyageurs. One who complains of hunger or indeed of hardship of any description, things that in any other country would be termed extreme misery, is hooted and brow-beaten by the whole party as a pork-eater or a young voyageur, as they term it; and although in many instances I have observed they will endure much privation through laziness, and not infrequently as a bravado, to have it said of them they did so-and-so, I found in this instance my men very willing to cook the fowls and still less averse to eating them. Heavy rain.

Wednesday, 15th – Light rain. In the morning I left the camp at daylight in search of game, leaving the men with the horses and being scarce of them and at the same time weak, I chose to walk.

On arriving at Sandiam River, which falls in the Multnomah, a stream of considerable magnitude, we found the village deserted and no canoes. A raft could soon have been made, but from the rapidity of the current we could not guide it across. Therefore we looked up and down for the most suitable place to swim. The men chose to swim on their horses, I alone. Fannaux in the midst of the stream, in spurring on his horse, imprudently gave the bridle a sudden jerk, when rider and horse went hurling down before the current. Fortunately he extricated himself from the stirrups, and of course had to adopt my plan of swimming alone. I had articles of my clothing and my bedding drenched, but what gave me most pain was the whole of my collection being in the same state. Proceeded on and found an Indian Village .only two miles further on, with plenty of canoes. Camped about three o'clock, being fain to give my collection and clothing time to dry, which employed me all the evening. Killed no game; gained about eighteen miles. To-night, from constant exposure to the wet and cold, my ankles are swollen, painful, and very stiff.

Even Douglas now began to falter. The cold was almost intolerable, the path uncertain, and Douglas almost lost himself when he ventured off alone to try to find help from a Canadian trapper whom they believed to be nearby. Eventually, on the 17th, he located two Calapooia lodges,

where I was kindly treated by the inmates. The only article in the way of animals food was a small piece of the rump of Long tailed Deer, which the good woman on seeing I stood in need of food, had without loss of time cooked for me. The greater part of it was only the bare vertebrae, which she pounded with two stones and placed it in a basket work kettle among water and steamed it by throwing red hot stones in it and covering it with a close mat until done. On this, with a few hard nuts and roots of the *Quamash*, I made a good breakfast. After paying my expenses with a few balls and shots of powder, and a few beads, I resumed my walk towards the end of my journey, five miles distant.

Finally, help came from a brigade of men on their way to the Umpqua River, from where Douglas and his companions had just come. The famished explorers were given venison steaks, potatoes and a basin of tea, and were sent off on the correct path to Fort

Vancouver, which they reached on the evening of 19 November. 'Fatigue and constant exposure to the rain and cold' had exhausted Douglas, and painful swollen ankles 'obliged me to remain within doors for nine days'. He used the time to dry the seeds and arrange the plants that had survived the fall in the river and to pack them for the long journey to England. Though this had not been the happiest or most productive of treks, Douglas had at least found the sugar pine he had sought for so long and had collected its seeds.

Chapter Eight

HUDSON'S BAY EXPRESS

'Sky beautiful at sunset, the snowy summits of the hills tinted with gold; the parts secluded from his rays are clothed with cloudy branches of the pine wearing a darker hue, while the river at the base is stealing silently along in silvery brightness or dashes through the dark recesses of a rocky Dalle.'
Douglas' journal, 19 April 1827, as he travelled up the Columbia River

Lesser men might have put their feet up and rested for the winter. That was not Douglas' way. Barely three weeks after his return, he was ready and eager to venture out again, deciding to travel down the Columbia to its mouth. Douglas was not a man to sit back idly – he drove himself hard, and as the time for the return journey home approached he felt impelled to search for anything of interest. He was also keen to set the Chenook language down on paper.

December 9th to 25th – My time lying heavy on my hands, I resolved on visiting the ocean in quest of Fuci, shells, or anything that might present itself to my view. Hired a canoe of some Chenooks who were here on a trading excursion. Mr McLoughlin sent one of his men with me, who with two Indians formed my party. Two days took me to Fort George, the old establishment where I slept and waited until the wind abated, before I could cross the river to the north side. Scarcely had I been ashore when the wind began to blow a strong gale from the south-west amid the rain falling in torrents – one of the most dreadful nights I ever witnessed.

About midnight I was awakened by the breaking of the surge on the shore and the crashing of the drift-wood pile above pile; and the sea rising so suddenly and so unusually high, in an instant dashed my canoe to pieces and obliged me to strike my tent at midnight, and retire back into the wood. In the morning when the storm abated I went to the house of Cassicass, son of the chief Com Comly, and borrowed a canoe and proceeded along Baker's Bay; crossed the portage over Cape Disappointment to the bays near Cape Shoalwater of Vancouver, which I gained in two days' march, both rainy.

The trip now proved a great disappointment. Another day's walking brought Douglas to the 'house of my old Indian friend, Cockqua, who greeted me with that hospitality for which he is justifiably famous'.

He regretted that dry salmon and berries of *Gaultheria Shallon* was all the variety he could offer me. The boisterous weather had obliged the wildfowl to seek more sheltered situations than his neighbourhood afforded and it was too rough to venture on fishing.

Cockqua's offering – different types of berries and dry salmon pressed together into cakes and dried for winter storage – made Douglas violently ill, so much so that he abandoned his expedition and turned back to Fort Vancouver. Perhaps he was lucky to have not been offered fresh berries mixed with salmon eggs and roe, and bound together with eulachon oil, or soapberries whipped into a frothy treat known as 'Indian ice-cream'; Indians considered this a real delicacy and ate it with specially carved wooden spoons, but it did not appeal to the European palate. Douglas continued in his journal:

The salmon is very bad, lean in the extreme, killed in the small creeks in September, October, and November, in the spawning season: when dried resembles rotten dry pine-bark. Having nothing but this to subsist on, I was seized with a most violent diarrhoea which reduced me in four days unable to walk. The weather giving no proofs of improvement – and from my increasing weakness I became alarmed lest it should prove dysentery – I abandoned the idea of prolonging my stay. Therefore in the morning I set off for the Fort, having obtained one duck to make a little broth. Three days took me to the

The original 'Mother' Douglas fir on Scone Estate which supplied seed for many of the first plantations of the tree in Britain. *(Photo courtesy of Forest Life Picture Library)*

(Left) 'Portage on the Hoarfrost' by Sir George Back, 1833. *(Courtesy of the Glasgow Institute)*

(Right) Mount Hood, with fir noble growing in the foreground. *(Photo by Alan Fletcher)*

(Below) Canoeing on the waterways of Oregon. *(Photo courtesy of Oregon Tourism Commission)*

(Left) A giant Douglas fir in the Pacific North West, recently felled. *(Photo courtesy of Alan Fletcher)*

(Right) Old growth Douglas fir in Washington State. *(Photo courtesy of Alan Fletcher)*

(Far right) A typical early Hudson Bay Company trading post west of the Rockies. *(Reproduced courtesy of the Hudson's Bay Company Collection)*

(Below) The 'Committee's Punchbowl' in the Athabasca Pass in the Canadian Rockies. *(Photo courtesy of James Ogilvie)*

(Top left) Mount Hooker, Canadian Rockies. *(Photo courtesy of James Brown)*

(Bottom left) Typical Cascade Mountain scenery around Mount Rainier in Washington State. *(Photo by Alan Fletcher)*

(Above, inset) Early specimen of Sitka spruce (then called *Abies Menziesii*). *(Photo by Alan Fletcher)*

(Above) The tallest tree in the British Isles – a Douglas fir growing at the Hermitage, Perthshire. *(Photo courtesy of Forest Life Picture Library)*

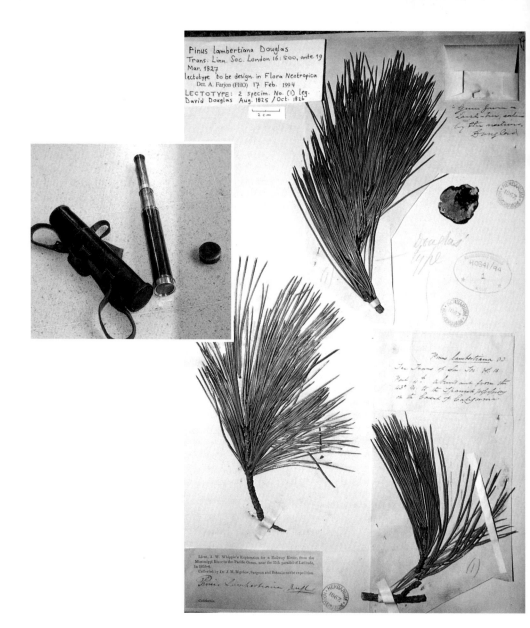

Pinus lambertiana Douglas
Trans. Linn. Soc. London 16 : 500, ante 19
Mar. 1827
lectotype to be design. in Flora Neotropica
    Det. A. Farjon (FHO) 17 Feb. 1994
LECTOTYPE: 2 specim. No. (1) leg.
David Douglas Aug. 1825 / Oct. 1826

1847.
ERECTED BY THE LOVERS OF BOTANY IN EUROPE
IN MEMORY OF
DAVID DOUGLAS,
A NATIVE OF THIS PARISH,
WHO, FROM AN ARDENT LOVE OF SCIENCE AND
A DESIRE TO PROMOTE THE IMPROVEMENT IN BOTANY,
VISITED THE UNEXPLORED REGIONS ON THE BANKS
OF THE COLUMBIA AND SOUTHWARD OF CALIFORNIA,
WHENCE HE TRANSMITTED A GREAT VARIETY OF THE SEEDS
OF VALUABLE TREES AND FLOWERING PLANTS
ADAPTED TO THE CLIMATE OF GREAT BRITAIN
AND WHO, AFTER DEVOTING TEN YEARS OF THE PRIME OF LIFE
IN ADDING TO THE ARBORETUM AND FLORA OF EUROPE,
SUFFERED AN ACCIDENTAL AND LAMENTED DEATH
IN ONE OF THE SANDWICH ISLANDS,
ON 13TH OF JULY, 1834, IN THE 35TH YEAR OF HIS AGE.
ENDOWED WITH AN ACUTE AND VIGOROUS MIND,
WHICH HE IMPROVED BY DILIGENT STUDY,
THIS EMINENT BOTANIST
UNIFORMLY EXEMPLIFIED IN HIS CONDUCT
THOSE CHRISTIAN VIRTUES WHICH INVESTED HIS CHARACTER
WITH A HIGHER AND MORE IMPERISHABLE DISTINCTION
THAN HE JUSTLY ACQUIRED
BY HIS WELL-EARNED REPUTATION FOR SCIENTIFIC KNOWLEDGE.
A DUTIFUL SON, A KIND AND AFFECTIONATE BROTHER
A SINCERE FRIEND, HE SECURED BY THE RECTITUDE
OF HIS MORAL AND RELIGIOUS PRINCIPLES,
NOT LESS THAN BY THE BENEVOLENCE OF HIS DISPOSITION,
THE ESTEEMED REGARD OF ALL WHO KNEW HIS WORTH.

(Above) David Douglas's original Sugar
Pine Collections. *(Reproduced courtesy
of the Royal Botanic Gardens, Kew)*

(Inset) Douglas's telescope, now kept at
the Royal Botanic Garden, Edinburgh.
(Photo by Syd House)

(Left) The memorial to Douglas in the
grounds of Scone Old Parish Church,
Perthshire.

village of Oak Point, where the Indians had that day caught ten sturgeon.

Learning I stood in need of some, they instantly told me I could have none unless I should give either my hatchet or coat. Being neither willing nor could I encourage such on principle, I declined bargaining. I offered tobacco, powder, and ball, and my knife for as much as would be one meal for myself and people, which they refused, but as I was a good chief and liked them they would let me have it if I would give the handkerchief from my neck for one small bit, and seven buttons off my coat for a second bit of the same size, which I did! I have heard of people put to many shifts to live, but never in my life was I in such a hard case in bargain-making. He had my blessing and promise of a sound flogging should I ever meet him in a convenient place. I slept half a mile above the village and the following morning started early with the tide and a light air of wind.

Douglas reached Fort Vancouver at midday on Christmas Day, 'having gleaned, like my trip in the same quarter last year, less than any journey I have had in the country'. Here, 'soon recovered from my sickness by a change of food', Douglas spent the harsh winter months arranging his plants, writing up his notes and organizing seeds and specimens to be sent to London. Letters arrived, including one from Joseph Sabine and another from John Douglas, who was now Clerk of Works at the Duke of Buccleuch's Drumlanrig Castle. Interesting companions also helped to pass the time and relieve the winter gloom. Among the Fort's residents during these frozen months, in which horses and cattle succumbed to the cold, were Captain Aemilius Simpson, who was in charge of the Hudson's Bay Company's Pacific trade, James McMillan, who went on to establish Fort Langley, further north on the Fraser River, and George Barnston, who later became responsible for Fort Walla Walla.

To Aemilius Simpson, the kinsman of Governor Simpson, head of the Hudson's Bay Company, goes the credit for seizing the lucrative trade in pelts and silk, tea and cloth between China and America and also (perhaps more surprisingly) for bringing the first apple trees to America's Pacific coast. At dinner one evening in London, he was impressing on his pretty table companion the lack of home comforts he would enjoy in the American west. Slicing open her dessert apple, she shook out the ripe seeds and tucked them into his waistcoat pocket. Months later, he discovered the forgotten seeds, which had survived the passage round the Horn, and promptly had them planted.

As a keen naturalist, George Barnston was inspired and amused by Douglas. Much later, he recalled that winter and the Californian condors that wheeled above the Fort.

> One morning a large specimen was brought into our square, and we had all a hearty laugh at the eagerness with which the Botanist [Douglas] pounced upon it. In a very short time he had it almost in his embraces fathoming its stretch of wings, which not being able to compass, a measure was brought, and he found it full nine feet from tip to tip. This satisfied him, and the bird was carefully transferring to his studio for the purpose of being stuffed. In all that pertained to nature and science, he was a perfect enthusiast.

The time for Douglas' long-postponed homeward journey, overland to York Factory on Hudson Bay and thence by sea to England, was now fast approaching. On 20 March two boats left Fort Vancouver. One carried the Hudson's Bay Company men, the other acted as a support to watch for hostile natives and to help when porterage was required at the narrow rapids and waterfalls further up the Columbia River. Edward Ermatinger, a Swiss/English fur trader who had joined the Hudson's Bay Company in 1818, was to join Douglas in the long trek to York Factory; the others would divert at Fort Colville for an expedition to explore the interior. (Ermatinger subsequently wrote an account of his travels, which was eventually published by his son in 1912 as *York Factory Express Journal*.) Each of the flat-bottomed boats, which tapered at the bows and stern, was paddled by a seven-strong crew of French Canadian and Iroquois voyageurs.

> 19th March 1827 – ... commenced packing my collections to go by sea in the first vessel for England, and have made a tin box for as large a portion of the seeds as I could think of carrying on my back across the mountains; in this one will go my journal. Three boxes packed by the 17th, and should any occur in the interim, Mr McLoughlin will cause an additional one to be made. Left room in one for my plants that were omitted to be sent down in the autumn.
>
> Had my very small clothing made ready, paid my debts, and received a copy of the amount. Weather fine until the 17th. March, Tuesday, 20th – Showery all day. Preparations being made for the annual express across the continent; by five o'clock in the afternoon I left Fort Vancouver in company with Mr

Edward Ermatinger for Hudson's Bay, Messrs McLoughlin, McLeod, Annance, and Pambrun for the interior. We were accompanied to the riverside by the few remaining individuals who constituted my little society during the winter, where we wished each other a long farewell – I glad that the time was come when my steps should once more be bent towards England. I cannot forbear expressing my sincere thanks for the assistance and hospitality, and strict attention to my comfort which I uniformly enjoyed during my stay with them – in a particular manner to Mr McLoughlin (Chief Factor).

Douglas decided to walk along the riverbank in order to study the early spring flowers that were already braving the elements. Geology was another new interest, and he had had a mineral hammer made for him at the Fort during the winter. Although he had already travelled the river several times, there were still new plants to discover. The boat was packed, so his decision to walk was welcome. However, his feet suffered badly and he wrote much of his blisters. Indeed, trouble with his feet was an omen of hardships to come.

Saturday, 24th – Started at five and crossed the Falls portage at nine, where we breakfasted. Mr McLoughlin and Mr McLeod started on foot and were shortly followed by Mr Pambrun and myself. Early in the day the boats being favoured with a following breeze enabled them to use a sail, which gave great assistance, the stream being rapid and very strong.

Embarked at one o'clock, as the road was bad and unable to keep pace with the boat. Came up with those who started in the morning, but did not embark, horses being promised by Indians residing twelve miles above the Falls. Camped on the north side of the river, seven miles above Day's River, at dusk. Were joined by our friends, who walked all day.

The servant, Overy, who had waited behind for the purpose of bringing up the horses, came to us two hours after dark, having in his hand eight or ten broken arrows which he wrested from an Indian who threatened to put one through him if he did not allow himself to be pillaged. He might have laid him dead on the spot, but prudently chose to allow him to walk away, being rewarded previously with a heavy flogging and deprived of his bow and arrows. Five horses at the camp and the owner agreed to go to Wallawallah. Very high wind from the south-west during the night.

Sunday, 25th – The Indian who was engaged last night chose

this morning to change his mind. He got a comfortable supper and a whiff of the pipe, which perhaps was all he wanted. Three of us went off on foot and three in the boat until nine o'clock, when I took my turn until dark. High wind in the morning, calm at noon. Saw many butterflies and swallows. Camped on the north bank, nine miles below the big island.

Monday, 26th – At daylight want off on foot over a point of land and met the boat at the lower end of the big island at nine o'clock, when we took breakfast; and having to cross over to the south channel, the north being too shallow, I embarked for the remainder of the day. Put ashore at two at the upper end of the island, where we discovered that Mr McLoughlin's gun had been left at our breakfast-place, and being loath to lose it, having some celebrity attached to it (Sir Alexander McKenzie used it on both his former journeys), Overy, another Canadian and an Indian were dispatched for it in the morning: in the meantime halted for them.

That the entire expedition had to halt so that McLoughlin's gun could be retrieved owed much to the fame of its previous owner. It transpired that two Indians had gone off with it, and although they were chased, the weapon was never recovered. Eventually, the journey resumed, and on the 28th the party reached Walla Walla, where they were joined by the others who had been searching for the gun. This was familiar country, for Douglas had travelled here regularly in 1826. He still found much to interest him, whether in early flowering plants or in geese starting their courtship rituals.

Wednesday, 28th – Started at five and reached the establishment at eleven, where we found our friends, who came overland and arrived there last night. Stayed until three o'clock during which time I changed what few plants I had gleaned and put my grouse in order. Camped three miles below Lewis and Clark's River [Snake River]. Evening fine.

Saturday, 31st – Morning fine and pleasant. Crossed the river to the low gravelly grounds below the rapid, where clouds of grouse were flying round us. At this season they appear to be more shy than in the autumn. Observed them in groups as before, dancing. The males spread the tail like a fan and puff up their breast or pouches to as large a size as the whole body, and like the pigeon singing their song, which I listened to with much pleasure. The voice is 'hurl-r-r-r, hoo-hiurr-r-r-r boo,' a very hollow, deep, melancholy sound. The female I have heard call only when rising from the ground, which is 'cack cack-cack,' like the common pheasant.

The flesh is fine, but not so white as many others. Four cocks were killed, two by Mr McLeod with his rifle and two by myself with heavy shot, all too much injured for preserving. Met Mr A. McDonald from Thomson's river, who returned with us to go to Okanagan. The river being lower than ever it has been observed by Baptist the guide, considerable difficulty was experienced dragging the boat over the shallow rocks. While they were in the rapid I took a turn round the ground and found a species of *Allium*, 2 to 6 inches high, pink and white flowered, in gravelly and rocky places. ...

April Monday 2nd to Thursday 5th – The river flowing through a more mountainous country, and further to the north, scarcely a vestige of vegetation can be seen, only the gravelly bank and north side of the river, all the ground covered with snow. Walked along the banks of the river picking up any mineral that seemed curious – found some very fine pebbles. Arrived at Okanagan on Thursday, a little before dusk.

Friday, 6th – Fine, clear, and pleasant. At two o'clock I alone embarked in the boat to go round the big bend, a day and a half's journey, being much fatigued and my feet very painful, blistered, and blood-run, having walked eleven days. My fellow-travellers remained to come over the point on horseback.

On the 12th, Douglas, McLoughlin and McLeod reached Fort Colville, near the Kettle Falls, on foot, the rest of the party arriving later by boat. Here Douglas retrieved the seeds he had left at the Fort the previous autumn.

We were most cordially welcomed by my old and kind friends, Messrs Dease and Work. Hung out my papers, examined the seeds found my box with all my articles quite safe which was omitted to be sent down last autumn.

April Friday 13th to Tuesday 17th – Weather changeable hail, snow and rain, wind northerly. The first night of my arrival, I had the great misfortune to get my pair of grouse devoured, the skins torn to pieces by the famished Indian dogs of the place. Although they were closely tied in a small oilcloth and hung from time tent-poles, the dogs gnawed and ate the casing, which were leather thongs. Grieved at this beyond measure. Carried the cock bird 457, and the hen 304 miles on my back, and then unfortunately lost them.

Wrote a note to Mr Archibald McDonald at Okanagan to endeavour to procure for me a pair against the sailing of the first vessel for England. Mr Work showed me a pair of *Mouton Blanche* [white mountain sheep] of the voyageurs, male and female, skins in a good state of preservation. It is the same animal which I saw in Peall's Museum at Philadelphia, brought by Lewis and Clarke. The male is large, 200 to 250 lb weight. The female considerably smaller, a purer white colour, at the same time finer, the beard less, and the horns shorter. Also a pair of Black-tailed Deer, male and female, likewise in a good state.

The same gentleman had a solitary skin of the small wolf of the plains, a singular variety and curious from its being time deity or god of the Flathead tribe of Indians. ...

Took a single specimen of each plant not already sent to England, and packed in one of my old journals to save room. Packed the remainder to be sent to England and left the few minerals collected on my journey upward in charge of Mr Work.

Made a memorandum for Mr McLoughlin regarding the final packing of two boxes at Fort Vancouver to be placed on the ship's invoice as dry plants, seeds, preserved animals, and articles relating to natural history, for the Horticultural Society of London. Made a note to be read to my Chenook friend Cockqua, regarding a kind of *Arctonys*, which I was unable to get when there. In order that Mr Sabine may know of the ship's arrival in England, that the collection may come to hand without delay, wrote the following note to him to go by sea.

Fort Colville, Columbia River
April 16th, 1827

Dear Sir, beg to inform you that the Hudson's Bay Company's ship has arrived, on board of which are four boxes for the Society, containing the total collection made by me in N.W. America. – I am dear Sir, your most-obedient servant, D. DOUGLAS.

To Jos. SABINE, Esq., &c. &c.

Made a note to the commander of the vessel as to treatment.

Douglas now parted from the party travelling to the interior on Hudson's Bay Company business. His journal conveys the bond that had grown up between these travellers and their sadness at parting. It was time to set out for the headwaters of the Columbia and the pass over the Rockies.

Having now just bid farewell to my Columbian friends, I cannot in justice to my own feelings refrain from acknowledging the kindness shown to me during my stay among them, a grateful remembrance of which I shall ever cherish. My society now is confined to Mr Edward Ermatinger, a most agreeable young man who goes to Hudson's Bay with us, and seven men – four Canadians and three Iroquois Indians. Our next stage is Jasper House, in the Rocky Mountains, distant about 370 miles. Laid down to sleep at 2 A.M.

Douglas and his party were travelling across the present-day border with Canada towards the headwaters of the Columbia, and on through the Lower and Upper Arrow Lakes. The countryside was (and remains) beautiful, and captured Douglas' imagination.

Wednesday, 18th – Overslept ourselves this morning and were not up until daylight, when we hurriedly pushed off lest we should be seen by our old friends, who left us last night. A shower of snow fell during the night, which continued throughout the morning. Thermometer 28°, wind northerly and very piercing. General course of the river northerly, bounded on both sides by high mountains many places rugged, granite, iron, and trap rock. ... The only plants in flower are *Lilium pudicum* [*Fritillaria pudica*, or mission bell] and a species of *Pulmonaria* already in the collection. Camped at dusk ... on the left-hand side of the river. Travelled twenty-nine miles. Mr Ermatinger, during the time of boiling the kettle, favoured me with some airs on the flute, which he plays with great skill. Noon cloudy.

Thursday, 19th – Just as I laid down my pen at midnight a heavy shower of snow commenced and continued for two hours, three inches deep in the morning. Found it very local, for five miles higher up there was none. Like many others, this day's journey admits of little variety.

Country more mountainous and rugged, the timber smaller. Ten miles from our camp, about eight o'clock A.M. passed Flathead River, a stream not more than 30 yards broad at its entrance, but throws a large body of water into the Columbia. The entrance is cascades, 9 or 10 feet high, over which the water is dashed, which has a fine effect, assuming as it were from a subterranean passage, both sides being high hills with large pines overhanging the stream.

The headwater of this stream was passed by Lewis and Clarke in their tour across the continent. I am informed ... that its source is a small lake in the Rocky Mountains, which discharges water to both oceans from the east – and is the head-water of one of the branches of the Missouri, and one, as I have observed, is a feeder of the Columbia. Took breakfast two miles and a half above it on the opposite side at nine, when we stayed our usual time – half an hour.

From the high grounds on the bank of the river, as far as the eye can behold, nothing is to be seen but huge mountains, ridge towering above ridge in awful grandeur, their summits enwrapped in eternal snow, destitute of timber, and no doubt affording but a scanty verdure of any sort. Lower down the scene is different – rugged perpendicular cliffs of granite and scattered fragments which from time to time have been hurled from their beds in masses too large and weighty for anything to withstand.

General course of the river northerly scarcely a mile without a rapid. Camped on the right at the foot of a high mountain remarkable for its being circular.

Douglas wrote lyrically of the grandeur of the scenery on the Upper Columbia and of the play of sunlight on the snow and the river. He also attempted some sketches – evidently without great success, as his terse note to himself reveals ('when you get home, begin to learn'). All the time he observed and collected – not only plants, but also animal and bird life: 'Not a day passed but brought something new or interesting either in botany or zoology.'

April 19th – Morning cool; noon clear, fine, and pleasant. Sky beautiful at sunset, the snowy summits of the hills tinted with gold; the parts secluded from his rays are clothed with cloudy branches of the pine wearing a darker hue, while the river at the base is stealing silently along in silvery brightness or dashes through the dark recesses of a rocky Dalle. How glad should I feel if I could do justice to my pencil (when you get home, begin to learn).

Friday, 20th – Slight frost in the morning. The tent being wet and partly covered with snow from the preceding night, a small fire had to be kindled in it before it could be folded. Passed, about a mile above our camp, McGillivray's or Cootanie River

[Kootenay River], also a stream of some magnitude, rapid, and very clear water. This is said to be a good route across the mountains, but from the hostile disposition manifested by the natives inhabiting the higher parts of the Saskatchewan, the Athabasca portage is preferred being free from such visitors. Five miles above it the Columbia gradually widens to a lake, one to two and a half miles broad, some places very deep, having bold perpendicular rocks; at other places small bays with gravelly or sandy beach with low points of wood. The scenery to-day is fine, but not so broken, the hills fully as high and more thickly wooded; high snowy peaks are seen in all directions raising their heads to the clouds.

Douglas had now entered the Lower Arrow Lake, where the Columbia River widens considerably.

Took breakfast at 8 A.M., gained then nine miles. Course of the river then north-west and by north-west, and north-east. About 10 A.M. a light breeze sprang up which enabled us to use a sail, which slackened during the middle of the day, but freshened up again in the afternoon. Noon clear and fine. Intended to have arranged a few words of the Chenook language, but was molested out of my life by the men singing their boat-songs.

Douglas admired the boatmen, if somewhat grudgingly, for their stoicism and certainly appreciated their navigational skills. But the noise of their singing drove him to despair, distracting him as he searched the river bank for plants and drowning the birdsong.

Saturday, 21st – Shortly after dusk last night an Indian and his two children came to our camp and sold a small piece of venison and a few small trout, 10 to 14 inches long, of good quality, and some small suckers, so common in the lower parts of the river.

I learn that sturgeon is in the lake, but is not fished by the Indians. Morning clear and fine, wind easterly, which greatly impeded our progress. Started at daylight and continued our route along the north shore. At seven passed a camp of Indians, consisting of three families, from whom three pair of snow-shoes, such as I obtained at Kettle Falls, were purchased. ...

Here were four Indians gathering from the pines a species of lichen, of which they make a sort of bread-cake in times of scarcity. In their camp were horns of Black-tailed deer and one pair of Red, or stag, the first I have seen since I left the coast.

The last eleven miles of the lake due east. Drift-wood is seen on the rocks, 10 feet above the present level. On leaving the lake the river returns to its natural breadth about 150 yards, and continues with a swift current for a mile, when it again gradually widens out into a second lake [Upper Arrow Lake], neither so broad nor deep as the one already mentioned. For fifteen miles the shores are low sand and gravel, with low points or necks of land chiefly wooded with *Pinus Larix* and *P. canadensisi*; under their shade a Species of *Lunarza* is just peeping through the ground. The timber is of more diminutive size and the lake widens out into bays on both sides, about three to four and a half miles broad. The canoes of the natives here are different in form from any I have seen before. The under part is made of the fine bark of *Pinus canadensis* (Pine), and about one foot from the gunwale of birch-bark, sewed with the roots of *Thuya* (Cedar) and the seams neatly gummed with resin from the pine.

They are 10 to 14 feet long, terminating at both ends sharply and bent inwards so much at the mouth that a man of middle size has some difficulty in placing himself in them. One that will carry six persons and their provisions may be carried on the shoulder with little trouble.

Sunday April 22nd – ... A river seems to flow into the bay on the east. At the end of the lake, at the foot of a high and steep hill, were three Indian lodges. Camped on the land. Purchased of them a little dried reindeer-meat and a little black bear, of which we have just made a comfortable supper.

They seem to live comfortably, many skins of Black-tailed, Reindeer, and Red deer being in their possession. I purchased a little wool of *Mouton Blanche* as a specimen of the quality of the wool; gave seven balls and the same number of charges of powder for it. (Get a pair of stockings made of it.)

Continued our route, leaving the lake at 4 P.M., the river being due north. Very shallow, 2 to 3 feet deep, 200 yards broad, with a fine gravelly bottom; the banks low and covered to the water's edge with wood poplar and birch of large dimensions on the brink, with brushwood of *Cornus* and *Symphoricarpos*.

This part of the river has low banks and in many places long sandbanks with large quantities of dead timber buried and bound together in the sand. Observed flocks of a small bird fluttering in the pines resembling the English wren but somewhat smaller; has a sweet chirping voice and hangs by the claws, head down, from the cones of the pines.

Camped at dusk on a high point of wood (the channel of the river being here covered with snow) on the right hand. A Sunday in any part of Great Britain is spent differently from what I have had in my power to do. Day after day without any observance (except date) passes, but not one passes without thoughts of home.

The immense landscape, the isolation of the little party of travellers amid boundless forests and mountains, homesickness – all these sentiments came together in Douglas' mind. Never before had he written about his feelings so openly and with such emotion. He was also keenly aware of the difficulties that lay just ahead. The challenge was another set of Dalles, a sequence of treacherous falls and rapids where the river foams for 40 miles, just above the modern city of Revelstoke (and now disappeared under a damn and lake). Douglas and his companions took three days to traverse these particular Dalles – Douglas carried his precious notebooks and every single item of his collection himself. The French-Canadian boatmen called the area the *Dalles des Morts*, the path of death, following an incident in 1817 when a seven-strong party of travellers had their canoe wrecked in the rapids, with all their possessions – food, clothing, blankets, tools, firearms – dashed to pieces. All they could do was to set off to walk to Fort Spokane, 300 miles distant. One by one they died. Eventually, Indians found the sole survivor. Nearby was a body; the survivor claimed that he had killed him in self-defence, a claim given short shrift at Fort Spokane. He was considered lucky, in a brutal age, to escape with being dismissed from the Hudson's Bay Company. Rumours of cannibalism abounded, and the episode made Douglas perturbed and uneasy. But, down to earth as ever, he finished his diary entry on a practical note: 'Progress nineteen miles. Nothing in the way of plants this day. The rocks micaceous granite. Warm during the day. Will prove, I hope the dividing ridge of the continent.'

Monday April 23rd – As usual, started in the grey of the morning, about four o'clock. Breakfasted on the right-hand side at nine; gained nine miles. Purchased some fish of a woman, consisting of three kinds – grey and red suckers, and white mullet, the latter of fine quality. Continued our journey at ten. The river and country the same until five o'clock P.M., being then about fifteen miles further, where the river takes a sudden bend to the north-east and to all appearance loses itself in the mountains.

At this place and for two miles higher a scene of the most terrific grandeur presents itself; the river is confined to the breadth of 35 yards – rapids, whirlpools, and still basins, the water of a deep dark hue, except when agitated. On both sides high hills with rugged rocks covered with dead trees, the roots of which being laid bare by the torrents are blown down by the wind, bringing with them blocks of granite attached to their roots in large masses, spreading devastation before them.

The Dalles safely negotiated, the boat was dragged ashore for repairs and to await the autumn, when the westbound Express would arrive, carrying Hudson's Bay men and goods to the forts downriver. From now on, Douglas and his party would travel on foot, through what was new country for Douglas. It seemed a good time to take stock.

Friday, 27th – Examined the seeds in my tin-box and found them in good order and repacked them without delay and at the same time tied up all my wardrobe, toilet, &c., which is as follows:

> four shirts (two linen and two flannel),
> three handkerchiefs,
> two pair stockings,
> a drab cloth jacket, vest and trousers of the same,
> one pair tartan trousers, vest and coat
> bedding, one blanket
> seven pairs of deerskin shoes, or as they are called, moccasins
> one razor, soap-box, brushstrap, and one towel, with half a cake of Windsor soap.

In addition to these I was presented with a pair of leggings by Mr Ermatinger, made out of the sleeves of an old blanket-coat or capot of the voyageurs. This, trifling as it may appear, I esteem in my present circumstances as very valuable. When the half of these my sole property is on my back, the remainder is tied in a handkerchief of the common sort. Now that I conceive my wanderings on the Columbia and through the various parts west of the Rocky Mountains to be over, I shall just state as near as possible their extent.

In 1825

	Miles
From the ocean to Fort Vancouver, on my arrival in April	90
In May, to and from the ocean to Fort Vancouver	180
In June, to and from the Great Falls	210
In July, to and from the ocean and along the coast	216
In August, journey on the Multnomah [Willamette] River	133
In September, to the Grand Rapids	96
On the mountains of the Grand Rapids	47
In October and November, to the sea	90
In the same, trip to Cheechmeeler River or Whitbey Harbour	53
Ascending said river	65
Portage from it to the Cowahidsk River	35
Descending the latter	40
An allowance of my daily wanderings from Fort Vancouver, my headquarters	850
	2105

In 1826

	Miles
In March and April, from Fort Vancouver to the Kettle Falls	620
In May, journey to Spokane	150
In June, from Kettle Falls to the junction of Lewis and Clark's River [Snake River]	414
In June, journey to the Blue Mountains	190
In July, a second to the same	137
In July, ascending Lewis and Clark's River to the north and south branch	140
A third journey to the Blue Mountains from that place	103
From Lewis and Clark's River to Spokane	165
From Spokane to Kettle Falls	75
In August, from Kettle Falls to Okanagan by land	130
From Okanagan to Fort Vancouver	490
In September, October, and November, from the Columbia to the Umpqua River and the country continuous thereto	593
To the ocean and the bays north of the Columbia in December	125

Daily allowance from my places of rendezvous	600
	<u>3932</u>

In 1827
In March and April, the whole chain of the
Columbia from the ocean to the Rocky

Mountains	995
Total	<u>7032</u>

Douglas and his companions had now left the Columbia at the 'Big Bend' in the River and climbed day by day towards the high peaks of the Rockies. Their immediate destination was Fort Assiniboine, some 250 miles distant, but first they had to ascend the Wood River towards the Athabasca Pass. Although it subsequently fell into disuse as easier routes across the Rockies were located, the Pass was the one then favoured by the Hudson's Bay Company. Douglas floundered in the snow, which was often covered in a crust of hard ice that was not strong enough to support him, and cursed his snowshoes with their flapping laces. He had almost no experience of this type of travel, and was, literally and metaphorically, out of his depth. Ermatinger offered to distribute Douglas' load among the other travellers, but, worried that his precious seeds might be lost, Douglas turned down his suggestion. After seven thousand miles of backbreaking endeavour, he was loath to risk any loss, even though his baggage weighed at least 45 lb (20 kg).

Sunday, 29th – Found the cold piercing. At 9 A.M. entered a point of wood where the snow was 4 to 7 feet deep, with a weak crust not strong enough to support us.

Obliged to put on my bears' paws (snow shoes); path rough, and in addition to the slender crust, which gives the traveller more labour, were dead trees and brushwood lying in all directions, among which I was frequently caught.

Towards noon, the snow having become soft and we weary with fatigue, camped on the brink of a river, where no time was lost in making a little breakfast, every person's appetite being well sharpened by our walk. Travelled in the wood four and a half miles, course north. Progress to-day fifteen miles.

In the twilight last night the Wolverene paid us a second visit, when I gave a few shots which he thought he could carry, which I did in consequence of it being dark, he secreting himself in some hole under the root of a tree. Evening fine. Made a pair of socks out of the legs of a pair of old stockings; the feet being worn, took the skirts of my coat to wrap round my toes instead of socks.

Strict economy here is requisite – my feet, ankles and toes very painful from the lacing of my snowshoes; otherwise, well and comfortable, lying in a deep hole or pit among the snow on a couch of pine branches with a good fire at my feet.

If good weather visits us, we are thankful; if bad, we make the best of a bad situation by creeping each under his blanket, and, when wet, dry it at the fire.

Although game was far from plentiful, Ermatinger managed to shoot a grouse. However, Douglas snatched this unusual addition to the party's diet and set about preserving it and packing it on his backpack. Named *Tetrao franklinii* after Captain John Franklin, the Arctic explorer, the creature still resides in the Royal Scottish Museum in Edinburgh. The grouse also featured in one of Douglas' finest hours, when he lectured to the august Linnean Society in London in November 1827.

Monday, 30th – The ravines or gullies unmeasurable, and towards noon becoming sinking, ascending two steps and sometimes sliding back three. No water; melted snow, which makes good tea; find no fault with the food, glad of anything. The remainder of the day is spent as follows: on arriving at a camp, one gathers a few dry twigs and makes fire, two or three procuring fuel for night, and as many more gathering green soft branches of Pine to sleep on, termed 'flooring the house', each hanging up his wet clothing to the fire, repairing snowshoes, and arranging his load for the ensuing day, that no time may be lost; in the morning, rise, shake the blanket, tie it on the top, and then try who is to be at the next stage first. Dreamed last night of being in Regent Street, London! Yet far distant. Progress nine miles.

Though Douglas might dream of the sophisticated delights of London, astonishingly, the challenges of the trek were not sufficient to absorb all his energies. Mountains had drawn him ever since the far-distant days when he had climbed in Perthshire with the Brown brothers and had explored the peaks of Scotland's west coast with Hooker. Now some immense summits stood immediately before him.

Tuesday, 1st May – After breakfast at one o'clock, being as I conceive on the highest part of the route, I became desirous of ascending one of the peaks, and accordingly set out alone on snowshoes to that on the left hand or west side, being to all appearances the highest. The labour of ascending the lower part, which is covered with pines, is great beyond description, sinking on many occasions to the middle. Half-way up vegetation ceases entirely, not so much as a vestige of moss or lichen on the stones. Here I found it less laborious as I walked on the hard crust. One-third from the summit it becomes a mountain of pure ice, sealed far over by Nature's hand as a momentous work of Nature's God. The height from its base may be about 5500 feet: timber, 2750 feet; a few mosses and lichen, 500 more; 1000 feet of perpetual snow; – the remainder, towards the top 1250, as I have said, glacier with a thin covering of snow on it. The ascent took me five hours; descending only one and a quarter. Places where the descent was gradual, I tied my shoes together, making them carry me in turn as a sledge.

Sometimes I came down at one spell 500 to 700 feet in the space of one minute and a half. I remained twenty minutes, my thermometer standing at 18° night closing fast in on me, and no means of fire, I was reluctantly forced to descend. The sensation I felt is beyond what I can give utterance to. Nothing, as far as the eye could perceive, but mountains such as I was on, and many higher, some rugged beyond any description, striking the mind with horror blended with a sense of the wondrous works of the Almighty. The aerial tints of the snow, the heavenly azure of the solid glaciers, the rainbow-like hues of their thin broken fragments, the huge mossy icicles hanging from the perpendicular rocks with the snow sliding from the steep southern rocks with amazing velocity, producing a crash and grumbling like the shock of an earthquake, the echo of which resounding in the valley for several minutes.

Douglas paid a price for these exertions in terms of his health. In particular, his eyes were affected by snow blindness.

A number of errors about mountain heights stem from Douglas' account of his ascent. He was the first person known to have climbed any of the peaks of the Northern Rockies – the voyageurs preferred to circle round mountains rather than climb them. Douglas chose what he thought was the highest peak, and estimated its height as about 5500 feet (1700 metres) above its base and some 16,000 feet (4900 metres) above sea level. He named this peak 'Mount Brown' in honour of the first Keeper of the Botanical Department of the British Museum. From the summit of Mount Brown, Douglas saw another peak 'nearly the same height; this I named "Mount Hooker" in honour of my early patron', though he was not able to climb it. Douglas' measurements meant that for over seventy years the two mountains were considered to be the tallest in North America. No one challenged Douglas' calculations; nor, since the Athabasca Trail fell into virtual disuse, did anyone climb the mountains again. When the true heights were established (Mount Brown is 9156 feet (2791 metres), Mount Hooker 10,782 feet (3286 metres)) as late as the 1920s, Douglas was accused of falsifying his measurements. However, it is generally agreed that his sole error was to accept the British Admiralty estimate of the height of the Athabasca Pass. This placed the Pass at about 11,000 feet (3350 metres), whereas its true height is just over 5750 feet (1750 metres). When this error is taken into account, Douglas' estimates of the heights of the two mountains above the Pass appear remarkably accurate.

On 2 May, Douglas reached the so-called 'Committee's Punch Bowl', the half-way point of the journey across the Rockies at the continental divide. Now the challenge of the most difficult part of the journey had been overcome, and the travellers descended into warmer weather as the spring drew on.

Wednesday, 2nd – At three o'clock I felt the cold so much, and the thermometer only stood at 2 degrees below Zero, that I was obliged to rise and enliven the fire, to get myself comfortably warmed before starting. Through three hundred yards of gradually rising open low Pine-woods, we passed, and about the same distance of open ground took us to the basis of this mighty river – a small circular lake, twenty yards in diameter, in the centre of the valley, with a small outlet on the West end, namely the Columbia, and another at the East end, namely, one of the branches of the Athabasca, which must itself be considered one of the tributaries of the Mackenzie River. ... This, the 'Committee's Punch Bowl', is considered as being half-way, and we were quite glad to know that the more laborious and arduous part of our journey was accomplished. The little stream Athabasca, over which we conveniently stepped, soon assumed a considerable size, and was dashed over cascades and formed cauldrons of limestone and basalt seven miles below the pass; like the tributaries of the Columbia on the west side, the Athabasca widens to a narrow lake and has a much greater descent than the Columbia.

As the sun was edging on the mountains, I descried about a mile off to the east behind a low knoll, a curling blue smoke rising from above the trees, a sign which gave me infinite pleasure. Without any undue loss of time I soon made up to it and found Jacques Cardinal [a guide and packer working in the Jasper area] with eight horses, who had come to meet us. An hour after one of the men came up and shortly afterwards we heard several shots fired, which I knew to be signals for me, which obliged me to send the man on horseback to say that I had arrived at the Moose encampment.

Old Cardinal roasted, on the stack before the fire, a shoulder of *Mouton gris*, which I found very fine. He had a pint copper kettle patched in an ingenious manner, in which he was boiling a little for himself; this with a knife was all the cooking-utensils. He observed he had no spirit to give me, but turning round and pointing to the river he said 'This is my barrel and it is always running.' So having nothing to drink out of, I had to take my shoulder of mountain sheep and move to the brook, helping myself as I found it necessary. ...

Finding none of my travellers come up, Cardinal gave me his blanket, reserving for himself the skin of a Reindeer. Mountains on all sides still as high and uneven, but with less snow; no glaciers and more wood. Crossed the river fifteen times in three places; two half full of water, very rapid and full of large stones. This day marched twenty-five miles.

Thursday, May 3rd – ... Intended to put up at the usual camp, but finding the horses and land better than expectation, they proceeded to the end of the portage on horses, I following with the gun in search of birds. Arrived at a small hut called the Rocky Mountain House at half-past six o'clock much fatigued. Thirty-four miles.

They were now over the worst of the journey and were descending, at first on horseback, then by canoe, towards Jasper House. This was situated about 35 miles north of present-day Jasper, famous for the National Park named after it.

Friday, May 4th – This morning I was glad and somewhat relieved to know that the mountain portage was completed and our journey for three days would be water communication namely, to Fort Assiniboine. Embarked at daybreak in two birch canoes, and being light went down the stream rapidly. The river banks are low, many places narrow, and widens out to long narrow shallow lakes full of sand shoals.

Arrived at Jasper House, three small hovels on the left side of the river, at two o'clock, where we put up to refresh ourselves for the remainder of the day. Minimum heat 29F, maximum 61F. Fine and warm. The country to the south undulating and woody; on the north low and hilly, with even surface, also woody, with a most commanding and beautiful view of the Rocky Mountains on the west and east. The difference of climate is great and the total change of verdure impresses on the mind of the traveller an idea of being, as it were, in a different hemisphere more than in a different part of the same continent, and only a hundred miles apart.

Obtained from J. Cardinal a pair of ram's horns which he considers the largest, and the skull, but I regret the lower jaw is wanting. Had some of the much talked-of white fish for supper, which I found good, although simply boiled in water, eaten without sauce or seasoning, hunger excepted, not so much as salt, afterwards drinking the liquor in which it was boiled; no bread. To-night comfortable.

Saturday, May 5th – Last night an old violin was found at our new lodgings, and Mr E.'s [Ermatinger's] servant being something of a performer nothing less than dancing in the evening would suit them [the voyageurs], which they kept up for a few hours. This may serve to show how little they look on hardship when past; only a few days ago, and they were as much depressed as they are now elated.

Sunday, 6th – Wind continuing throughout. Started at sunrise and resumed our voyage with progress until breakfast, having gained about twenty-seven miles. Found the current less and more ice on the banks of the river. Proceeded only three miles further when we overtook Mr George McDougall and four men on their way from Western Caledonia. Had suffered great hardship passing the mountains from hunger; had been nine days coming from Jasper House, which we left yesterday following the ice as it cleared.

To describe McDougall as having suffered 'great hardship' was an understatement. He and his companions had almost died from the severe cold as they travelled in search of Caribou hides, which they bought and then later sold again for making shoes and saddle bags. A few days earlier, one of McDougall's men had stolen some precious pemmican. Turning judge and instant executioner, McDougall took his gun and shot him dead. Perhaps news of the incident had already spread. In any case, Douglas, who by now had grown into a judicious diplomat, would not have wanted to risk setting down such a story on paper. However, he did add a jarring note: 'obliged to put up with him until four o'clock, when the ice made a rapid move and we embarked and made six miles more'.

Douglas and his party were now travelling by canoe down the Athabasca River towards Fort Assiniboine, some 184 miles downriver from Jasper House. After the grandeur of the Rockies, Douglas found the country rather flat, and its botany was disappointing. They arrived at the Fort on 7 May, but had to wait for provisions and also for re-inforcements to counter any threats from hostile natives. Douglas now joined a party travelling further down the Athabasca, where he met John Stuart, the Hudson's Bay Company's chief factor for the area. Stuart, who had accompanied Simon Fraser in 1808 on his expeditions further west, was extremely familiar with the country and knowl-edgeable about its natural history. Douglas took to him immediately and gleaned much advice about his future route across country. He also learned that Thomas Drummond, another Scottish botanist who was collecting in Canada, had travelled downriver shortly before, accompanying a party that had been transporting, among other things, some of Douglas' collection of seeds to Fort Edmonton.

Returning rather wearily to Fort Assiniboine, the party, now larger and including Stuart, set out overland for Fort Edmonton. It was a tough trip. Douglas walked virtually the entire 100 miles, and provisions for both men and horses were scarce. Anxious to inspect his seed collection, Douglas hurried ahead of the main party, and on 21 May arrived at the Fort, where he was met by John Rowand, the chief factor. When, the next day, he inspected his collection, he realized that Drummond had dried out the damp from his precious seeds. For Douglas, initial wariness that another botanist had had access to his collection turned into gratitude. Fortunately, Douglas had packed his spare shirts with his collection, and these had helped to absorb the damp; to Douglas it was no doubt small matter that the shirts themselves were ruined.

Douglas received a present while he was at Fort Douglas.

Wednesday May 23rd to Saturday 26th – A fine young Calumet [golden] Eagle, two years old, sex unknown, I had off Mr Rowand; brought from the Cootanie lands situated in the bosom of the Rocky Mountains near the headwaters of the Saskatchewan River. His plumage is much destroyed by the boys, who had deprived him of those in the tail that were just coming to their true colour. Many strange stories are told of this bird as to strength and ferocity, such as carrying off young deer entire, killing full-grown Long-tailed deer, and so on. Certain it is, he is both powerful and ferocious. I have seen all other birds leave their prey on his approach, manifesting the utmost terror. By most of the tribes the tail feathers are highly prized for adorning their war-caps and other garments. The pipestem is also decorated with them, hence comes the name. Abundant at all seasons in the Rocky Mountains, and in winter a few are seen on the mountainous country south of the Columbia on the coast. Are caught as follows:

A deep pit is dug in the ground, covered over with small sticks, straw, grass, and a thin covering of earth, in which the hunter takes his seat; a large piece of flesh is placed above, having a string tied to it, the other end held in the hand of the person below. The bird on eyeing the prey instantly descends, and while his talons are fastened in the flesh the hunter pulls bird and flesh into the pit. Scarcely an instance is known of failing in the hunt. Its ferocity is equal to the grisly bear's; will die before he lose his prey. The hunter covers his hands and arms with sleeves of strong deerskin leather for the purpose of preventing him from being injured by his claws. They build in the most inaccessible clefts of the rocks; have two young at a time, being found in June and July. This one had been taken only a few days after hatching and is now docile. The boys who have been in the habit of teasing him for some time past having ruffled his temper, I took and caged him with some difficulty. Had a fresh box made for seeds and another for my journals, portfolio, and sundry articles.

The unremarkable stay at Fort Edmonton soon came to an end. At the end of May, Douglas and his party set off down the North Saskatchewan River (in present-day Saskatchewan) towards Fort Carlton House, the next stop on the journey. Douglas travelled in Mr Stuart's boat.

Saturday May 26th to Thursday 31st – Last night, before we should part with our new friends, Mr Ermatinger was called on to indulge us with a tune on the violin, to which he readily complied. No time was lost in forming a dance; and as I was given to understand it was principally on my account, I could not do less than endeavour to please by jumping, for dance I could not.

The evening passed away pleasantly enough; breakfasted at five o'clock and embarked in Messrs Stuart and Rowand's boat with all my baggage and went rapidly before the stream.

Day warm and pleasant. Put ashore in the dusk to cook supper, and as the Stone Indians had for the last twelve months manifested hostile intentions it was deemed unsafe to sleep at a camp where fire was.

Danger of attack by unfriendly Indians prevented Douglas botanizing on his own. Instead he had to keep with the others as they hunted large game. Some unpleasant surprises were in store.

We therefore embarked, had the boats tied two and two together, and drifted all night. Finding this mode of travelling very irksome, never on shore except a short time when cooking breakfast, always dusk before a second meal, I began to think this sort of travelling ill adapted for botanizing. The country here changed much for the better; small hills and clumps of poplar and small rocks. Just in the dusk of the evening had a fine chase after two Red deer swimming in the Water, and on following in the boat both were killed; smaller than those West of the mountains. Saw a huge grisly bear (unsuccessful in killing him) and a number of small plain wolves. Passed Fort Vermilion, an abandoned establishment, and Bear and Red Deer Hills, where the country becomes pastoral and highly adorned by Nature. Soil dry and light, but not infertile.

On Wednesday at sunrise five large buffalo bulls were seen standing on a colour of the river. Mr Harriott, who is a skilful hunter, departed and killed two, and wounded two more; all would have fallen had not some of the others imprudently given them the wind, that is on the wind side. ...

June 1st – A party of hunters went out at daylight after the herd of animals seen last night. Most willingly I followed them, not for the purpose of hunting but gathering plants. Mr Harriott and Ermatinger and three hunters went of to the opposite side to a herd and killed two very large and fine animals.

Seeing their boat at the side of the river and no one in it, gave us to know they had all gone for the meat and we put to shore. A party from our boats was sent off to help them. Accompanied by Mr F. McDonald, they readily were guided to their companions by calls, and found Mr H. and E. pursuing a bull that had been wounded, in which he joined. The animal, which had suffered less injury than was expected, turned and gave chase to Mr McDonald and overtook him.

His case being dreadful coming in contact with such a formidable animal and exasperated, seeing that it was utterly impossible to escape, he had presence of mind to throw himself on his belly flat on the ground, but this did not save him. He received the first stroke on the back of the right thigh and pitched in the air several yards. The wound sustained was a dreadful laceration literally laying open the whole back part of the thigh to the bone; received five more blows, at each of which he went senseless.

Perceiving the beast preparing to strike him a seventh, he laid hold of his wig (his own words) and hung on; man and bull sank the same instant. His companions had the melancholy sensation of standing to witness their companion mangled and could give no assistance – all their ball being fired.

Being under cloud night, and from what had taken place, his life could not be expected. One returned and acquainted the camp, when each with his gun went off to the spot. On arriving some of the half-breed hunters were in a body to discharge their guns at him, when I called out to Mr Harriott not to allow them to fire all together; that one well-directed shot was enough and by firing more Mr McDonald if alive might fall by one, being close, if not under the bull. He agreed to it, but while giving orders to some that he depended on, a shot went off by accident without doing any injury to anyone, and had the unexpected good fortune to raise the bull, first sniffing his victim, turning him gently over, and walking off.

I went up to him and found life still apparent, but quite senseless. He had sustained most injury from a blow on the left side, and had it not been for a strong double sealskin shot-pouch, with ball; shot, wadding, &c., which shielded the stroke, unquestionably he must by that alone have been deprived of life, being opposite the heart. The horn went through the pouch, coat, vest, flannel, and cotton shirts, and bruised the skin and broke two ribs. He was bruised all over, but no part materially cut except the thigh – left wrist dislocated.

My lancet being always in my pocket like a watch, I had him bled and his wounds bound up, when he was carried to the boat; gave twenty-five drops of laudanum and procured sleep. In hopes of finding Dr Richardson no time was lost to convey him to Carlton. The following day several more were killed, but from what I had seen my desire of seeing such dreadful brutes cooled.

Finan McDonald was a red-haired, red-bearded Scot, 6 foot 4 inches tall, who gloried in his larger-than-life reputation. He had already staked a formidable claim to the Snake Bay region for the Hudson's Bay Company, and had engaged in desperate battles with the Blackfoot tribe, who lost sixty-eight warriors for a dozen Hudson's Bay men. The incident with the bull left him badly injured, but, at least partly thanks to Douglas' rapid decision-making and ministrations, he lived for many years, and eventually became a member of the Canadian Parliament.

Douglas and his party, including the injured McDonald, arrived at Carlton House on 3 June. Here Douglas met Thomas Drummond. The two men warmed to each other immediately. Drummond's collection greatly impressed Douglas, and this took the edge off his disappointment at the abandonment, because of aggressive Indians, of his much-anticipated trip down the Red River. Drummond was another redoubtable Scottish plant-collector; later he botanized in Texas and New Mexico, dying in Havana in 1835.

> In the evening had an account of [Drummond's] travels and progress and informed me had received a note from Mr Sabine concerning *Phlox Hoodii*. He appears to have done well. I must state he liberally showed me a few of the plants in his possession – birds, animals, &c., in the most unreserved manner.

After a day or two, the party set off again, canoeing down the Saskatchewan River and then across Cedar Lake and the Grand Rapids first to Cumberland House and then to Norway House at the northernmost tip of Lake Winnipeg. Arriving at Norway House on 16 June, he found, much to his delight, letters awaiting him from, among others, his brother and Dr Hooker. His brother wrote with the sad news of his father's death – 'news of a melancholy cast', he recorded in his journal. Subsequent correspondence from Joseph Sabine revealed that Douglas instructed that £40 of his salary – a major portion of his annual income – should be sent to his mother.

On 17 June, George Simpson, Governor of the Northern Department of the Hudson's Bay Company, arrived at Norway House *en route* from Montreal to Hudson Bay. Simpson was developing into one of the legends of early Canada. A tough, hard-driving Scot, he was much feared on his tours of inspection of Company outposts. He was unscrupulous and extremely cunning, and his determination and energy led him to the top of the Company and to huge political influence both in Montreal, where he was based, and beyond. Governor Simpson noted Douglas' exertions from his journey, and offered him 'some linen ... which I refused, at the same time extremely indebted to him'.

Douglas stayed at Norway House until 2 July, when he embarked on another exploration following a chance invitation. At Norway House, Douglas had also met Sir John Franklin, the Arctic explorer. Franklin offered him a passage in his canoe across Lake Winnipeg and down to the Red River. Douglas was glad to accept. On 12 July, he finally reached the Red River Settlement, where he stayed with Donald McKenzie, 'Governor of the Colony, a most kind and excellent man, who during my whole stay showed me great hospitality, and afforded me much valuable assistance'. At the thriving Settlement, which eventually grew into the city of Winnipeg, Douglas made the acquaintance of the Reverend Provenchier, the Roman Catholic Bishop, 'a person of liberal disposition and highly cultivated mind, who lives only to be useful and to be kind' and took every opportunity for botanizing – in his month's stay he formed 'a small Herbarium of two hundred and eighty-eight species, many of them new to me'.

On 10 August, Douglas left the Settlement and started on the eighteen-day journey north-east to Hudson Bay through a succession of lakes and rivers. The trip was uneventful, and Douglas noted merely that the stormy weather made sailing uncomfortable and that he had discovered a specimen of *Linnaea borealis*, the twinflower, in fruit. Unfortunately, Douglas' pet calumet eagle, which had travelled with him for two thousand miles, accidentally strangled itself on its cord just before they reached York Factory, the hub of the Hudson's Bay Company operations and the transit-point for goods to and from Britain. Here *Prince of Wales*, the ship that was to carry him home, was already waiting in the Bay. Douglas was 'kindly received' by John McTavish, the Chief Factor, who thoughtfully provided new clothes for the worn-out traveller.

Douglas had spent almost two and a half years in North America, and by his own calculations had travelled nearly 10,000 miles on foot or horseback or by canoe. He had explored and botanized constantly, and for the most part had remained out of contact with his fellow-men. The culmination of this massive human effort – physical and mental – was the trek across the continent from the Pacific to Hudson Bay. While the arduous route was already familiar to fur trappers, Douglas was the first outsider to succeed in making the land crossing. A final adventure remained before he sailed for England. Meeting Thomas Drummond again, they joined a party rowing out to visit the ship anchored in Hudson Bay. A tremendous storm blew up and drove their rowing boat some 70 miles out, well out of sight of land. Those on the shore gave them up for lost, but after enduring the storm for two days and two nights, Douglas and his companions managed to row back to land.

Worn out from his epic travels, Douglas was now very ill and lost all power in his limbs. He spent the entire voyage back to England, from 15 September to 11 October, confined to his cabin, unable to move or to write up his journal. However, an entry made shortly before he sailed captures his mood at the end of his trip.

Here ended my labours, and I may be allowed to state, that when the natural difficulties of passing through a new country are taken into view, with the hostile disposition of the native tribes, and the almost insuperable inconveniences that daily occur, I have great reason to consider myself a highly favoured individual. All that my feeble exertions may have affected, only stimulate me to fresh exertions.

Chapter Nine

FAME IN LONDON

'Qualified, as Mr Douglas undoubtedly was, for a traveller, and
happy as he unquestionably found himself in surveying the wonders
of nature in its grandest scale, in conciliating the friendship (a
faculty he eminently possessed) of the untutored Indians, and in
collecting the productions of the new countries he explored; it was
quite otherwise with him during his stay in his native land.'
William Hooker, 'Brief Memoir of the
Life of Mr David Douglas', 1836

D ouglas reached London on 11 October 1827. That he had
managed to survive, and had come home to tell the tale, was
relief enough for the Horticultural Society. For a long time the
Society and its officials had been apprehensive about his chances of
returning alive. Thomas Andrew Knight, the Society's President, had
gloomily prophesied that:

Our collector proposes, when he has sent all he can home by a
ship, to march across the continent of America to the country of
the United States on this side, and to collect what plants and
seeds he can in his journey: but it is probable that he will perish
in the attempt. Mr Sabine says, that if he escapes, he will soon
perish in some other hardy enterprise or other. It is really lamen-
table that so fine a fellow should be sacrificed.

At first, Douglas, ill and tired, could not enjoy the Society's
excitement and the adulation heaped upon him. He was too sick even
to address the Linnean Society, and Joseph Sabine, the Society's

141

Secretary, had to read his carefully prepared paper on his treasured sugar pine on his behalf. Gradually, however, his battered body grew stronger, and eventually he rose from his sick bed to glory in his triumph and the universal praise. Sabine gushed to the Society's Council that 'Mr Douglas throughout his mission acted in the spirit with which he had executed the trust he had undertaken'.

The plants and seeds he had sent home were evidence of Douglas' success. He had despatched more material than any collector before him – the Society was swamped. The seeds of large trees were sent off to the many members with estates big enough to grow them. The two hundred or so varieties of smaller plants – shrubs and herbaceous and annual flowers – were nurtured in the Society's garden, where Douglas could watch tenderly over their progress. Many proved hardy enough to grow in the British climate and went on to become staples of English gardens, among them lupins and penstemons. The December 1830 edition of the Horticultural Society's *Transactions* reported that Douglas had brought home with him an even greater number of plants and seeds than previously, and that from them 210 distinct species had been raised in the Society's gardens. Of these, eighty were 'abandoned' as 'botanical curiosities', while the remaining 130 were grown and distributed to all parts of the world.

Honours were heaped on Douglas. He was awarded fellowships (which had the attraction of free membership) of the Linnean, Geological and Zoological Societies. He was lionized by fashionable society – his stories of escapes from grizzly bears, near-starvation, canoe dashes down roaring waters, the rugged men of the Hudson's Bay Company and parleys with Indian 'savages' were listened to avidly in drawing-rooms and lecture halls.

The Society was particularly thrilled by the cost of the expedition, which amounted to less than £400, including Douglas' pay. George Bentham, a prominent member, blustered that:

> His whole expenses for food, etc whilst among the Indians, three years, amounted to £66 including a wager of £5 he lost to an Indian chief. He used to pay the Indians by drafts on the Hudson's Bay Company for little articles such as a few nails etc. which makes the detailed account transmitted by the Company to the Horticultural Society a very curious document.

Yet, as John Lindley of the Society wrote a few months later, the flowering currant, *Ribes sanguineum*, earned the Society the cost of the entire trip. Not surprisingly, as time passed and the Society continued to trot Douglas out on display, the initial flattery palled and dark thoughts intruded. Perhaps it was the comparison between the value to the Society of the plants he had brought back after such titanic efforts and his salary (which was less than the porter at the Society's office earned); perhaps it was the materialistic and class-ridden society in which he now found himself, or maybe even the anti-climax of adjusting to a more mundane life in contrast with his independence, self-reliance and adventures in the Pacific North West – whatever the reasons, Douglas now became increasingly ill at ease and difficult in his dealings with the Society and with London life in general. He took to dressing as though he were still in the wilderness, and was disagreeable and discourteous to nearly everyone. Invited by the Society to write up his diary for publication, with the singularly munificent offer to keep the profits for himself, he vacillated endlessly and turned down offers of help from Sabine and Lindley. (The manuscript lay forgotten for decades in the Society's vaults, and was eventually published in 1914.) However, he did compile a descriptive list, headed 'Some American Pines', of the seventeen species of conifer he had found in the Pacific North West.

Hooker – the only person who could influence Douglas, and perhaps the only person for whom Douglas felt much regard – understood the situation well, and summarized it succinctly in his 'Brief Memoir':

Qualified, as Mr Douglas undoubtedly was, for a traveller, and happy as he unquestionably found himself in surveying the wonders of nature in its grandest scale, in conciliating the friendship (a faculty he eminently possessed) of the untutored Indians, and in collecting the productions of the new countries he explored; it was quite otherwise with him during his stay in his native land.

Mr Booth [an old friend of Douglas] remarks, in his letter to me on the subject, 'His company was now courted and unfortunately for his peace of mind he could not withstand the temptation of appearing as one of the Lions among the learned and scientific men in London. ... Flattered by their attention and by the notoriety of his botanical discoveries, which were exhibited at the meetings of the Horticultural Society, or published in the leading periodicals of the day, he seemed for a time as if he had attained the summit of his ambition. But alas! when the novelty had subsided, he began to perceive that he had been pursuing a shadow instead of a reality.'

Douglas' feelings were understandable. He rapidly realized that the accolades were superficial, especially since membership of the learned societies of the time was confined to the rich and titled. His achievements may have been revered; his person was not. He was furious that many of his animal specimens, obtained at great personal cost in dangerous terrain, remained rotting in corners of the Society's offices, still unpacked and eaten away by moths. On the far-off Pacific coast he might have longed for home. Now, back in Britain, he found he no longer felt at home there. Hob-nobbing with London's rich and privileged exposed his unease and lack of sophistication; his social position and underprivileged background left him uncomfortable.

In the Douglas papers in the Royal Horticultural Society's Lindley Library a memo records an episode, on 16 April 1828, in which Douglas was chastised in front of Hooker for speaking out of turn. Lindley was 'quite disgusted with the manner in which he [Douglas] spoke to Mr Sabine ... [and considered] that he must either be insane or that he was conducting himself very ill. ... Mr Douglas appeared to be quite ashamed of his conduct.'

Douglas now took a perverse pleasure in favouring Hooker with as much information as possible. 'Everything goes to Glasgow, Dr Hooker gets all, is in everyone's mouth,' he wrote smugly in a letter to Hooker. Hooker's great work *Flora Boreali-Americana*, which he published between 1829 and 1840, took much botanical information from Douglas' diaries, along with the recollections of Thomas Drummond and Dr John Richardson, whom Douglas had met during his journey home. Hooker insisted on including a map of Douglas' route; when he was shown the proof, Douglas roundly castigated the publisher for showing his journeys in a 'sickly yellow', which he thought inappropriate for a 'culler of weeds'. Green replaced the yellow. Information provided by Douglas also appeared in James Wilson's *Illustrations of Zoology* (1831).

Douglas finally travelled to Glasgow in the autumn of 1828 to visit Hooker, who was Director of the Botanic Garden; Douglas was astonished at the transformation his old friend and mentor had achieved. Hooker arranged for Douglas to have his portrait painted by Sir Daniel MacNee, the society artist who worked mainly in Glasgow. Several lithographs were produced from the painting, and this small portrait, 14 inches by $12^1/_2$, is now the principal image we have of Douglas, although his niece, Miss Aitkinson, also made a small pencil drawing of him.

On his return to London, he met Archibald Menzies, and on one memorable evening the pair were joined by Dr John Scouler. The three

Scotsmen, each of whom had travelled to the Pacific North West, would have enjoyed swapping stories and recollections. For Menzies in particular it must have been a stirring moment when his compatriot arrived home with many of the plants he himself had discovered. Douglas was suitably deferential to his senior colleague. In the paper he wrote that year – 'An Account of some new, and little known Species of the Genus Ribes' – he described Menzies as his 'esteemed friend'.

Menzies had retired from the Navy and had settled down in London to practise as a doctor. He had twice circumnavigated the globe; one of the principal inspirations behind the Society's desire to explore in the Pacific North West, he was the father of botanical exploration in that part of the world. He eventually died in 1842 at the age of eighty-eight. Scouler also travelled around the world before returning home to practise medicine in his native Glasgow. He then became Professor of Mineralogy in Dublin, subsequently transferring to geology and zoology. When he retired, in 1853, he settled back in Glasgow, where he was one of the leading scientific lights until his death in 1871.

The Colonial Office asked Douglas to give his opinion on the location of the north-west boundary between the USA and Canada. This was a flattering task, and Douglas wrote to the Colonial Office on 27 November 1828:

> There is not any natural boundary which would give a plea to the American Government to claim this fine country up to the 49 degree. Neither have they priority of discovery either on the Coast or in the Interior. The boundary line ought to extend (from my observations on the spot) from the 'Lake of the Woods' keeping the same parallel to the Rocky Mountains, from thence south on the Eastern Base, to the pass of Lewis and Clark 46 degree North Latitude and then cross over the dividing side of the continent to the sources of the Solomon (Salmon) River which stream those travellers descended until they came on the Columbia in 46 degrees 37 North latitude 119 degrees West long and from that point to the sea on the Columbia leaving the river open to both powers.

Douglas also explained the huge importance of the fertile Columbia River and the valuable timber in the area.

These were prophetic opinions. Had the boundary been drawn where Douglas suggested, Britain would have controlled the Columbia River area, with its massive timber supplies. Douglas foresaw the time when, stripped of beaver by the rapacious Hudson's Bay Company, the Columbia River would grow rich on timber exports. Gratifying as it was to be singled out in this way as an expert, Douglas still had no prospect of a worthwhile job. The Horticultural Society was experiencing one of its periodic crises and was unwilling to send plant-collectors on expensive missions. Douglas may have been brilliantly successful, but all he could now reasonably expect was a curatorship at a botanical garden. He turned on his friends. Of a lecture by Lindley he wrote in barbed style that 'the beginning was bad, the end was bad and the middle worthy of the beginning and the end, not one sentence worth repeating, and the manner of delivery shockingly ill'. Lindley was eager to share Douglas' American plant collections with Hooker, but Douglas was reluctant to agree. He wrote to Hooker:

> Certainly for the present I should not give him any. I am not certain but I shall manage to keep him out of my collections. ... He shall not have the pleasure of picking of them as before of my former collection and then to toss me overboard when he obtained it all. I trust you will not think me spiteful but really after the usage I have received, and if you knew all, I am confident you would in one moment say I was right, and would advise me to be more cautious for the future.

Thomas Nuttall, whose gardens he had visited in Philadelphia, came in for much the same treatment.

Douglas found himself friendless and unhappy in London. Everything was disagreeable – the noise, the smells, the society and especially the climate, which, he grumbled to Hooker, 'kills me'. The Society was in a real dilemma about what to do with their famous yet troublesome plant-collector. Douglas himself wished to return, but to begin with the Society was not inclined to agree to a further trip, probably on the grounds of expense. Eventually, the obvious solution was adopted, however, and Douglas was asked to return to the west coast of America. This time, however, he was to concentrate his botanizing on California, where the climate allowed quite different species from further north to flourish.

The prospect changed everything. Once again, Hooker had been at work in the background, persuading the Society that Douglas should be despatched. Hooker himself was eager to obtain the botanical treasures that he was certain lay within the soil of California. Both the Horticultural Society and Hooker urged Douglas to pack up and travel out as soon as possible. The Hudson's Bay Company offered

Douglas a berth on one of their ships – he was now benefiting from the good impression he had made on senior members of the Company. And Douglas' Spanish, which Hooker had encouraged him to learn, would finally be of use.

Douglas himself was hugely excited by the whole project. He wrote to Hooker on 6 August 1829 that 'my principal objects are to make known the vegetable treasures of the Interior of California'. Douglas was already ambitiously mapping out even more extensive travels – to the Sandwich Islands and also to Russia.

> I am not quite certain, but when I have completed my expedition on the Continent of America, I may cross to the opposite shore and return ... near the Russian frontier with California. What a glorious prospect! ... The work of the same individual on both Continents, with the same instrument under similar circumstances and in corresponding latitudes.

Existing information about California was sketchy, and so Douglas was to survey as well as botanize. Captain Edward Sabine, Joseph Sabine's brother, agreed to teach Douglas the basics of surveying and the techniques of computing results into accurate map data. As Douglas had only limited mathematical training, he had to learn the trigonometry of planes and spheres for global positioning and also how to use the instruments. Sabine decided to concentrate on the practicalities in the three months that remained before Douglas left; the basic mathematics he could learn later during the long sea voyage. At Greenwich Observatory, Sabine taught Douglas to use a sextant, barometer, hygrometer, thermometer and compass, and also a chronometer and instruments for calculating the irregularities of the earth's magnetic field.

Douglas grasped the challenge – and his attitude to the world was transformed. He worked up to eighteen hours a day; his ability to absorb knowledge quickly greatly impressed his teacher. 'I have had only one or two very slight outbreakings as Mr Sabine calls my fits since I saw you,' he wrote to Hooker in August 1829. He became totally dedicated to his work.

Perhaps because of Douglas' behaviour, or perhaps because of its uncertain finances, the Horticultural Society was not inclined to generosity, and was only prepared to pay for the instruments he needed for botanizing, meagre though his other requirements were. However, the Colonial Office made a grant of £80 for surveying instruments, whereupon Sabine went out and ran up a bill for £231 eight shillings and six pence in order to equip his pupil for the tasks demanded of him. The Colonial Office also agreed to pay Douglas' expenses for his trip as well as an additional sum for the charts he was to make for them, while the Zoological Society gave him a good double-barrelled shotgun worth £18. In contrast with his first two voyages, on this expedition Douglas was well supplied with good instruments and equipment. Of course, the amounts being invested in him – together with free travel provided by the Hudson's Bay Company – put him under an even greater obligation to study hard, and later to come up with the desired results.

Nonetheless, Douglas had to ask the Horticultural Society for a £40 advance on his salary in order to buy his personal equipment. At the last moment, private donations made up the necessary money. Douglas' attitude to money was typically Presbyterian. He felt that he should be rewarded fairly for his endeavours, yet, as he wrote to Hooker: 'If I had a good salary I might fold my hands and become lazy, therefore I can feel no objection to being paid according to my labour.'

Another worry was finding a Bible of 'good bold legible type' – Douglas' sight was already beginning to fade as a result of the ophthalmia and snow blindness he had suffered on his previous expedition. Douglas failed to find a suitable edition in London, and eventually Hooker bought one for him in Glasgow.

Revitalized at the prospect of travel and at the chance to botanize once again, Douglas set off on a farewell trip to his mother in Scone and to his brother at Drumlanrig Castle in Dumfriesshire.

As a final, touching, present to himself, and ever the animal-lover, he bought a small Scotch terrier, Billy, which now became his constant companion on his travels. The pair returned to London, collected Douglas' equipment, and boarded the Hudson's Bay Company ship the *Eagle*, bound, under the ominously named Captain Grave, for the Columbia River.

Chapter Ten

CALIFORNIA

'The ladies are handsome, of a dark olive brunette, with good teeth, and the dark fine eyes, which bespeaks the descendent of Castille, Catalan or Leon. They (sweet creatures) have a greater recommendation than personal attractions. They are very amiable. On this head I must say, *Finis*, otherwise you will be apt to think, if ever I had a kind feeling for man's better half, I left it in (*Calida Fornax*) California.'
Letter from Douglas to Hooker, 1831

Fresh from his intensive studies with Captain Sabine at Greenwich Observatory, Douglas sailed on the *Eagle* on 31 October 1829. His scientific instruments were his main preoccupation during the long voyage, and every day he recorded the latitude and longitude. Writing to Captain Sabine, he claimed that, 'I never suffered an opportunity to pass without endeavouring to perfect myself in the use of my instruments. During my whole passage, my days were only moments.' The tedium of his first voyage, six years before, was forgotten. His instruments were of the best quality and functioned very well, and at every port of call Douglas found that the chronometer was giving the time accurately. In addition, the Colonial Office had furnished him with letters of recommendation directing any of Her Majesty's ships in the Pacific North West to afford him 'such facilities as they may have in their power to grant him'. All in all, despite the inadequate financial reward offered by the Horticultural Society, he described his journey as 'not [that] of a commonplace tourist', and began to feel that he was embarking on a royal tour.

Unfortunately, Douglas' diary did not survive this trip, and so the main sources of information about Douglas' last years are his letters to his family, friends and associates, of whom Hooker is the most important. Contemporary accounts by others who met and recollected Douglas are also important. A.G. Harvey's extensive research into these records, published in his excellent book *Douglas of the Fir*, provided much of the missing detail about Douglas' activities during this period. Subsequent commentators on Douglas, including the present authors, who have relied heavily on his work, are much indebted to Harvey.

Making landfall on Honolulu, Douglas started taking barometric measurements of several mountains, and climbed Mauna Parii, the seat of Akua, the God of Fire. The constant motion and the large quantities of metal in the vicinity had distorted his instrument readings on board the *Eagle*; once on land he hoped to obtain more accurate readings. The botany of the island fascinated him – ever-observant, he noted over five hundred species of fern alone – and he resolved to try to return. Before his ship sailed, he bought a present for Hooker, a set of all the books that had been published on the Hawaiian Islands, elegantly bound in tortoiseshell.

Much to his disappointment, the *Eagle* did not call at the big island of Hawaii, so depriving him of the opportunity to climb the two famous volcanoes, Mauna Kea and Mauna Loa, but headed instead across the Pacific towards America. On 3 June, seven months after leaving London, Douglas arrived for the second time at the mouth of the Columbia. The fur traders of the Hudson's Bay Company were happy to see him again, and 'pleased to find that his stature as a disciple of science had greatly increased'. Improvements had continued at Fort Vancouver, especially in the garden, and the farm had been extended. There were also a number of new residents, one of whom described Douglas as 'a fair florid partially bald-headed Scotsman of medium stature and gentlemanly address about forty-eight years of age'. Douglas was in fact thirty-one – clearly the life of a botanical collector had exacted a heavy toll. Douglas found willing assistants for his surveying work in the boys sent out to be trained by the Hudson's Bay Company. One of them, George B. Roberts, who later became treasurer and probate judge of Wahkiakum County in Washington State, recalled that assisting Douglas helped to 'furbish up my school acquirements'. Douglas found a number of changes in the Columbia region. Fever had decimated the native population, while greater contact with Europeans had inevitably led to conflict and clashes; Douglas would now be travelling and botanizing in a much more hostile environment.

Although Douglas' ultimate destination was California, it was six months before he could complete his journey, largely because there was

no boat to take him south. In the meantime, ever inquisitive and energetic, he seized the opportunity for botanizing, secure in the knowledge
that its gentler climate made California suitable for travel and plant-
collection during the winter. He journeyed up the Columbia to Fort
Walla Walla, taking one William Johnson with him as a personal
servant and assistant. Johnson, an old man-o'-war hand with a roving
disposition, was well suited to the task; later he became the first resident of present-day Portland. At Walla Walla, Douglas renewed his
friendship with George Barnston, with whom he had passed the cold
winter of 1826–27. Once again, Barnston, according to Harvey, was
struck by Douglas' enthusiasm and – a vital characteristic for any
collector – his 'quickness of sight . . . in the discovery of any small object
or plant on the ground over which we passed'. His problems with his
sight were perhaps still confined to print. Barnston recalled that:

> When in the boats, as they proceeded along, he would frequently
> spring up in an excited manner, and with extended arms keep his
> finger pointed at a particular spot on the beach or on the shelving
> and precipitous rocks, where some new or desirable plant had
> attracted his notice. This was the signal to be put on shore, and
> we would then be amused with the agility of his leap to the land,
> and the scramble like that of a cat upon the rocks to the object he
> wished to obtain, happy if he achieved this without slipping and
> falling into the deep water alongside the boat.

Barnston also recalled that he and Douglas employed young Indian
boys to catch lizards with a horse-hair noose. Lying flat on the hot
sand, the boys would lasso the lizard as it emerged from its hole.

This was a productive expedition. In the Blue Mountains,
Douglas wrote to Hooker on 11 October, 'I again found my *Paeonia*'.
This was the *Paeonia brownii* which he had found there four years
previously. In all, Douglas sent Hooker three chests of seeds. These
included

> one bundle of six species, exceedingly beautiful, of the genus
> *Pinus*. Among these, <u>*P. nobilis*</u> is by far the finest. I spent three
> weeks in a forest composed of this tree and could not cease to
> admire it; in fact my words can be only monotonous expressions
> of my feeling. I have added one new species during this journey,
> *P. grandis*, a noble tree … growing from one hundred and
> seventy to two hundred feet high.

When they reached Britain, Douglas' seed and the resulting

specimens proved extremely popular. Plants of the noble fir were sold to fellows of the Horticultural Society for as much as 15 to 20 guineas each. These two trees, the noble fir and the grand fir, became some of the most popular and finest specimen trees grown in British collections in the nineteenth century, and are now firmly established as forest trees. Noble fir, now renamed as one of the silver firs, *Abies procera*, is the largest of the true firs. Very tolerant of extreme temperatures, it is popular as a Christmas tree; in Germany and the Netherlands, its attractive blue-green foliage is used for decoration.

Turning downstream again on July 23, Douglas reached the Cascades, 'the land of my little vain Indian Chumtalia', who had accompanied him on an expedition four years previously. He hoped to persuade Chumtalia to join him again, but this proved out of the question as it was the time of the Potlatch, the present-giving ceremony, of Chumtalia's young daughter – Douglas considered that it would have been ungracious to press him to travel at such a time. Continuing downstream, Douglas reached Fort Vancouver in time for the kail harvest, which no doubt reminded him of his native cuisine, kail being a humble and disparaged brassica much grown and eaten in Scotland.

During August, Douglas voyaged up the Santiam and Willamette Rivers, and made his first observations of Mount Jefferson. He calculated its height as 11,320 feet (3450 metres) – a reasonably accurate estimate given his inexperience. (It is now thought to be 10,495 feet (3200 metres) high.) As presents, Douglas took four jew's harps, three pounds of assorted beads, three bundles of barleycorn beads, four dozen plated coat buttons, and a whole gross of finger rings, all purchased at the Company's store in Fort Vancouver for nineteen shillings and four pence. Unfortunately, Douglas lost all his specimens on the return trip on the Santiam, at exactly the same spot where he had lost everything in 1826: 'a kelpie or elf is the charm of that stream'.

Back at Fort Vancouver, he discovered that Chumtalia had died: 'Poor Chumtalia is since dead. He was blown up by his own powder horn which was on his person, and falling on his side, his knife entered about the fifth rib so that he died. He is now laid with his fathers.' Worse still, a fever, probably influenza, had broken out. It spared neither Indians nor Europeans – twenty-four of the Company's men died, and activity in the Fort came to a virtual standstill. In his letter to Hooker, Douglas wrote:

> A dreadfully fatal intermittent fever broke out in the lower parts of this river about eleven weeks ago, which has depopulated the country. Villages, which had afforded from one to two hundred active warriors, are totally gone; not a soul remains! The houses

are empty, and flocks of famished dogs are howling about, while the dead bodies lie strewed in every direction on the sands of the river. I am one of the very few persons among the Hudson's Bay Company people who have stood it, and sometimes I think, even I have got a great shake, and can hardly consider myself out of danger.

Originally, Douglas had planned to travel south to California by land, making his way through the difficult terrain where in autumn 1826 he had sought and found the sugar pine. The tree still intrigued him, and he wanted to collect more cones and seeds. But his previous experience with hostile Indians, who continued to threaten explorers, decided him against the journey. The forts of the Hudson's Bay Company were vulnerable and ill-defended as so many Company men had died from fever. Douglas wrote to Hooker:

You may judge my situation, when I say to you that my rifle is in my hand day and night; it lies by my side under my blanket when I sleep, and my faithful little Scotch terrier, the companion of all my journeys, takes his place at my feet. To be obliged thus to accoutre myself is truly terrible. However, I fail not to do my best, and if unsuccessful in my operations can make my mind easy with the reflection that I used my utmost endeavours.

As overland travel was impossible, Douglas sailed in late November in the Company's brig *Dryad*, arriving at Monterey, California, on 22 December. Before he left Fort Vancouver, Harvey tells us, he drew a comprehensive list of supplies from the store.

Cod line, candles, shot, lead, cotton, etc., plus;

	£	s	d
10 lbs Hyson Tea	3		
60 lbs loaf sugar	1	15	
9 gals Madeira wine	7	1	
1 Faustian Coattee		1	1
1 pair bedford trousers		14	3
9 gals brandy	2		6
2 large black silk Handkerchiefs		17	6
2 Bernagore silk Handkerchiefs		2	6
1 large moose deer skin	5	8	
3 prime chev. skins		6	9

	£	s	d
2 pairs Nankeen trousers		11	6
1 Jews harp			2
150 Spanish dollars	46	8	1

Douglas' visit started inauspiciously. California was still under notional Mexican control, and the first governor under the newly established Mexican republic had just resigned. His replacement was suspicious of Douglas' claim that he wished to explore, survey and collect plants. He refused to grant Douglas a passport until 20 April, and refused him permission to draw the fortifications at Monterey.

Douglas stayed with William Hartnell, an English trader who had married into a prominent local family and become a Mexican citizen. Hartnell, a fluent Spanish-speaker, helped Douglas to bring his own Spanish up to scratch. While he waited for his passport, Douglas botanized extensively in the pleasant early spring weather. He found a beautiful wild gooseberry, *Ribes speciosum* – 'a flower not surpassed in beauty by the finest Fuchsia' – and later the same day the baby blue eyes, *Nemophila menziesii*, which today is one of the most popular garden flowers worldwide. (While baby blue eyes was a true discovery, the wild gooseberry had already been found by Menzies.) From February onwards, Douglas travelled north and east on El Camino Real (the King's Road) to visit the Franciscan missions at San Juan Bautista, Santa Clara and Santa Cruz.

Douglas' true journeying began once he was in possession of his passport. He set off south towards Santa Barbara, where he arrived in mid-May, visiting missions *en route*. Writing to Barnston he described the missionaries as an 'excellent class of men'.

I lived almost exclusively with the fathers who without exception afforded me the most essential assistance, hospitality to excess, with a thousand little courtesies which we feel and cannot express. I had no bickerings about superstition, no attempts at conversion, or the like, the usual complaints of travellers, indeed so much to the contrary, that on no occasion was an uncharitable word directed at me. When there I was under no restraint; my time was entirely my own, feast day and fast all the same, the good men of God gave me always a good bed, and plenty to eat and drink of the best of the land. A more upright and highly honourable class of men I never knew. They are well educated; I had no difficulty from the beginning with them, for saving one or two exceptions, they all talk Latin fluently, and though there be a great difference in the pronunciation between one from Auld Reekie and Madrid, yet it gave us but little trouble. They know and love the sciences too well to think it curious to see one go so far in quest of grass.

Writing to Hooker, he displayed impressive religious tolerance:

> Any man who can make himself well understood by [the fathers], either in Castilian or Latin, will discover very shortly that they are people who know something more than their mass-book, and who practise many benevolent acts, which are not a little to their credit, and ought to soften the judgement of the stranger, who has probably had the opportunity of seeing more men and things than the poor priests of California. Their errors are the errors of their profession, and I thus make bold to say so, having had reason to know the individuals in question are honourable exceptions to priests in general. I am no friend to Catholicism, still I should desire to maintain my own opinion without hurting the feelings of others.

In the Gabilan range of mountains Douglas found a new pine, 'one of the most beautiful objects of nature', which he named *Pinus sabiniana*, after Joseph Sabine. He sent home cones, leaves and a description, which was read to the Linnean Society. Seeds from this tree were planted at Kew, but did not thrive in the English climate. The tree is commonly known as the digger pine, after the Digger Indians who ate the large sweet oily nuts and chewed the gum. North of Santa Cruz, Douglas came upon the giant coast redwood *Sequoia sempervirens*, 'the great beauty of Californian vegetation', in what is now the California State Redwood Park. The tree did not please Douglas, who wrote that it 'gives the mountains a most peculiar, I was almost going to say awful, appearance – something which plainly tells that we are not in Europe'. He measured standing specimens at 270 feet (82 metres) long and 32 feet (10 metres) in circumference and collected seeds and foliage. However, these failed to arrive, and the tree was not introduced in Britain until 1847.

Now Douglas travelled to San Francisco to botanize in the Mount Diablo region. His aim was to enter from the south the area he had explored for the sugar pine four years before. Having reached the Russian settlement at Fort Ross, 200 miles north of Monterey, he reluctantly decided that the risk of pressing on alone into unknown territory was too great. It was a fortunate decision – while he believed that he was only 65 miles short of his goal, he was in fact some 300 miles away.

Writing to George Barnston from Monterey at the end of August, Douglas was struck by the aridity of the climate, especially the intense drought in the summer months.

In no part of the world have I experienced such a dryness in the atmosphere, nor can I call to my memory having read of greater. Even the deserts of Arabia and Egypt, the plains of Sin and Ispahan in Persia, I mean the driest places on the globe, when satisfactory observations have been made, are more humid than California. Often when the thermometer Fahr., stand at 80° or 100°, 30° or 40° of dryness is by no means infrequent. On some occasions I have sunk the thermometer below zero, and after repeated trials, with all the care I am capable of bestowing on such a delicate operation, not the least particle of moisture could be detected. But Nature ever kind and varied in her operations compensates for the extreme dryness of the daytime by copious dews during the night, at all times proportionate to the dryness of the preceding day. Otherwise animals or plants could not live; the lost would only be existence, and that for but a short period. In 1831, the rain was only .700 of an inch, the 39th part of the mean of the English climate. Notwithstanding these drawbacks to this beautiful country, it is the land of the vine, the olive, the fig, the banana and in the southern parts the sugar cane, and a variety of the usual fruits seen in semi-tropical climates. The vine is cultivated to a large extent, from 10,000 to 100,000 in one vineyard. The wine is excellent, indeed, that word is too small for it; for it is very excellent.

The aggressive glare of the sun brought on further attacks of ophthalmia. To Hooker he wrote: 'I can never read what I write, so do pardon my blunders and if you can fathom what I wish to say I am for once happy.' But his enthusiasm for wildlife and the outdoors remained undiminished – 'tell Joseph [Hooker's son] I caught two fine trout yesterday, twenty seven pounds each.' Douglas now planned to take the next ship that called back to Fort Vancouver and the Columbia River. Little did he know that his wait would be a long one: until August the next year.

Douglas busied himself cataloguing his finds in preparation for their journey home. In this task he was helped by another plant-collector, Dr Thomas Coulter, who had arrived in California from Mexico, thinking it still unexplored. Coulter was working for his professor, De Candolle of Geneva, and was the first person to botanize in the Colorado desert. The two men got on famously, putting aside any professional rivalry for the pleasure of the company of another specialist. A third naturalist, a German named Ferdinand Deppe, also arrived in California at this time; he too combined exploration with trading in specimens and seeds. Through his friendship with Coulter, Douglas obtained plants from Colorado for Hooker. Douglas and Coulter made many botanizing expeditions together, searching unsuccessfully for the eggs of the Californian condor and observing sea otters being hunted. Douglas commented to Sabine that 'Hides and Tallow is the wealth of California', one of the few comments he made about the slaughter of fur-bearing animals.

Douglas was developing into a philosophical thinker with ever-widening interests. Unusually for his time, he did not explore in order to exploit but to gather seeds and plants that nature would take but a short time to replace. This ran contrary to the policy of the Hudson's Bay Company, which trapped out one area and then proceeded to the next. At first, Douglas made no comment – his ability to fulfil the Horticultural Society's brief and the aims he had set himself largely depended on the Company's goodwill. But, now that he was several years into his work in the Pacific North West, critical remarks occasionally crept into his accounts of his travels. He had come to question the policy of trapping great quantities of wildlife, and had perhaps also started to wonder what would happen to those areas where the balance of nature was being destroyed before his eyes.

In January 1832, Douglas was compelled to join a 'Company of Foreigners' formed to help keep the peace during uprisings against the Mexican authorities in California. Guard duty did not please a man of Douglas' disposition, especially since he wanted to use the brief spring for plant-collecting. Shirking his responsibilities, he left for the Santa Lucia Mountains towards the South, but was careful not to travel too far from Monterey lest a ship should arrive. On this trip, Douglas found the rare and beautiful bristlecone fir, *Abies venusta* ('charming fir'). Probably the mission fathers told him where to look for it, for they used its resin as incense. He also found the Monterey pine, *Pinus radiata*, with its brilliant, grass-green foliage, and *Pinus coulteri*, the big-cone pine. The Monterey pine was destined to become one of Douglas' most important discoveries in terms of economic value, and it is now grown as a major timber tree across the world in warm temperate or Mediterranean-type climates. Its natural range is limited to the Monterey peninsula, where it is found in rather unremarkable groves.

Back in Monterey, Douglas packed two consignments, one for the Horticultural Society, the other for Hooker, still his favoured mentor, to whom he wrote, 'you will begin to think that I manufacture

Pines at my pleasure'. His discoveries from California rivalled his collections from the Columbia River, and for a time the Society was overwhelmed by the work of sorting and cataloguing the seeds and plants. Besides the pines, Douglas sent seaweeds, mosses and sixty new plants, including five mariposa lilies: the white fairy lantern *Calochortus albus*, the yellow *C. luteus*, the golden fairy lantern *C. pulchellus*, the lilac *C. splendens* and the butterfly *C. venustus*.

Douglas' most unusual find was an entirely new order of plant, *Garrya elliptica*, or quinine bush, although he himself thought the grey-ball sage *Audiberta incana* more interesting. He also introduced the unusual *Gilia tricolor* and the delicate feather *G. androsacea*, as well as the scarlet bugler penstemon, *Penstemon centranthifloius*. Among the poppy family, Douglas found *Platystemon californicus*, or buttercup-like creamcup, the bush poppy, *Dendromecon rigidum*, and the magnificent blazing-star, *Mentzelia lindleyi*. Also included in the consignments for England were many lupins and new *brodiaea*, together with the wild heliotrope, *Phacelia tanacetifolia*. It seems that Douglas may also have come across gold, some sixteen years or so before its official discovery in California. On the Columbia Douglas told incredulous traders that he had found enough gold flakes in the roots of the plants he had collected in California to have a watch seal made; however, he thought so little of the discovery from a geological point of view that he did not write about it.

Douglas made many friends in California. Among them were George Kinloch, a fellow Scot, and his wife, Roger Cooper, a pioneer wine-maker, and the Reverend Patrick Short, who was the first British priest west of the Rockies. Don Estevan Munras, a prosperous Spaniard, used to entertain the entire Company of Foreigners to fabulous Sunday dinners at his immense villa known as 'La Granga', which remains a Monterey landmark to this day. When he finally left California, Douglas wrote of his admiration for the local women:

> The ladies are handsome, of a dark olive brunette, with good teeth, and the dark fine eyes, which bespeaks the descendent of Castille, Catalan or Leon. They (sweet creatures) have a greater recommendation than personal attractions. They are very amiable. On this head I must say, *Finis*, otherwise you will be apt to think, if ever I had a kind feeling for man's better half, I left it in (*Calida Fornax*) California.

Douglas won a reputation as a medicine man when one day a local boy fell into the hold of a boat in the harbour and broke his arm. The unconscious boy was taken to Douglas, who splinted the arm; so well did Douglas care for the lad that thereafter he became known as Dr Douglas.

Douglas had hoped to take a Hudson's Bay Company ship direct to the Columbia River, but it failed to arrive because of the captain's death. Eventually, Douglas managed to leave in August 1832 on a vessel bound for Honolulu, where he arrived on 7 September, hoping to find another ship to take him to Fort Vancouver. In Honolulu he made numerous astronomical observations – but 'the vile Cockroaches ate up all the paper, and as there was a little oil on my shoes, very nearly demolished them too!' – and managed to procure a brace of Sandwich Island geese from high on the volcanic mountains. These survived the journey to London and were given to the Zoological Society.

It was on Honolulu that Douglas learned of the resignation of Joseph Sabine from his post as Secretary of the Horticultural Society. Overspending on lavish fêtes and beautifully illustrated publications, combined with a failure to collect subscriptions, had put the Society some £3000 in debt. Although relations between Douglas and the Society had been very poor during his last stay in London, Douglas remained very loyal to Sabine, and on 9 September wrote to resign his membership in protest. The collections he sent home from California and Honolulu were therefore the last to be divided between the Horticultural Society and Hooker. Thereafter everything went to the Professor in Glasgow. Now a freelance roving plant-collector, Douglas suggested to Hooker that it 'may be worth your while to set about a Flora of these Islands which, with what I can furnish, a handsome something can be made, at all events'. Douglas must have been aware that in resigning he was putting at risk future opportunities for travel, given his reliance on the Society's standing and contacts. Presumably he was counting on the fact that it would take a long time for his letter of resignation to reach London and even longer for the news to be sent back to the Pacific North West. By now he had built up a reputation and a network of contacts throughout California and the Pacific North West. He also had the contacts he had made at the Colonial Office when he was last in London, he had been trained in the use of his scientific instruments, and he possessed the all-important letters of recommendation to Her Majesty's ships. All these, he must have reckoned, would see him through.

After a brief and violent rheumatic illness, Douglas left for the Columbia River on *Lama*, a forty-six ton American ship. He reached Fort Vancouver on 14 October, less than two months after leaving Monterey. The speed of travel greatly impressed him: 'What would have been thought, forty years ago of passing over more than half of the great basin of the Pacific with such a craft?'

Chapter Eleven

DISASTER ON THE FRASER RIVER

'This disastrous occurrence has much broken
my strength and spirits.'
Douglas writing to Hooker, 6 May 1834

Douglas passed the winter – an exceptionally harsh one, as it had been six years previously – at Fort Vancouver. Dr John McLoughlin, who was still chief factor, continued to welcome visitors and travellers such as Douglas. The Fort itself was developing fast. The farm now extended to 200 acres, vines had been planted, a 70-ton ship was being constructed on the riverside, and a school had been established to educate the mixed-race children of the Fort and the surrounding area.

Douglas used the peaceful, star-spangled nights to make no less than eight thousand astronomical observations. These he wrote up in detail and sent back to Captain Sabine in London.

Taking advantage of better weather in February, Douglas, accompanied by the ever-reliable William Johnson, headed north towards Puget Sound. His aim was to survey and position the headlands and mountains and to calculate the heights of the summits. He also collected over two hundred species of moss and several seaweeds – for some time Douglas had been keen to collect seaweeds and had written to all his friends up and down the coast asking them to collect 'everything in the shape of a seaweed' for him. On 26 February, during the return journey, Douglas found some enormous examples of the Grand Fir near Mount St Helens – 'a forest of these trees is a spectacle too much for one man to see', he wrote. He then met Archie MacDonald, the Hudson's Bay Company chief trader, at Fort

Nisqually, and they returned together to Fort Vancouver, arriving in the first week of March.

Douglas had long dreamed of returning to Britain through Alaska and Siberia, crossing the icy sea that divides the north American and Asian landmasses. Perhaps he now felt himself capable, both physically and mentally, of such a feat, and perhaps also, now that he was free of the Horticultural Society's shackles, he felt that this bold and exciting journey would bring him fame and fortune on his return to London. He had worked out his plan in some detail before leaving London, and had received an invitation from Baron von Wrangel, the Russian Governor of Alaska, to travel to Sitka, on the coast of what is now British Columbia. Alaska had been under Russian control since 1799, and since the early 1820s, Russia had been trying to extend its southern border south towards Vancouver Island, a move strongly resisted by the Hudson's Bay Company.

Douglas wrote excitedly to Hooker about how he hoped to compare the two continents, America and Asia.

> What a glorious prospect! Thus not only the plants, but a series of observations may be produced, the work of the same individual on both Continents, with the same instruments, under similar circumstances and in corresponding latitudes! I hope I do not indulge my hopes too far. ... People tell me that Siberia is like a rat-trap, which there is no difficulty entering, but from which it is not so easy to find egress. I mean at least to put this saying to the test. And I hope that those who know me know also that trifles will not stop me.

Fever struck Fort Vancouver just before he set off; Douglas was lucky – 'only three individuals out of one hundred and forty escaped it, and I was one of that small number'. But the years of exploration were taking their toll in other ways. Though he was not yet thirty-four, he suffered repeated, debilitating attacks of rheumatism, and his sight was failing. His right eye was entirely blind, while he suffered from double vision and blurring in the left. Purple eye-glasses were supposed to help, but he used them 'most reluctantly, as every object, plant and all, is thus rendered of the same colour'.

Equipped with such boundless optimism and self-belief, Douglas departed for Sitka on 20 March. From here he planned to take a boat across to Otosk in Siberia. He had taken the precaution of approaching the Russian authorities in London, who were supportive. The Russians based at Sitka were already planning a party in his honour, he had been told, while those he had met in California (where they had established farms to supply their settlements further north with food) had impressed him as 'a set of people whose whole aim is to make you happy'. The Russians were keen to support scientific exploration, while the Tsar, Nicholas I, was a fellow of the Horticultural Society and as such had benefited from Douglas' plant-hunting adventures.

Once again, our knowledge of this expedition owes much to the work of A.G. Harvey, whose account was first published in the *British Columbia Historical Quarterly* in October 1940. After leaving the Hudson's Bay Express at Fort Okanagan, Douglas travelled on horseback with the New Caledonia Brigade, who were aiming to trade in the region. He had with him his servant, Johnson, and his terrier, Billy.

Travelling up the Okanagan Valley and Lake, they then took the trail to Fort Kamloops. During the evening here, Douglas was unwise enough to offend the Chief Trader, a fellow Scot named Samuel Black, an enormous, powerfully built man. Douglas voiced his low opinion of the Hudson's Bay Company – it was a mercenary enterprise that put pursuit of profit above the lives of its employees; none of its traders had a soul above a beaver skin. This was one of the few occasions when Douglas seems to have fallen out with his hosts. No doubt Douglas deplored much about the Company. The ruthless exploitation of men, both employees and the indigenous peoples, and wildlife would have appalled him, but he was always able to set this on one side. On this occasion, he was dealing with a particularly tough and ruthless individual. Samuel Black had been intimately involved in much of the rough stuff during the period of bitter rivalry between the Hudson's Bay Company and the North West Company, and several murders and foul deeds were ascribed to him. Black was by no means uneducated or unsympathetic to Douglas' views. But he was on his feet in a second, responding in a similarly insulting manner and demanding satisfaction. The challenge was accepted, but the duel itself was postponed until the following morning.

Come the dawn, Douglas realized that discretion was the better part of valour, and declined Black's demand that he fight. He had spoken too hastily. He was the first man who was not a fur-trader to travel in the region, and over the years the Company's officers had shown him much kindness. This incident dogged Douglas' reputation for many years. In reality, Douglas was merely voicing the fears of many of the more enlightened men within the Company, who realized that Governor Simpson's short-sighted policy of eliminating all the beaver would make the area valueless for trapping. Perhaps Douglas was also repelled by the scale of the slaughter. William Hooker had always deplored the needless maiming or slaughter of wildlife, and his views may well have influenced Douglas.

Of course, we do not have Douglas' side of the story. One suspects that the legend that grew out of this incident owes much to the character and story-telling of Black and to the lack of any counter-views from Douglas.

From Fort Kamloops the Brigade, together with Johnson and Douglas, made their way up the Fraser River towards Fort Alexander, where they swapped their horses for boats. Douglas walked until they reached the Quesnel River, and then took to the boats. The strong current in the Upper Fraser slowed the travellers, and the boats had to be hauled by rope and pulley. Leaving the Fraser, they travelled up the Nechaco and Stuart Rivers to Fort Fraser, and then struck out overland to Fort St James. Here they arrived on 6 June, having covered 1150 miles in two and a half months, thankful for the hospitality of Peter Warren Dease, the chief factor.

Taking stock, Douglas now realized the magnitude of what he was attempting and that his chances of fulfilling his ambition of crossing to Siberia were minimal. To reach Sitka and Russian America, still some 800 miles distant, he would have to travel 500 miles to the coast, where Fort Simpson was the nearest Hudson's Bay post. This journey would be on scarcely charted rivers running through barren terrain and with large and difficult portages. Douglas described the land as 'nothing but prodigious mountains ... not a deer comes, say the Indians, save once in a hundred years – the poor natives subsist on a few roots'. From Fort Simpson Sitka lay a further 300 miles north along the coast, and the local Indians were known to be hostile to American traders. Douglas wrote regretfully to Hooker that their chances of taking 'a fine jaunt to the Highlands' together had vanished.

With no other options open to him, Douglas had to return to the Columbia and try to negotiate a sea passage north to Sitka. Douglas and Johnson set off on their own in a small birch-bark canoe on the long journey back to the Columbia River. Having negotiated the Stuart and Nechaco Rivers, they stayed at Fort George for a few days before starting down the Fraser. On 13 June, disaster struck at Fort George Canyon, when the canoe was wrecked in the rapids on the Stony Islands. Douglas was trapped in the whirlpools and swept down stream for an hour and forty minutes. Amazingly, he managed to recover his instruments and his astronomical observations, notes, charts and barometric readings; his dog Billy also survived. Food, clothing and blankets were all lost, and, worst of all, so too was the sole copy of his diary, which he had been keeping for Hooker, and over four hundred species of plants.

They made their way back to Fort George, and, having obtained another canoe, descended the Fraser and the Columbia uneventfully, stopping at Fort Walla Walla to allow Douglas to botanize in the Blue Mountains and replace some of his lost plants. On their return to Fort Vancouver in August 1833, Douglas was shattered, both physically and mentally. Perhaps for the first time, despite all the privations of his previous explorations, exposure and near-starvation had forced him to confront his own mortality. He wrote to Hooker:

> I cannot detail to you the labour and anxiety this occasioned me, both in body and mind, to say nothing of the hardships and sufferings I endured. Still I reflect, with pleasure, that no lives were sacrificed. This disastrous occurrence has much broken my strength and spirits. Such are the not infrequent disasters attending such undertakings. On the whole I have been fortunate, for considering the nature and extent of the Country I have passed over (now 8 years here) and the circumstances under which I travelled my accidents have been few.

Remembering the dangers they had passed through together, Douglas resolved that 'should I live to return', he would reward 'my old terrier, a most faithful and now, to judge by his long grey beard, venerable friend, who has guarded me throughout all my journeys' with a pension of 'four pence-worth of cat's-meat per day'.

Two new arrivals at Fort Vancouver provided companionship, and perhaps helped Douglas to recover his equilibrium. William Tolmie and Meredith Gairdner were both former medical students of Hooker, who had recommended them to help McLoughlin deal with the fever epidemic. Both doctors were also interested in botany, and Douglas was glad to have their help in replacing his losses. He wrote to Hooker:

> It reconciles somewhat to the loss, to reflect that you now have friends in that country, who will probably make up the deficiency. I have given Dr Gairdner my notes on some more new species of *pinus*. This gentleman and Mr Tolmie will have a good deal to contend with. Science has few friends among those who visit the coast of North West America, solely with a view to gain. Still with such a person as Mr McLoughlin on the Columbia, they may do a great deal of service to Natural History.

Douglas also shared his passion for mountaineering with the two newcomers. He and Gairdner planned to climb Mount St Helens, but as the volcano had recently erupted, the Indian guides refused to take them. When they tackled Mount Hood, deep snow forced them to turn back short of the summit. Tolmie had a similar experience on Mount Rainier.

His long-cherished Siberian ambitions abandoned, Douglas now flung himself into planning an exploration of Hawaii. His two previous visits to the Islands, at that time still known as the Sandwich Islands, had made him curious. The potential for botanizing, and also for exploration and mountaineering, seemed great. Furthermore, Mauna Kea, the mighty and as yet unmeasured volcanic peak, was reputed to be the highest mountain in the world. Here was a challenge that would truly wipe away the memory of the Siberian fiasco.

Chapter Twelve

HAWAII, VOLCANOES
AND THE FINAL
ADVENTURE

'Man feels himself as nothing – as if standing
on the verge of another world.'
*Douglas writing in his journal in
January 1834 at Mauna Kea on Hawaii*

Douglas set out from the Columbia River on 18 October 1833 on the brig *Dryad* accompanied by two Hudson's Bay Company employees, Duncan Finlayson and John Ball. The Company had just established an outpost on the Sandwich Islands, so named by Captain Cook in 1778 in honour of the Earl of Sandwich. The Islands had strategic value not only as a staging-post but also for trading timber and salted salmon from the Company's territory in the Pacific North West. Senior Company employees also took leave on the Islands, appreciating the warmer weather and the beautiful women, and their relaxed approach to personal relationships. The Company's operations were controlled by one George Pelly, who (characteristically for the Company) was a cousin of the British governor.

We know more about this expedition, Douglas' last, because his journal survived. He also wrote several long letters to Hooker, parts of which Hooker reproduced in his 'Brief Memoir' of Douglas.

Before venturing down the coast, *Dryad* waited in a bay at the mouth of the Columbia for eleven days while storms and gales subsided. The high winds and huge seas continued, and even Douglas, by now a seasoned sailor, confessed that he was 'nearly a wreck'. *Dryad* finally reached San Francisco on 4 November, anchoring off Point de los Reyes. The captain wanted to sail again as soon as the

166

ship had been provisioned for the long voyage, but the storms showed
no sign of ceasing, and they did not leave until 28 November. As
usual, Douglas managed to fit in some exploring, though he could not
stray too far lest the ship sail at the short notice.

> I accompanied Mr Finlayson in a small boat to Whaler's
> Harbour [present-day Sausilito], near the neck of the bay which
> leads to the hill of San Rafaele, the highest peak in the immedi-
> ate vicinity of the port. We landed at Mr Read's farmhouse,
> placed on the site of an old Indian camp, where small mounds
> of marine shells bespeak the former existence of numerous
> aboriginal tribes. A fine small rivulet of good water falls into the
> bay at this point.

Conditions at last improved enough to allow *Dryad* to sail, but
there was severe weather in the Pacific before she arrived in Honolulu
on 23 December. Douglas went on shore with Mr Spaulding, one of
his fellow passengers and an American missionary, to visit the school.
He also met Richard Charlton, the British consul, with whom he spent
Christmas Day. When they sailed again on 29 December for Hawaii
Island, Mauna Kea, the object of Douglas' voyage, could be seen very
clearly in the distance, 'a few small stripes of snow lying only near its
summit, which would seem to indicate an altitude inferior to that
which has been commonly assigned to this mountain'.

At 13,796 feet (4205 metres) above sea level, Mauna Kea is the
highest mountain in Hawaii, with a height off the ocean floor of
18,200 feet (5550 metres). Caves where ancient Hawaiians dug basalt
for tools dot the upper slopes, which today are used by skiers; here,
too, is the modern Mauna Kea Observatory, much used for deep-space
observation. On the lower slopes are large cattle ranches and coffee
plantations. The Islands are volcanic in origin, having thrust up from
the floor of the Pacific Ocean. Mauna Kea is probably, though not
definitely, extinct, while the other two volcanoes, Mauna Loa and
Kilauea, are still actively erupting. Thousands of miles from any continental land mass, the Islands have evolved a unique flora and fauna,
which has sadly been much reduced since Europeans first landed. In
Douglas' day, of course, they were much more pristine.

Douglas landed at Byron's Bay (now called Hilo) on 2 January,
where he stayed with the Reverend Joseph Goodrich, an American
missionary. An enthusiastic geologist, Goodrich had climbed Mauna
Kea several times, and helped Douglas with all his arrangements,
including hiring guides and interpreters. On 7 January, Douglas and
his party began the 27-mile ascent. As usual, Douglas refused to

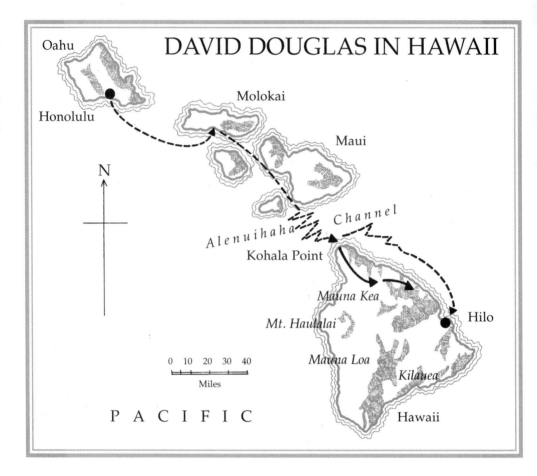

DAVID DOUGLAS IN HAWAII

Oahu

Honolulu

Molokai

Maui

N

Alenuihaha *Channel*

Kohala Point

Mauna Kea

Mt. Haulalai

Hilo

0 10 20 30 40

Miles

Mauna Loa

Kilauea

P A C I F I C

Hawaii

entrust his precious instruments to native bearers and carried most of them himself – a load weighing some 60 lbs (27 kg). The going was slow and hard, and was made worse by fog, heavy rain and swollen rivers that proved dangerous to cross. Though soaked to the skin and numb with cold, Douglas noted the large timber trees and tree ferns; when he pitched camp he observed the constellations Orion and Canopus shining intensely in the night sky. Douglas was also exasperated by his local guides:

> Everything being arranged, some of the men were despatched early, but such are the delays which these people make, that I overtook them all before eight o'clock. They have no idea of time, but stand still awhile then walk a little, stop and eat, smoke and talk, and thus loiter away a whole day.

It took Douglas four days to complete the ascent – 'though exhausted with fatigue ... yet such was my ardent desire to reach the top that the last portion of the way seemed the easiest'. He immediately set about making barometric observations to gauge the heights of the mountains.

> One thing struck me as curious, the apparent non-diminution of sound, not as respects the rapidity of its transmission, which is of course, subject to a well known law. ... Snow is doubtless a non conductor of sound; there may be something in the mineral substance of Mauna Kea which would affect this.
>
> The great dryness of the air is evident to the senses. Walking with my trousers rolled up to my knees, and without shoes, I did not know there were holes in my stockings till I was apprised of them by the scorching heat and pain in my feet, which continued throughout the day; the skin also peeling off my face. While on the summit I experienced violent head ache, and my eyes became blood shot, accompanied with stiffness in their lids.

Despite physical discomfort, he collected many specimens, including some 'beautiful species mosses and lichens'. The landscape was spectacular.

> Still the magnificence of the scenery commanded my frequent attention, and I repeatedly sat down in the course of the day, under some huge spreading Tree fern which more resembled an individual of the Pine family. ... On the higher part of the mountain I gathered a Fern identical to the *Asplenium viride* of my own native country, a circumstance which gave me inexpressible pleasure, and recalled to my mind many of the happiest scenes of my life.

Having conquered Mauna Kea, Douglas now set his sights on Kilauea, the sister mountain, 4000 feet (1247 metres) high, and then famous as the world's greatest active volcano. After paying off the men he had hired for the Mauna Kea expedition, he set off once more on 22 January after just a few days' rest.

> Paid off the whole of the sixteen men who had accompanied me, not including Honori and the King's man, at the rate of two dollars, some in money and some in goods; the latter consisted of cotton cloth, combes, scissors and thread etc.; while to those

who had acquitted themselves with willingness and activity, I added a small present in addition. Most of them preferred money, especially the lazy fellows. The whole of the number employed in carrying my baggage and provisions was five men, which left eleven for the conveyance of their own Tapas and food. Nor was this unreasonable, for the quantity of Poi [a starchy food made from the taro plant and the islanders' main food] which a native will consume in a week nearly equals his own weight! Still, though the sixteen persons ate two bullocks in a week, besides what they carried, a threatened scarcity of food compelled me to return sooner that I should have done. . . . No people in the world can cram themselves to such a degree as the Sandwich Islanders.

At the hut where the Kilauea party halted for the night, an old woman was feeding her four cats with fish. Billy the terrier succeeded in annoying the household by disrupting things. But the situation was smoothed over.

A well looking young female amused me with singing, while she was engaged in the process of cooking a dog on heated stones. I also observed a handsome young man, whose very strong stiff black hair was allowed to grow to great lengths on the top of his head, while it was cut close to the ears, and falling down the back of his head and neck had all the appearance of a Roman helmet. . . . The following day a little before daybreak my host went to the door of the lodge and after calling over some extraordinary words which would seem to set orthography at defiance, a loud grunt in response from under the thick shade of some adjoining Tree ferns was followed by the appearance of a fine black pig, which coming at his master's call, was forthwith caught and killed for use of myself and attendants.

Douglas gained the summit in less than two days, outstripping most of his companions, and spent the night close to the edge of the crater. The sight of the volcano overawed Douglas, even though it was comparatively inactive.

The nearly full moon rose in a cloudless sky and shed her silvery brightness on the fiery lake (of the crater) roaring and boiling in fearful majesty, the spectacle became so commanding that I lost a fine night for making astronomical observations, but gazing at the volcano.

Douglas made extensive calculations and observations before retreating down the mountain. Climbing down into the crater, he encountered a lava flow. Walking across this was most alarming – the lava felt hollow beneath the feet, almost as if it would crack and then open up to engulf them. Douglas offered shoes to his native guides, but they preferred 'a matt sole, made of touch leaves and fastened round the heel and between the toes which seemed to answer the purpose entirely well'.

> Of all the sensations of nature, that produced by earthquakes or volcanic agency is the most alarming. . . . On the black ledge, the thermometer, held in the hand, five feet from the ground indicated a temperature of 89F . . . on the lava if in sun 115F and at the South end 124F. . . . I remained on the rim of the crater for upwards of two hours and suffered from an intense headache, my tongue parched . . . and the intense heat corroded my shoes so much they barely protected my feet from the hot lava.

Kilauea crater, with the fire pit Halemaumau on the crater floor, remains active today, with lava flows extending for up to 50 miles.

By 28 January, Douglas was ready to attack Mauna Loa (13,678 feet, 4,169 metres), the third of the great volcanoes of Hawaii and the world's largest single mountain mass. The lava flows made the ascent hard and treacherous, but Douglas and his companions reached the summit on the 29th; heavy snow near the top made the climb even more arduous. They started to descend in the late afternoon and, poorly equipped as usual – Douglas had no change of clothes, food, water or fuel for a fire – had to continue downwards until 2 a.m., when they chanced on some scrubby trees. Here they spent the rest of the night huddling around a small fire.

Douglas had now climbed three great volcanic mountains in less than one month – indeed, he was probably the first person to climb both Mauna Loa and Mauna Kea. He had also made innumerable observations and calculations, and had as always collected a mass of plants. The combination of overwork and physical stress once again left him exhausted in both body and mind. For too long he had neglected his own comfort – the huge loads he carried contained much scientific equipment but little food or clothing – and had pushed himself beyond normal endurance, keeping himself short of food and water and setting a punishing pace. Now he was suffering the physical consequences. The strong sunlight and the glare from the snow made his rapidly deteriorating sight even worse; on Mauna Loa his eyes became so inflamed that blood discharged from them. He was also in poor shape mentally, and some of his letters, which confuse the various mountains, suggest that at times his mind was becoming unhinged.

Returning to Honolulu in April, Douglas had energy enough to tour the island and observe the local customs while waiting for a passage back to Britain. During this period he struck up a friendship with John Diell, a chaplain from the seaman's mission. Diell was keen to see something of the spectacular volcanic mountains, and Douglas agreed to take him up Kilauea. The two men set off in July, but soon became separated when Diell made a detour to visit the island of Molokai. Typically, Douglas did not turn back, but continued with Diell's manservant and Billy, his terrier. They intended to walk to Hilo, some 90 miles, but Diell's servant dropped out after developing 'lameness'. Douglas was now alone, with only Billy for company. On 12 July, he arrived at the huts of Ned Gurney, a cattle-hunter who made his living by trapping wild cattle in pits on the hillside and selling the meat, hides and tallow to passing ships. Gurney, who was English, had been found guilty of theft in 1818 and had been deported, at the age of nineteen, to Australia. He had managed to reach Honolulu in 1822 – whether he escaped or was pardoned is uncertain – and had decided to stay there.

Gurney was almost certainly the last man to see Douglas alive. According to Gurney, the two had breakfast together, after which Douglas asked him for directions. The cattle-hunter accompanied Douglas a little way up the track and, warning him about the three cattle pits about 2¹/₂ miles further up the track, turned back at about 10 a.m. About two hours later, two natives found Douglas' body in one of the pits together with a trapped bull, which was still alive. They rushed to find Gurney, who returned, shot the bullock, and rescued Douglas' body. Billy the dog was still close by, guarding Douglas' bundle, which he appeared to have left on the path to Hilo. Gurney claimed that he traced Douglas' footprints from one pit to the second and then to the third; he must, Gurney said, have slipped and fallen in, perhaps while peering down. The infuriated and possibly injured beast trapped in the pit would have trampled him to death.

Gurney had the body wrapped in hide, and engaged a party of Hawaiians to carry it the 27 miles to Hilo, where Diell and Goodrich (Douglas' American missionary friend) were awaiting his arrival. Both men were immensely shocked at the sight of the mutilated corpse. Sarah Joiner Lyman of Hilo, wife of missionary David Lyman, recorded the events in her diary:

July 14th 1834. This has been one of the most gloomy days I ever witnessed. . . . Mournful to relate Mr Douglas is no more. . . . Just as Mr Diell was about to go down to the beach to meet Mr Douglas, we were informed that his corpse was at the water's edge in a canoe. . . . His clothes are sadly torn and his body dreadfully mangled. Ten gashes on his head. . . . A carpenter was engaged to make a coffin and a foreigner to dig his grave under a breadfruit tree in Mr Goodrich's garden. Whilst engaged in digging the thought occurred to him that Mr Douglas was murdered. He suggested it to Mr Goodrich and Mr Diell. Their suspicions were at once excited. They left digging the grave and concluded to preserve the body in salt and send it to Honolulu that it might be more satisfactorily determined how the wounds were inflicted. . . . The whole is involved in mystery.

The suggestion of murder came from Charles Hall, an experienced American cattle-hunter, who thought that Douglas' injuries were inconsistent with the way he was supposed to have died. The attempt to preserve the body in salt was not very successful, and by the time it reached Honolulu it was decaying rapidly. There it was examined by four doctors from *Challenger*, a British vessel in port, whom Richard Charlton, the British consul, had hastily called in. They found nothing to suggest foul play.

Hall later argued that Gurney and Douglas had quarrelled, Gurney had killed the botanist and had then disposed of his body in the wild bull pit, anticipating that the bullock would maul Douglas' body and so disguise any signs of a struggle. Hall pointed out that the bullock was elderly, and that its blunt and battered horns could not have inflicted injuries of the kind Douglas had suffered. Hall and another white man were sent to the bullock pits to investigate. They heard several reports that cast doubt on Gurney's story. The most compelling was that Douglas was said to have been carrying 'a large purse of money' to pay for guides and also for his passage home; the purse had subsequently vanished. Heavy rainfall had washed away the footprints Gurney described, and there was no other evidence to support his account.

It fell to Richard Charlton to organize Douglas' funeral in Kawaiaho Church, one of Honolulu's oldest and most distinguished buildings, on 4 August. Every foreign resident of the island was present, as were the *Challenger*'s officers, one of whom read the service. Douglas' body was laid to rest in the burial ground.

The belief that Douglas had been murdered persists to this day. The finding of the post-mortem did nothing to dispel it. The chief suspect was Ned Gurney, whose past was no doubt enough to generate suspicion. But John Diell's servant, who disappeared before

Douglas' death, was also regarded as a possible culprit. It was also suggested that Douglas' relationship with native Hawaiians had deteriorated, mainly because of his increasing irritability, and that he might have been killed during a quarrel.

There were many loose ends. One was the missing purse. No one knew for sure if it ever existed, although a few dollars were found on Douglas after his death. The chronometer in his breast pocket had smashed, yet its case was intact. However, his second chronometer was still functioning, although the fob on which he carried it had been destroyed. Some people doubted that, bad eyesight notwithstanding, anyone could have fallen into a pit whose cover had already been broken by a bullock.

Many Hawaiians continued to believe that Douglas had been murdered. In 1896 a report was published in the *Hilo Tribune* claiming that a native hunter named Bolabola knew this for certain.

> A noted hunter and trailer, now over 70 years of age, and familiar with every inch of ground around the Mauna Kea slopes, took up the narrative. It was noticed that he lowered his voice, with now and then the older men nodding in approval. ... We all felt so [that Douglas had been murdered] at the time, but were afraid to say so and only whispered it among ourselves. And when my father and the old Kaline [another noted Hawaiian] died, they both repeated the story to me.

No one will ever know for certain the true circumstances surrounding the death of Douglas. Inevitably, the doubts and lack of certainty invite theories of murder and deliberate killing. Yet many of the facts seem to support the theory that Douglas died in a tragic accident. It was not unknown for people to fall into cattle pits; Douglas' sight was poor; and his dog Billy was still guarding his bundle by the path. All these facts are consistent with Douglas, curious as ever, getting too close to the edge of the pit, slipping and falling in. In addition, if there had been a struggle, the dog would probably have tried to defend its master and would have been injured or killed.

In 1841, two scientists, Dr Charles Pickering and Mr J.D. Brackenridge, visited the site of Douglas' death. They noted that local rumour accused Gurney of murdering Douglas. However, they also pointed out that the pits, which cattle crossed on their way to the water, were covered with pulled-up 'fragile plants' such as raspberries, and that this covering was in turn concealed by earth. They also recounted the story of a Hawaiian who, excited that a large bullock had fallen into a pit he had prepared, slipped and fell in himself.

Although he managed to kill the bullock with his knife, by the time he was found, he, too, had died from his injuries.

Richard Charlton, the consul, asked T.C. Ryde Rooke, a friend of Douglas in Honolulu, to undertake the gloomy task of dealing with Douglas' affairs. In a letter dated 10 August 1835 to George Bentham of the Horticultural Society, Ryde gave a detailed account of what he had done:

> I consider it my duty to inform you of the steps I have already taken and the course I intend pursuing. Capt. Seymour of H.M. Ship *Challenger* has been kind enough to take charge of the most valuable of the remaining instruments ... in order to forward them to you by the first opportunity and also the Journal of Mr D's discoveries ... which are highly interesting. The remaining books, M.S.S. papers, Instruments etc of which I enclose an inventory are left in charge to be forwarded to you by the first safe conveyance.

The inventory made by Ryde included two mountain barometers ('one of them spoiled'), one magnet, one portable compass ('Broken'), one pocket thermometer, various journals dealing with his chronometer, meteorological measurements, magnetic variation, lunar observations, as well as two volumes of the *Botanical Journal*. Those of Douglas' clothes and other personal effects that were not considered important enough to be sent to England were sold at public auction, and the money raised was used to pay his local debts.

Inevitably, given the distances involved and the length of time needed for a sea voyage, the news of Douglas' death took some time to reach Britain. Hooker found out in a roundabout way, as he recalled in his 'Brief Memoir':

> The first knowledge of his [Douglas'] decease, which reached one of the members of his family in this country, was in a peculiarly abrupt and painful manner. It was seen in a number of the *Liverpool Mercury*, by his brother Mr John Douglas, when looking for the announcement of the marriage of a near relative. He immediately set out for Glasgow to communicate the unwelcome tidings to me; and in a few days these were confirmed on more unquestionable authority, by letter from Richard Charlton Her Majesty's Counsul at the Sandwich Islands to James Bandinel Esq [a Foreign Office official in London].

Hooker received much of Douglas' collection, including several preserved birds, while on reaching England, Billy the dog was cared for by Mr Bandinel. Douglas' family and Hooker himself were probably the people closest to Douglas and therefore most directly affected by the news. John Douglas corresponded in some detail with Hooker, lamenting his brother's death – 'my loss is irrecoverable'. At Hooker's request, he wrote a detailed account of Douglas' early days which

Hooker included in his 'Brief Memoir'. John Douglas settled his brother's affairs, especially his dealings with the Society, collected the proceeds of the sale of some of his collections and paid some debts. The episode was an unhappy one, and left Douglas considering legal action against the Society, though in the end he did not proceed.

No record or headstone was made to commemorate Douglas' burial place. When one Reverend Julius Brenchley from California visited Hawaii in 1855, he was so dismayed at the lack of a memorial that he paid for a white marble gravestone to mark the burial site, which was in danger of being lost. Decades later, the Royal Horticultural Society organized the restoration of the now crumbling white stone, and the monument was moved inside the church. The exact location of Douglas' grave in the churchyard remains unknown.

Brenchley had a Latin text engraved on a bronze plaque affixed to the stone.

HERE LIES MASTER DAVID DOUGLAS, BORN IN SCOTLAND A D 1799. AN INDEFATIGABLE TRAVELLER, HE WAS SENT OUT BY THE ROYAL HORTICULTURAL SOCIETY OF LONDON AND GAVE HIS LIFE FOR SCIENCE IN THE WILDS OF HAWAII, JULY 12, 1834.

E'N HERE THE TEAR OF PITY SPRINGS, AND HEARTS ARE TOUCHED BY HUMAN THINGS. – VIRGIL

One hundred years after Douglas' death, on 12 July 1934, a group of seven men and a boy climbed Mauna Kea to dedicate a monument to Douglas at the place of his death. Many Scots people have lived and worked on Hawaii, and a small group from the Robert Burns Society of Hilo decided to raise money for a monument. Some two hundred Douglas firs were planted, forming a grove around the monument. In 1942, a Judge Wood wrote in the journal *American Forests*:

Standing in Kaluaka today, 6000 feet up the side of Mauna Kea, one sees no water in the crater. The wall around it is still in place, except where the roots of a giant koa have crowded the stones away. The sides are overgrown with wild raspberry bushes. The entrances may still be seen, where wild cattle came to drink. Quite a number of lovely evergreen trees have been planted inside the wall, in memory of the good and great man whose name they bear.

Chapter Thirteen

THE MAN AND HIS ACHIEVEMENTS

'His worth as a useful member of society and practical botanist
will live and be felt while the study and cultivation of plants and
flowers remain pleasing and beneficial to mankind.'
*George Barnston, a contemporary of Douglas at Fort Vancouver,
writing in 1860 (quoted in A.G. Harvey,* Douglas of the Fir, *1947)*

How do we measure the success and achievements of this tough
Scot who died so tragically? And why does his tale inspire
such great interest and affection?

There is no doubting the strength of the Douglas 'legend', which,
even two hundred years after his birth, continues to attract people as
the magnitude of his achievements is increasingly recognized. Because
his employers at the Horticultural Society obliged him to keep a
journal, we know much more about him than we do about the many
other plant-collectors who travelled in the Americas and the Pacific. In
Sir William Hooker he also benefited from a distinguished patron and
champion.

The legend is based largely on Douglas' own writings, though it
is difficult to know how far they can be relied on. His journal was not
edited and published until some eighty years after his death, by which
time none of his contemporaries was still alive to verify, or challenge,
the contents. Like most people, Douglas was probably unable to resist
overstating some of his achievements, and some of his mountaineering
feats have been questioned. Nevertheless, by and large, both his
accounts of his travels and his botanical observations stand up well
wherever they can be tested. Perhaps the best testimony is that of his
contemporaries, those who knew him and worked with him. The

recollections of these men – Willie Beattie, the head gardener at Scone, William Hooker, Governor De Witt Clinton of New York State, and the many characters in the 'wild west' of the Columbia River such as Meredith Gairdner, the doctor, and George Barnston, who spent a winter with him at Fort Vancouver – are universally warm and affectionate. Admittedly, Douglas could be single-minded, even stubborn, but a plant-collector working in difficult circumstances had to develop these qualities in order to survive and succeed.

How then should we sum up Douglas' life and work? Perhaps his achievements are best assessed in three ways: as a plant-hunter; as one of the first European explorers in the American north-west; and as an individual who, from humble beginnings, attained remarkable things.

Douglas was one among many eminent plant-hunters who between them created the gardens and landscapes of Britain, and many other countries, as we know them today. The importance of the region he explored in terms of plants suitable for the British climate and the tenacity and success of his collecting put him among the most influential of these remarkable men. He was also one of the few who survived and returned to talk about his discoveries. And because he was one of the first, he was also among the most influential and therefore inspired others.

A casual look at any British suburban garden will reveal the extent of Douglas' horticultural contribution. Lupins, flowering currant, *Mahonia*, Californian poppies, penstemons, clarkias and sunflowers, among many others, all bear testimony to his determination. The numbers are immense. He collected and sent to the Horticultural Society the seeds of more than 880 species. Of these, well over 200 were original introductions, and about 130 proved hardy in Britain.

Douglas did have a fair amount of luck on his side. He collected in a region where the climate is similar to that of western Europe and where there is a rich diversity of plants. He was also fortunate that so many of his specimens reached London safely. However, this was also the result of his diligence and care – he packed his specimens well and sent them home by different routes in order to reduce possible losses.

It is possible to argue that Douglas merely happened to be in the right place at the right time. But this ignores the extraordinary tenacity that he brought to his collecting. Would any one else have been so determined and so diligent? Many others followed Douglas, but were overcome by the scale of the task and by the physical difficulties and hardships of travelling in such a vast country.

It is Douglas' contribution to the business of forestry that is perhaps most valued today and is the main reason why his legend has endured. In the early nineteenth century, Britain was largely a de-forested land. For generations, the native forests had been exploited, so much so that most had vanished and Britain was becoming increasingly reliant on imported timber. Even for a great seafaring and trading nation, this was potentially risky; in times of conflict, timber supplies could easily be blockaded. Thus interest in reafforestation was growing – and nowhere more than in Perthshire, where the pioneering 'planting' Dukes of Atholl initiated major programmes of tree-planting in the Tay Valley.

Britain is poor in native trees, especially those suitable for timber; there are only three native species of conifer, and only one of these, the Scots pine, has any significant commercial value as timber. Douglas' achievement was to increase significantly the choice of trees available to foresters who wanted to improve the productivity of their woodlands, just as, at the same time, farmers were 'improving' the productivity of the land for growing food. The trees Douglas introduced to Britain therefore stimulated considerable interest among the great landowners eager to improve their landholdings and landscape their parkland. The great houses of Scotland – Scone Palace, Blair Castle, Murthly and Drumlanrig, among many others – are surrounded by landscaped amenity or 'policy' woodlands that invariably contain 'Douglas introductions'. Usually these are among the largest and most outstanding specimens. Similarly, in England, Ireland and Wales, many of the great houses have excellent collections of Douglas introductions. The Forestry Commission has inherited two of the best of these, at Westonbirt Arboretum in Gloucestershire and Bedgebury Pinetum in Kent, and now operates them as specialist tree collections open to the public.

Douglas' comments on the potential suitability of his tree introductions showed remarkable foresight. The Douglas fir was soon found to grow well in the British Isles, and quickly became fashionable. It is now an important timber tree in Britain and continental Europe, and is also one of the most important specimen trees, grown for its grandeur and size. Douglas firs are now the tallest trees in Europe, and the tallest examples are to be found at The Hermitage at Dunkeld, only a few miles from Douglas' birthplace. The other silver firs that Douglas introduced, the noble fir and the grand fir, have also grown remarkably in Britain, and almost match the Douglas fir in scale and height.

In the commercial timber trade, the Sitka spruce has become the most important timber tree in Britain. It forms the backbone of the domestic forestry industry, particularly in the wetter western parts of the country, the very places that Douglas predicted it would grow well. Douglas wrote up his field observations of his tree discoveries, and these were published as an appendix to his journal in 1914. His predictions of the use and value of the Sitka spruce proved remarkably accurate:

> It may nevertheless become of equal if not greater importance [than the Douglas fir]. It possesses one great advantage by growing to a very large size ... in apparently poor, thin damp soils. ... This unquestionably has great claims on our consideration as it would thrive in such places in Britain where *P. sylvestris* [Scots pine] finds no shelter. It would become a useful and large tree.

During the twentieth century, the Douglas fir was the most important timber tree in the international forestry trade. As Audrey Grescoe wrote in *Giants: The Colossal Trees of Pacific North America,*

> It has been used to build houses and other buildings throughout the world, has been laid down as sleepers to carry goods and people across the world's railroads, and to build the piers and jetties from which have sailed ships and boats on the world's oceans. It is the construction timber *par excellence*. This century Douglas fir has been quoted as the 'greatest lumber source the world has ever seen'.

In the twenty-first century, another 'Douglas tree', *Pinus radiata*, the Monterey pine, which Douglas introduced from California, is likely to replace the Douglas fir in international trade, having been planted extensively in New Zealand, Australia, Chile, South Africa and southern Europe. Is it any wonder then that Douglas is viewed as one of the greatest influences on the present-day practice of forestry in Britain and beyond?

Douglas' single most important achievement was to widen enormously the availability of suitable trees for planting in Britain. In 1919, shortly after the end of World War I, the British government decide to create a timber reserve to protect the nation from over-reliance on timber imports. The foresters of the fledgling Forestry Commission, entrusted with the task of replanting, turned principally to the trees Douglas introduced, which had already been observed and trialled for some eighty years. The resulting predominantly conifer woodlands have had arguably the single biggest impact on the landscape of rural Britain in the twentieth century.

Amid the many voyages of discovery made by Europeans during the eighteenth and nineteenth centuries, Douglas' travels are remarkable. Here was a man driven to travel and to explore. He twice undertook the long sea voyage to the Pacific North West via Madeira, Rio, Cape Horn and the Galapagos Islands. He travelled overland on foot and by canoe from the Pacific to Hudson Bay; he climbed in the Rockies; he ascended the volcanoes of Hawaii; and he planned to walk through Alaska and to Siberia and thence to Europe. Douglas' energies were also fuelled by an enthusiastic inquisitiveness that extended far beyond his professional botanical expertise. He was interested in everyone and everything. His accounts of his overland trips around the Columbia River show enormous insights into the life of the early European settlers and traders. He was also the first person to describe, often in sympathetic detail, the way of life of the native Americans, and his accounts form an important historical record of the time before European immigration and disease changed those societies for ever. His was a pragmatic approach. Whenever possible he made sure that he got on well with the people through whose country he was travelling, if only because they were often the only people who could help him track down the seeds and specimens he was determined to collect. Warm feelings were often reciprocated, and his nickname – 'Grass Man' – suggests that he was regarded with equal interest.

Reading Douglas' journal, it is easy to become blasé about the difficulties of travel at that time. Bill Bryson, the American travel writer who lived for many years in Britain, provided a modern-day perspective on travel in a forested wilderness when wrote about his own experiences in walking through the North American woods on the Appalachian Trail:

> The American woods have been unnerving people for 300 years. ... To begin with they are cubic. The trees surround you, loom over you, press in from all sides. Woods choke off views, and leave you muddled and without bearings. They make you feel small and confused and vulnerable. ... Stand in a desert or a prairie and you know you are in a big space. Stand in a wood and you only sense it. They are a vast, featureless nowhere. And they are alive.

Douglas must have experienced a similar awe of these great forests. Yet he had confidence in his own ability to survive and to achieve his tasks, whether facing down hostile natives or hunting aggressive grizzlies.

And what of the man? Like so many, Douglas was an ordinary man who achieved extraordinary things. His assets were single-mindedness, a determination to achieve his objectives, physical toughness, huge quantities of courage, loyalty, and a great deal of ability. For all his humble origins and limited education, he wrote well and developed a broad scientific curiosity that extended way beyond his original botanical expertise.

It is evident that Douglas did not gladly suffer those whom he considered to be fools. He could be difficult and stubborn. He fell out with the Horticultural Society over the editing of his journals and then over the removal of Joseph Sabine from his post as Secretary. Douglas lived in a hierarchical society, and at times his Scottish directness must have irritated. Even Hooker, his great ally, commented on his 'restless and dissatisfied' nature.

Yet there was clearly also a warmth to the man. Despite his commitment to his native Scottish Presbyterianism, of which there is little doubt, he was no bigot. He got on equally well with the Roman Catholic Fathers of California and with the 'heathen' natives of the Columbia region. He was also interested in medicine and healing, so much so that he came to be known as 'Doctor' wherever he travelled. The warm recollections of his friends on the Columbia and the testimonies of people such as De Witt Clinton all point to Douglas as someone who got on with, and was liked by, the people he dealt with.

When news of Douglas' death reached Britain, initial disbelief was succeeded by sadness among everyone who had met him or who knew of his work. In 1836, *Gardener's Magazine* wrote: 'If we only imagine the British Gardens deprived of the plants introduced by Douglas, we shall find them but little further advanced in point of ornamental production than they were a century ago.' It fell to Sir William Hooker to ensure that Douglas' achievements would be recognized. In 1836, he published 'A Brief Memoir of the Life of Mr David Douglas, with Extracts from His Letters', so that his 'name and virtues will long live in the recollection of his friends'.

In Douglas' native county, the Perthshire Royal Horticultural Society established a fund to raise money to build a stone memorial, which was erected in 1841 in the grounds of the Old Kirk in Scone. It is a fitting tribute: over 23 feet tall, it carries a portrait and a biographical notice describing Douglas' life and achievements and naming the plants he introduced to Britain. The long list of contributors to the monument recorded in the *Annals* of the Society is testimony to the high regard in which Douglas was held. All the great landowners of Scotland made donations, together with many from

England. Contributions also came from Austria, Germany, Denmark and France, from members of botanical gardens around Britain, and also from humble nurserymen and apprentice gardeners. One of the saddest must have been Willie Beattie, head gardener at Scone and Douglas' first mentor.

For a humble gardener from Scone, Douglas made a major contribution to the world of botany in general and to horticulture and forestry in particular. His memorial today is not just in the stones of the Old Parish Church but in the gardens, landscapes and forests of Britain and other temperate climates where his introductions are found today. His contribution is summed up in this tribute from *Gardeners Chronicle* in 1926, one hundred years after the beginning of his major plant-collecting expeditions:

> There is scarcely a spot deserving the name of garden, either in Europe or in the United States, in which some of the discoveries of Douglas do not form the chief attraction. The frequent mention of his name as the discoverer and introducer of some of the finest coniferous trees that adorn the lawns and parks of Great Britain affords abundant evidence that the above state-ment contains very much if not the whole truth, and to no single individual is modern horticulture more indebted than to David Douglas.

Appendix 1
THE TREE INTRODUCTIONS OF DAVID DOUGLAS

'It may nevertheless become of equal if not greater importance
[than Douglas fir]. It possesses one great advantage by growing to a
very large size ... in apparently poor, thin damp soils. ... This
unquestionably has great claims on our consideration as it would
thrive in such places in Britain where *P. sylvestris* (Scots pine)
finds no shelter. It would become a useful and large tree.'
Douglas' description of Sitka spruce in his journal

David Douglas is perhaps best remembered for his tree introductions.
He was fortunate to be one of the first Europeans to visit the Pacific
North West and discover its great store of natural wealth. What he
saw was a landscape of glacier-clad volcanoes, vast forests, wilderness, waterways, and jagged mountain ranges. On someone
accustomed to the sparse, if beautiful, tree cover of the Scottish hills
and straths, the vast forest and groves of huge trees must have made
an enormous impression.

The mountains in north-west America run north to south rather
than, as in Europe, east to west. As a result, during and after the last
Ice Age, some 10,000 years ago, trees and plants were able to retreat
before the glaciers to warmer refuges from which they could readily
recolonize after the ice fell back. This all took place quickly in geological terms, but more gradually from our human perspective. Over
thousands of years, the evolutionary process was helped as plants
drifted away from an increasingly inhospitable climate and drifted
back again to find new niches and habitats to exploit. When Douglas
arrived, this evolution was in full swing, as it still is today, even allow-
ing for the huge influence of man since the early nineteenth century.

Douglas was especially struck by the great variety of conifers.
When describing one of his discoveries, he commented to Hooker that
'you will begin to think that I manufacture pines at my pleasure'. And
so it must have appeared to his incredulous mentor as yet another new
conifer discovery had Douglas exclaiming with pleasure. When the
Royal Horticultural Society finally published Douglas' journal in
1914, it contained an Appendix entitled 'Some American Pines'. This

came from a document in Douglas' hand that was almost certainly written between his return from his first journey to the Pacific North West in 1827 and his departure for his second in 1829. In it Douglas lists and describes some seventeen species of conifer. At the time, botanists considered all conifers to be pines, and not until later in the century were the different families or genera recognized and given separate names. Looking over these descriptions and bringing the story of the trees up to date gives a real insight into why many contemporary foresters consider Douglas their 'patron saint'.

It is clear from his journal, notes and correspondence that Douglas saw, recorded and gathered seed and specimens from more trees than he has subsequently been credited with introducing. Some of his collections did not make it back to England; even if they did, not all were raised successfully from seed. Douglas mentions many trees common in the Pacific North West, such as western red cedar, *Thuja plicata*, and western hemlock, *Tsuga heterophylla*, yet seed of these did not reach London. However, it is hard to imagine so painstaking a collector as Douglas ignoring these magnificent giant conifers, particularly as he would have seen them in virgin forest. In fact, Douglas failed to distinguish between these western conifers and similar but different species of conifer found on the eastern side of the Rockies. Thus he called western hemlock *Tsuga canadensis*, which is the name given to eastern hemlock, and also mistakenly called western red cedar *Thuya occidentalis* after the white cedar found in the eastern USA and Canada. Thinking that these were the same species, he probably did not bother to collect their seed.

Douglas' discoveries and introductions whetted the appetite of many collectors and encouraged them to retrace his steps. Some succeeded in introducing the trees Douglas had observed and noted, but none was to come close to matching the achievements of this extraordinary young Scotsman.

Douglas fir (*Pseudotsuga menziesii*)

Being familiar with the description given by Archibald Menzies, who had voyaged with Vancouver in the 1780s and 1790s, Douglas found the Douglas fir almost as soon as he landed in the Pacific North West. Measuring one specimen some 227 feet (68 metres) long and 48 feet (15 metres) in circumference at 3 feet (1 metre) from the ground, he was impressed! On his return home he wrote that 'they form one of the most striking objects in nature. . . . It will prove a beautiful acquisition to English Sylva if not an important addition to the number of useful timbers. The wood may be found very useful.'

The natural range of Douglas fir is widespread, from Monterey in California in the south to Vancouver Island in the north and the western Rocky Mountains in the east, so Douglas would have encountered the tree regularly. Douglas' earliest seed collections were made in 1825 around the lower reaches of the Columbia River near Fort Vancouver, Washington State. These arrived in Britain in 1827, and many original specimens from them can still be found, for instance at Scone Palace, Dawyck Gardens and Drumlanrig in Scotland, where they form magnificent specimen trees. Plants raised by the Horticultural Society from these first collections were distributed to Society fellows. The subsequent demand for further specimens was so great that seed from Douglas fir trees growing at Lynedoch on Scone Estate realized some £500 between 1845 and 1853.

Douglas fir has become one of the most widely planted specimen conifers in the policy woodlands and designed landscapes of Britain as well as a significant timber tree in its own right producing high-quality timber. It is best grown on the fertile slopes and terraces of the glens and straths of Argyll, Perthshire and the Great Glen in Scotland, the valleys of the Welsh Marches and the south-west of England. The tallest tree in Britain is now reputedly a Douglas fir in Perthshire, growing on Forestry Commission ground adjacent to The Hermitage near Dunkeld (see p. 180); this measures some 212 feet (65 metres). Douglas fir has also been introduced to other European countries such as Germany and France, as well as to New Zealand, where it forms an increasingly important timber resource.

Douglas fir, which has been described as the world's greatest-ever timber source, has been the most significant timber traded throughout the twentieth century. Although conflict has recently arisen over the exploitation of the remaining stands of old growth, there are many places in British Columbia, Washington State and Oregon where magnificent stands of huge Douglas fir can still be seen in their natural habitat. The tallest Douglas fir in North America today is some 329 feet (100 metres) and is found in Oregon, which seems entirely appropriate, since the tree is the state's arboreal emblem. Intriguingly, much taller trees have been felled in the past, including a 415-feet (127-metre) monster recorded in 1902 on Vancouver Island that surpasses even the coastal redwoods of California.

Sitka spruce (*Picea sitchensis*)

Douglas rather cleverly spotted the potential for Sitka, though once again he was following in the footsteps of Archibald Menzies, who discovered and described the tree. Douglas wrote of Sitka that:

187

> It may nevertheless become of equal if not greater in importance [than Douglas fir]. It possesses one great advantage by growing to a very large size … in apparently poor, thin damp soils. … This unquestionably has great claims on our consideration as it would thrive in such places in Britain where *P. sylvestris* (Scots pine) finds no shelter. It would become a useful and large tree.

Douglas first collected seed from the mouth of the Columbia River, but this was lost. He made subsequent collections in 1826 and 1830, and some original specimens from these collections remain in Ireland. The last reputed original specimen in Britain was in Perthshire. Unfortunately, this was felled in 1998 when a tree cutter, unaware of the difference between the tree equivalent of a cold and a terminal condition, misdiagnosed the tree's health. However, there are many fine old specimen trees throughout the west of Britain in Wales, southwest Scotland, Argyll and the western Highlands, Perthshire and elsewhere. For those used to early thicket crops of Sitka spruce, the sight of stands of huge Sitka trees well thinned and spaced out is quite a revelation. Never popular in amenity woodlands, Sitka spruce is nevertheless a fine specimen tree, particularly in relation to the size to which it can grow. Modern forestry practice recognizes the benefits of leaving groves of trees to grow on in perpetuity; as early plantations evolve into true woodlands and forests, the number of such groves has increased.

Today, the ubiquitous Sitka spruce is a major feature of the upland landscape of northern and western Britain. After World War I, Sitka spruce was used to reforest bare land and so became the major instrument in developing a strategic timber reserve to replace Britain's depleted timber stocks. Sitka spruce is now the mainstay of the British forestry industry. It can grow on relatively inhospitable sites and produces a crop of timber where other trees struggle to survive. The quality of the timber is excellent for paper production and for higher-quality end-uses such as building construction. For a country such as Britain, which imports about 85 per cent of its timber requirement, mainly as conifer softwood timber, such an asset is worth developing. Sitka is the main tree component of about one third of Britain's forests, yet it accounts for about two thirds of timber production, a proportion that is likely to increase significantly between the years 2000 and 2020 as the forests planted during the 1960s and 1970s reach their optimum harvest. While the use of Sitka spruce to create large plantations in the uplands of Scotland, Wales and northern England once attracted much conflict and adverse publicity, foresters have now learned to be more discerning and sensitive in using the tree in forest design and planning.

In North America, timber from Sitka spruce has always been highly prized for its light weight yet relative strength. For this reason, it has had a number of specialist uses, such as aeroplane construction. Orville and Wilbur Wright used it to build their plane *Kitty Hawk*, in which they made the first successful powered flight. Sitka spruce forests took heavy casualties in providing timber for the first Sopwith Camels in World War I and the famous Mosquito fighter bomber of World War II. Sitka timber was also used in the biggest plane that has ever flown; this was *Spruce Goose*, which belonged to Howard Hughes, the millionaire recluse. The wood's ability to resonate sound means that it is highly prized for making musical instruments such as pianos, violins and guitars.

The tallest champion Sitka spruce in Britain is found in Perthshire at the remarkable height of 200 feet (61 metres). However, this is a mere stripling in comparison with the 'Camanah Giant' in British Columbia which, at 315 feet (96 metres), is the tallest Sitka spruce of all.

Douglas' words proved prophetic. A major domestic timber industry, providing jobs and creating wealth, based predominantly on the spruce that he introduced, has grown up in Scotland and beyond.

Noble fir *(Abies procera)*

Douglas clearly had a soft spot for noble fir, having spent three weeks in forests composed predominantly of *Pinus nobilis*, as he called the tree, while exploring the Willamette River in Oregon in 1825. All his collections from that expedition were lost. Seed from subsequent collections reached Britain in 1830, when Douglas described the tree to Hooker as 'by far the finest. I spent 3 weeks in a forest composed of this tree, and day by day could not cease to admire it.' In his note 'Some American Pines' he wrote:

> The present tree, among the many highly interesting species by which it is surrounded in its native woods, in point of elegance justly claims the pre-eminence. ... This if introduced would profitably clothe the bleak barren hilly parts of Scotland, Ireland, and Cumberland, besides increasing the beauty of the country.

Noble fir is found in the higher elevations of the Cascade Mountains in Washington State, Oregon and northern California. This is a relatively restricted range in comparison with other conifers from the area. Commonly recognized as a handsome tree, with large prominent cones and silvery blue foliage, it is the tallest growing of the true firs in the Pacific North West. The champion tree, 278 feet (85 metres) high, is found in the Gifford Pinchot National Forest in south-western Washington State.

In Britain, noble fir is very popular as an ornamental tree in large gardens, designed landscapes and policy woodlands. The size of the cones and the colour of the foliage make it stand out. It has also been planted as a forest tree, mainly in Scotland, where it thrives. However, the timber is not as strong or useful as Sitka spruce or Douglas fir; this now limits its use as a forest tree, although foresters still value its attractiveness and silvicultural qualities. It is also commonly planted as a Christmas tree, and commands a considerable premium over other types of tree. The foliage is also highly prized in continental Europe for making Christmas wreaths and decorations.

Two original trees from Douglas' collections survived until 1968. The tallest champion tree in the British Isles is now found at Ardkinglas, Cairndow, near the head of Loch Fyne in Argyll, and stands over 170 feet (52 metres) tall.

Grand fir *(Abies grandis)*

This is another of the true firs discovered by Douglas on his journeys around the Columbia River in 1830. Seed was despatched to Britain in the same consignment as noble fir. He described to Hooker specimens 'growing from one hundred and seventy to two hundred feet high' and on seeing grand fir growing at the base of Mount St Helens, he exclaimed that 'a forest of these trees is a spectacle too much for one man to see'.

Douglas' collections of these new trees were ultimately distributed among the fellows of the Horticultural Society. The vigorous growth and attractiveness of the young trees created such a demand that plants changed hands at fifteen to twenty guineas each. The profits helped to finance further seed-gathering expeditions in the 1840s and 1850s that followed in Douglas' footsteps. The nursery firm Veitch sent out collectors such as William Lobb, and a group of Scottish landowners who wanted to develop their tree and forest interests formed the Oregon Association and sent out John Jeffrey, a young Scotsman, to follow Douglas' trail to seek new trees and collect seeds.

One definite original from Douglas' seed survives at Curraghmore, County Waterford, Ireland. Other huge early specimens are found elsewhere, particularly at Diana's Grove, Blair Atholl, Perthshire.

Grand fir has a much wider range than noble fir, extending from California to Vancouver Island and east to Montana and Idaho. The tallest specimen, found in the Olympic National Park in Washington State, is almost 230 feet (71 metres) tall. In Britain, grand fir grows very rapidly, and there are many huge specimens, including the tallest champion tree. This is some 206 feet (63 metres) tall and is found at Strone House, on Loch Fyne, Argyll. The fastest-growing stand of trees in Britain is a grove of grand fir growing near Dunkeld, Perthshire; this is growing at about three times more volume over its area than the equivalent average stand of conifer trees in Britain. Like noble fir, the timber is not especially prized in comparison with other softwoods, so grand fir is now planted mainly for its amenity value, especially since it can withstand considerable shade and grow under existing matured trees. The bark of young trees contains resin blisters which, when pinched, squirt a fragrant, transparent resin.

Pacific silver fir or red fir (*Abies amabilis*)

Introduced and named by Douglas in 1830 (*amabilis* means 'lovely'), *Abies amabilis* has only ever been used as a specimen tree in large gardens and specialist collections. No original specimens survive. The tallest champion tree, found in the Scottish Highlands, stands 131 feet (40 metres) high, about two-thirds the height of the tallest tree in Washington State.

The tree ranges from the Alaskan border south along the coast to California and inland to the Rocky Mountain region in central Idaho.

Douglas called the Pacific silver fir 'another tree of singular beauty' that 'justly merits our further consideration'. For fifty years after its introduction, no one could find any trees to follow up Douglas' initial discovery. The suspicion was that Douglas had confused it with noble fir; the two are very similar and their range overlaps. But it was rediscovered in 1880, proving Douglas' observations correct.

Monterey pine (*Pinus radiata*)

Of the true pines discovered by Douglas, none has been utilized on a wider scale than Monterey or radiata pine. It can be recognized by its clusters of three-needled leaves and of large cones, which persist around branches for many years. Monterey pine has been planted all over the world and has proved a successful timber tree in Australia, New Zealand, South Africa, South America (particularly Chile) and southern Europe. It is set to become the major timber traded in the international timber market in the twenty-first century, taking over from Douglas fir, which was the twentieth century's most significant timber.

Douglas introduced the Monterey pine in 1833 from his travels in California. It is an oddity in that its surviving native habitat is a small area in Monterey County, in the part of California where the writer John Steinbeck lived and set many of his works. The Ice Age was probably responsible for pushing the tree to the relatively warmer Californian climes; for some reason it has been unable to move out from this refuge as the climate has improved. In its home territory, Monterey pine is an unremarkable tree in terms of size and form, yet elsewhere it is able to grow rapidly, reaching over 200 feet (61 metres) in fifty-two years in New Zealand.

In Britain, Monterey pine is very common in the south and south-west of England, where it can be seen on the edges of fields and large estates. It is also in large gardens and arboreta elsewhere. It is the most vigorous of all the conifers in Britain; shoots more than 5 feet (1.5 metres) are common, with one achieving 8 feet (2.5 metres).

There are no originals left from Douglas' collections, although one tree in Buckinghamshire has been raised from a cutting taken in 1839, presumably from an original seedling. The tallest British tree, in Hampshire, is 128 feet (39 metres) high, which compares rather well with the 121 feet (37 metres) North American champion, although it is much shorter than the New Zealand giant.

Western yellow pine *(Pinus ponderosa)*

In North America, western yellow pine has an enormous range, from British Columbia to Mexico and inland to Colorado, Nebraska and Texas. In Britain, where it is rarely found, it is more commonly called ponderosa pine. It was introduced by Douglas in 1827, probably from collections made near Spokane, Washington State, and has proved long-lived; a number of specimen trees date from the introductions. Douglas described the trees as 'tall, straight, seldom divided by large branches, very elegant, ninety to one hundred and thirty feet high'.

Trees grown from Douglas' original collections, and the best-growing specimens, can be found in the south and Midlands of England and in the Welsh borders away from coastal areas. The tallest champion tree is at Powis Castle, Montgomeryshire, Wales, where it stands over 134 feet (41 metres) tall; this is probably an original from Douglas' collection.

Ponderosa is an important timber tree in North America and was used in the development of dendrochronology, the science of tree-ring dating, in the early twentieth century.

Sugar pine *(Pinus lambertiana)*

Of all the trees introduced by Douglas, the sugar pine has been the greatest disappointment in fulfilling the promise he predicted when describing his epic search for the tree in Oregon in 1826. He wrote to Hooker: 'I rejoice to tell you of a new species of *Pinus*, the most princely of the genus, perhaps even the grandest specimen of vegetation.' When he found it, he noted in his journal: 'New or strange things seldom fail to make great impressions, and often at first we are liable to over-rate them; and lest I should never see my friends to tell them verbally of this most beautiful and immensely large tree.' Douglas also noted that the cones were the longest of any conifer, and that the seeds were a culinary delicacy of the local peoples.

Introduced into Britain in 1827 and initially cultivated with great excitement, sugar pine has unfortunately proved highly susceptible to a terminal condition caused by white pine blister-rust. As a result, there are no surviving originals, nor many mature specimens. The current champion tallest tree in Britain, in Shropshire, has only reached 75 feet (23 metres).

In its home range in the mountains of Oregon and California, sugar pine is a large tree, growing up to 164 feet (50 metres) tall, and plays an important part in the timber industry.

Western white pine *(Pinus monticola)*

Introduced by Douglas in 1823, western white pine ranges from British Columbia to Idaho and Montana, and is a major timber tree.

Although there are no originals surviving in Britain, some specimens from the 1840s and 1850s have survived. Unfortunately, the species, like all five-needled pines, is susceptible to rust. Specimens can be seen at Dawyck, Scone and the Royal Botanic Garden, Edinburgh.

Big-cone pine *(Pinus coulteri)*

Named for Dr Thomas Coulter, Douglas' travelling companion in California, the three-needled pine, big-cone pine, was introduced in 1832. It is found in southern California and Baja California in Mexico. Its cones are among the biggest and heaviest of all pine cones. The tree is relatively short-lived in Britain; the tallest specimen is in the Royal Botanic Garden, Edinburgh.

Digger pine *(Pinus sabiniana)*

Native to the dry foothills of the Californian mountains, Digger pine, introduced in 1832, is short-lived and rare, and is found only in specialist collections such as the Forestry Commission's Bedgebury Pinetum in Kent. Douglas discovered the tree inland from the Monterey peninsula near the San Juan Bautista Mission and named it in honour of Joseph Sabine of the Horticultural Society. He obviously thought sufficiently well of it to describe it as 'a noble new species' and, despite its small size, as 'one of the most beautiful objects in nature'.

Vine maple *(Acer circinatum)*

A small, broad-leaved tree, native to the Pacific coast from British Columbia to California, vine maple is a handsome ornamental with dramatic colours in the autumn. According to Douglas, it

> forms part of the underwood in the pine forests. ... [It] is called by the voyageurs *Bois de diable* (wood of the devil) from the obstruction it gives them in passing through the woods. The wood is very tough and is used by the natives for making hooks with which they take the salmon.

Hardy in Britain, vine maple is a good specimen tree for a small garden.

Bigleaf maple *(Acer macrophyllum)*

Bigleaf maple is one of the few large, broad-leaved trees of the Pacific North West. Introduced by Douglas in 1825, it was initially admired but quickly forgotten as a forest tree because of its unfavourable comparison with sycamore. In its home range, from British Columbia south to California, it is prized as the only Pacific maple of any commercial importance, and is used for veneer, furniture and wood-turning. Rock musicians value the timber highly for the back of electric guitars and will pay a considerable premium for it. Bigleaf maple is also used for the back, side and neck of violins and bass fiddles.

In his journal, Douglas described bigleaf maple as

> one of the largest and most beautiful trees on the Columbia River. Its large foliage and elegant racemes of yellow fragrant flowers contrast delightfully with the dark feathery branches of the lordly pine.

Specimens of bigleaf maple can be found in most arboreta. Its leaves, which occasionally extend to 2 feet (60 centimetres) wide, make it stand out.

Pacific madrona *(Arbutus menziesii)*

Like many of the plants introduced by Douglas, Pacific madrona was first collected and described by Archibald Menzies during his trips to the Pacific North West in the 1790s. The tree is one of the most beautiful broad-leaved flowering evergreens, and is reminiscent of eucalyptus with a reddish-brown trunk and orange-red fruits. Its range is on the Pacific coast from British Columbia to California, where it grows to almost 100 feet (30 metres). Menzies first saw Pacific madrona at the north-west tip of the Olympic Peninsula in Washington State. In his journal, Douglas reminded himself of the importance of collecting from it: 'Do not fail to put up a treble supply of its seeds: being evergreen it is the more desirable.'

Common in gardens in southern Britain, Pacific madrona will survive further north if protected from north and east winds. It is also frequently found in arboreta and botanical gardens. One extraordinary specimen grows adjacent to the wall of Farleyer House Hotel near Aberfeldy. The house is close to, and was once part of, the Castle Menzies estate, where Menzies himself was brought up.

The ones that got away ...

It is impossible to produce a definitive list of the trees Douglas discovered, introduced or merely recorded. Many of his notes were lost, and we cannot know how many seeds and specimens were lost *en route* to Britain. There has been some debate about whether Douglas missed, or failed to collect from, a number of common trees in the Pacific North West, such as western hemlock and western red cedar. Writing in the *Journal of the Royal Horticultural Society* in 1942, F.R.S. Balfour reported that the Society's archives contained unpublished sheets in Douglas' handwriting describing plants that he had collected. It is evident from these papers and from other notes in his journal and letters that Douglas recorded and collected many other trees besides those that he is credited with having introduced.

Lodgepole pine (Pinus contorta)

Douglas collected seed from lodgepole pine, but unfortunately, either it did not germinate in Britain or it was subsequently lost before being reintroduced in the mid-1850s. Lodgepole pine is now a staple of British forestry, although in the past it has fallen in and out of fashion. It has been used extensively as a pioneer crop in inhospitable sites with low fertility when afforesting deep peats in the Highlands; however, it has become less important as forest policy has moved away from utilizing this type of ground. Nevertheless, about 10 per cent of the new forests created in Scotland during the twentieth century have used lodgepole pine, and its distinctive deep-bottle-green foliage (quite distinct from the blue-green of the native Scots pine) is a frequent sight in the Highlands.

The tree has tremendous natural variability. Four distinct varieties are found across its wide range, which runs from Alaska down the coast to California and inland to Alberta and the Rocky Mountains of Dakota and Colorado, where it grows as a colonizer on marginal and inhospitable sites. Choosing the right source of seed is critical to its success as a forest tree in Britain. The tallest champion tree, found on the National Trust's property at Bodnant, Conwy, Wales, reaches 112 feet (34 metres).

Douglas, who saw lodgepole pine mainly on his travels along the coast, did not have a high opinion of its potential value: 'Little can be said in favour of this tree either for ornament or as a useful wood.'

Bristlecone or Santa Lucia fir (Abies venusta)
Bristlecone is rare in the north of Britain, and is largely confined to arboreta and collections in the south and west. Douglas found the tree in 1832 in the Santa Lucia Mountains of southern California, which is the extent of its limited range. He wrote to Hooker:

> When on the tree, being in great clusters, and at a great height withal, [its] cones resemble the inflorescence of a *Banksia*, a name which I should have liked to give to the species, but that there is a *Pinus Banksia* already. This tree attains a great size and height, and is, on the whole, a most beautiful object.

The tallest tree in Britain is in Devon, reaching some 125 feet (38 metres).

Western red cedar (Thuja plicata)
Western red cedar ranges from Alaska to California and inland to the Rockies, and so Douglas would have seen many of these valuable trees, which native Americans used for carving totem poles and for boat-building. Today, the highly prized timber is employed for making roof shingles, among other things. Douglas observed that:

> This is a rapid growing and very graceful tree, in magnitude far exceeding any other species. ... Their form frequently exceeding

one hundred and sixty feet in height and thirty-six feet in circumference six feet from the ground. ... No tree on the North West Coast is held in so much repute by the aborigines of the country as the present. Their canoes ... are made of the timber of this tree. ... The wood makes good shingles – the Hudson's Bay Company establishments are covered with it.

Common in large gardens and parks, western red cedar has only a minor place as a forest tree in Britain, although it has never lost its amenity appeal. The tallest champion tree in Britain, 151 feet (46 metres) high, is found on the side of Loch Fyne in Argyll.

Western hemlock (Tsuga heterophylla)
Western hemlock, one of the most common trees in the Pacific North West, is often found in association with Sitka spruce, Douglas fir and other conifers across its range from Alaska to northern California. Douglas, who called the tree *Pinus canadensis*, first mentioned it very soon after he reached the Columbia River for the first time: 'the ground on the south side of the river is low, covered thickly with wood, chiefly *Pinus canadensis*'. Subsequently, he referred to it frequently, but confused it with eastern hemlock, *Tsuga canadensis*, assuming that there was only one species across the continent. He noted that it was 'abundant on the woody parts of the North-West coast, fully larger than any found on the Atlantic side of the Continent'. On the Columbia River, in 1827, he saw 'lofty snowy peaks in all directions. Contrasted with their dark shady bases densely covered with pine, the deep rich hue of *Pinus canadensis* with its feathery cloudy branches quivering in the breeze.'

Why Douglas did not send seeds back is a small mystery. Perhaps he thought it unnecessary since, as far as he was concerned, this was not a new species, or maybe he did and the seeds were lost. It fell to John Jeffrey to introduce the tree to Britain in 1851. Many specimen trees date back to Jeffrey's introductions, particularly in the great tree collections of Perthshire. Western hemlock is also commonly seen in conifer woodlands, where it has found a small niche as a woodland tree. The tallest champion in Britain is found at Benmore, Argyll, where it tops 167 feet (51 metres); in contrast, the North American giant stands 240 feet (73 metres) high in the Olympic National Park in Washington State.

Coast redwood (Sequoia sempervirens)
Coast redwoods are the tallest trees in the world; the tallest reaches a staggering 370 feet (112 metres). Found along the coastal 'fog' belt

from central California to south-west Oregon, the coast redwood is also extremely long lived; some are as old as 2200 years, based on ring counts. Douglas found these trees just north of the Santa Cruz Mission in what is now the California State Redwood Park during the two years he spent in California. He wrote to Hooker:

> But the great beauty of the Californian vegetation is a species of *Taxodium* (Sequoia), which gives the mountains a most peculiar, I was going to say awful, appearance – something that plainly tells that we are not in Europe. ... I have repeatedly measured specimens of this tree 270 feet long and 32 feet round at 3 feet above the tree. Some few I saw, upwards of 300 feet high. ... I possess fine specimens and seeds also.

Douglas was the first field botanist to see and describe the redwood, although (inevitably) Menzies had got there before him and collected material that had been classified by academic botanists. The specimens and seeds Douglas collected must have been lost.

A valued timber, coast redwood is not grown much as a forest tree in Britain, although it is reasonably common in parks and large gardens. Viable seed was introduced in 1843, and a number of the original trees survive. The tallest champion tree, 154 feet (47 metres) high, is found at Bodnant.

Western larch (Larix occidentalis)
In its native range, southern British Columbia to Montana and northern Oregon, the western larch is the largest and finest of all the larches. However it has proved a relative failure in Britain because of frost and canker. Douglas mistakenly thought that the western larch was the same as the eastern larch, *Larix laricina*. However, he was unable to collect seed.

Douglas found the tree on 26 April 1826, near Kettle Falls on the Columbia River:

> *P. Larix* (Western larch) is found in abundance in the mountain valleys much larger than any I have seen on the other side of the continent or even read of. I measured some 30 feet in circumference, and several that were blown down by the late storms 144 feet long; wood clean and perfectly straight.

Giant or Golden chinkapin (Castanopsis chrysophylla)
Douglas discovered giant chinkapin and praised it fulsomely.

Unfortunately, he was unable to get seeds back to Britain. Eventually introduced in 1845, the tree remains rare. An evergreen up to 79 feet (24 metres) high, it is found along the Pacific coast from southern Washington State to California, and is remarkable for its showy white flowers and edible nuts which are like small chestnuts. When Douglas first saw it, on 9 October 1826, he wrote:

> What delighted me greatly was finding *Castanea chrysophylla*, a princely tree 60 to 100 feet high, 3 to 5 feet diameter, evergreen. ... Nothing can exceed the magnificence of this tree, or the strikingly beautiful contrast formed with the sable glory of the shadowy pine amongst which it delights to grow.

Subsequently, he described the tree at greater length:

> This princely tree occupies northern parts of California ... and by its rich varied verdure, eminently contributes to enliven the scenery, a relief as it were to the mind from the dull glossy but magnificently grand and imposing scenery of the pine tribe that decorate the higher latitudes of the north. ... The fruit is delicious and abundant and forests composed of this timber during the season of fruit teem with *Ursus* [bears], *Cervus* [deer] and *Columbae* [pigeons]. Of the latter I have killed several birds more than two hundred miles distant from the nearest point where they could obtain seed and have found in the crop abundance of fruit which I ate and found good. This fact led me first to the knowledge of this tree. ... How much beauty it would give English Sylva can be well imagined and I close this notice of it with regret at being compelled to say it yet remains to be introduced.

Garry or Oregon White Oak (Quercus garryana)
Douglas found Garry oak in 1825 on the Lower Columbia River:

> This is a handsome straight tree of considerable dimensions 40 to 100 feet high. ... For various domestic purposes the wood of the tree will be of great advantage, more especially in shipbuilding. Its hard, tough texture and durability, qualities of rare occurrence in the same species of oaks yet found in America, gives the present a decided superiority over every other native of that country. ... I have great pleasure in dedicating this species to N. Garry, Esq., Deputy Governor of the

Hudson's Bay Company, as a sincere though simple token of regard.

Garry oak, the only native oak in Washington State and British Columbia, has great commercial importance for the reasons Douglas stated. The name Douglas gave to the species might have faded into oblivion had not Hooker not accepted it into his great work *Flora Boreali-Americana*.

Unfortunately, the tree is very rarely grown in Britain.

THE FLOWER INTRODUCTIONS OF DAVID DOUGLAS

> 'On stepping on the shore *Gaultheria shallon* was the first
> plant which I took in my hands. So pleased was I that I could
> scarcely see anything but it.'
> *Douglas' journal, 8 April 1825*

Although probably best known for his tree introductions, Douglas was an all-round botanist and deserves also to be remembered as a collector of flowers and other plants. The Horticultural Society was hungry for any interesting seeds that would attract their members and sent Douglas off with a remit to collect as much as he could. He sent back thousands of seeds, and would assess each flower he found with an eye to its commercial potential: could this insignificant weed form the basis of a breeding programme and evolve into a much-desired garden flower? On all his trips to North America, Douglas sought and diligently catalogued many plants that subsequently become the mainstay of the gardening year in Britain. Today, Douglas' legacy is found in almost every suburban garden.

Salal (*Gaultheria shallon*)

This early discovery grows very well in Britain – indeed too well, as it quickly becomes naturalized and in some habitats takes over to the detriment of the native flora or other plants and so should be planted with care and forethought. Nevertheless, it produces masses of pale pink flowers in May and June and rapidly provides ground cover under shade in the garden.

Flowering currant (*Ribes sanguineum*)

Douglas' excitement at discovering the flowering currant in April 1825 was palpable. On 21 April 1829, while he was in London between his first and second trips to the Pacific North West, he presented a paper to the Horticultural Society entitled 'An Account of some new, and little known Species of the Genus Ribes'. His enthusiasm for this introduction is evident:

Few [species] possess greater claims on our attention as ornamental shrubs, than *R. sanguineum*. ... So long ago as the year
1787, my esteemed friend, ARCHIBALD MENZIES, ESQ.
during his first voyage round the world, discovered this species
near Nootka Sound, and, subsequently on his second voyage
with the celebrated Vancouver, in 1792, found it again on
various points of the coast of North West America. ... Whether
we consider the delicate tints of its blossoms which appear in
March and April, the elegance of its foliage, the facility with
which it is increased and cultivated, or its capability of enduring
the severest of our winters without the least protection, it may
be regarded as one of the finest and most interesting additions
that have been made to our shrubberies for many years.

While writing that *Ribes sanguineum* was 'an exceedingly handsome
plant', he ignored its scent. He was not given to noting the scents of
flowers. From his detailed reports, we know that the temperature on
the day he found the shrub was about 47 degrees Fahrenheit, so
perhaps the perfume was less evident in such chilly weather. The
Horticultural Society later estimated that the financial return on the
sale of this particular shrub was sufficient to cover the entire cost of
Douglas' two-year stay in the Columbia River area.

This early-flowering shrub appears to shrug off all types of
disease and has become a staple in gardens, heralding the end of
winter with its shivering racemes of pink or deep-rose flowers. In his
native Scotland, Douglas would have cheered at the enterprising use
of a phalanx of flowering currants in the windswept, almost tree-less
land south of Edinburgh. At a garden near Tarbrax, carved from hillside so cold in winter that the local inhabitants declare you can hear
the sheep stamping their feet to keep warm, the enterprising owners
have successfully planted 'walls' of flowering currant to create 'rooms'
for their different gardens. This plant is the ideal hedge. It propagates
easily and therefore inexpensively, reaches a convenient maximum
height of 6 feet (2 metres), and so never needs clipping on top. The
scent of the leaves, which some gardening books flatteringly describe
as 'aromatic' but others more truthfully declare to be ammonia-like or
pungent, makes a wonderful barrier to inquisitive sheep and maraud-
ing deer.

Camas lily (*Camassia quamash*)

'*Phalangium* [*Camassia*] *quamash*; its roots form a great part of the
natives' food.' So began Douglas' description of a plant that played a

very significant part in the lives of many native peoples of the West and of the settlers who arrived from the mid-nineteenth century onwards. The bulbs from this lovely blue-flowering plant that resembles a hyacinth were a staple part of the diet. To cook them, a pit was dug and filled with red-hot stones and layers of leafs from a thick-leafed plant such as *Lysichiton americanus* (skunk cabbage). The bulbs were then packed in and sealed with more leaves and a layer of soil. The whole bulbs were left to steam overnight and, when baked, were hung up to dry and stored for use during the winter. Douglas compared the taste of the cooked bulbs with that of baked pears, and speculated that they might also make 'a palatable beverage'. He also noted that 'assuredly they produce flatulence; when in the Indian hut I was almost blown out by strength of wind'.

The flowers of this Camas are blue. A very similar plant with white flowers is deadly poisonous. During the flowering season, native women would carefully weed out the white variety, leaving just the blue. Douglas once recorded that he was violently sick after a meal of mashed Camas – perhaps a rogue bulb had found its way into the meal.

Another bulb meal was concocted by boiling *Fritillaria pudica*, which Douglas named *Lilium pudicum*. Douglas sent home this delightful fritillary, whose nodding heads of yellow flowers gradually turn orange to bricky red with age, in a jar of sand. *Pudicum* means 'bashful', an apt name since when the flower emerges there is little hint of the glories to come.

Oregon grape (*Mahonia aquifolium*)

Major discoveries were the *Mahonia aquifolium*, or Oregon grape, and *Berberis nervosa*, which also proved a wonderful success in Britain. Douglas preferred the second of these – 'this is by far the more beautiful plant'. He despatched seeds of both these preserved in spirits, hoping that the alcohol would not disappear down the throats of those responsible for carrying them on the long land and sea journey back to London. In Britain, urban landscapers make extensive use of the Oregon grape's attractive prickly foliage and bright yellow flowers in early spring to brighten roadsides and town corners.

Menzies Island, called after the illustrious Scottish naturalist, lies in the centre of the Columbia River opposite Fort Vancouver. Here Douglas found a new form of bright-yellow forget-me-not, *Myosotis*, which he and his botanizing companion Dr Scouler promptly named after Hooker, *Myosotis hookeri*. He also sent back many varieties of another yellow flower, *Mimulus luteus* or monkey flower. Monkey flowers now grace greenhouses and gardens all over Britain, and have self-sown in numerous watery havens, including, astonishingly, in a ditch at the Butt of Lewis, on the far edge of the Hebridean island of Lewis, one of the last points of land on the eastern side of the Atlantic. Douglas found another version of this plant with yellow flowers with two streaks of purplish colour and two minute dots of the same colour in the upper petal. 'This interesting species I shall call *Mimulus scouleri*, after John Scouler'; it is now the most common in Europe.

Bulbs, alpines and evening primrose

In his journal, Douglas made detailed notes of his observations and collecting activities. Not all of them were new introductions, nor is it possible to confirm whether Douglas correctly identified every observation he made, but his enthusiasm was obvious. Into his collection went veronicas, species of chrysanthemum, 'a very strong species of Rumex', or docken, and a fragrant orange honeysuckle, *Lonicera ciliosa*. There was also a version of Solomon's Seal, *Smilacina*, a species of delphinium, and a marsh marigold such as *Caltha palustris*, which he noted was rare.

On 22 May 1825, he found a large-flowered hyacinth, whose blue flowers made it 'one of the finest and earliest flowering plants'. 'Will the bulbs keep in England?' he asked himself. Indeed they did, and one variety of the four he managed to sow in English soil was named after him in America; nowadays, it is known as *Brodiaea douglasii*, and is much sold as a summer-flowering bulb for suburban gardens. The genus *Brodiaea* is named in honour of James L. Brodie, another roving Scottish botanist.

Douglas collected plants from the *Umbellifarae*, or carrot and parsley, family, the thistle family and many buttercups, which nestled in the damp patches near the river. He also brought back the Saskatoon, or *Amelanchier alnifolia*, a spreading shrub whose delicate white flowers give way to berries of a deep, regal purple-black. The native people dried the berries for winter food, and used them for bartering; eight different variations of this shrub were familiar to native tribes. When he found *Anemone multifida*, a delicate little plant with simple creamy or yellow flowers, Douglas did not mention its local use for killing fleas and lice; an infusion of the leaves was used to drench clothing and the ground.

Between July and November 1825, Douglas found five species of evening primrose, *Oenethera*, with their yellow flowers. By the Grand Rapids he also discovered a species of *Chelone*, commonly known as turtle head, perhaps because of the pink flowers which, by a stretch of the imagination, have a hooded appearance like a turtle's head. Douglas was much pleased with this find, especially as it flowered in late September. Another fascinating find in eastern USA was a curious plant, devoid of any trace of green, called *Pterospora*, pinedrops. The tall, leafless stalks of this parasitic plant shoot up from decaying humus, often in shaded areas, as they do not require sun to 'flower'. The spikes stands up to 40 inches (1 metre) tall, often well into the winter, and were called 'coyote's arrow' by natives. Also nearby, and requiring plenty of humus on which to grow, were varieties of *Pyrola*, or wintergreen, which Douglas found soon after his arrival; 'some had said such a plant did not exist' – he proved otherwise.

Plants named after Douglas include a mound-forming rock plant with floppy yellow flowers, *Douglasia vitaliana*, even though it was probably not brought back by him. However, he did bring back a hawthorn that was given his name, *Crataegus douglasii*. Like many hawthorns, it is sprinkled with a multitude of white flowers in the spring, and clusters of berries in autumn, and possesses the usual vicious thorns. Native peoples used these to pierce ears and skin boils, and also made them into fish hooks. Yet another flower that bears Douglas' name is *Douglasia nivalis*, a ground-hugging mountain 'pink'.

In April and May 1826, Douglas found another exquisite lily, *Erythronium grandiflorum*, yellow glacier lily or dog-toothed violet, which blooms just after the snows melt. The glowing yellow petals furl backwards. For Douglas, its beauty was enhanced by its proximity to other flowers such as *Dodecatheon*, with its tiny pink and white flowers, and a small species of the spotted leafed *Pulmonaria*. The yellow glacier lilies were another root vegetable that could be eaten after prolonged steaming released sweet juices. *Sheperdia*, known locally as Soopallie, Chinook for 'soap', also had practical uses. The white flowers give way to brilliant scarlet berries, which since time immemorial had been made into what Europeans called 'Indian ice-cream'. The juicy, bitter berries were whipped up with water into a froth, but could also be eaten fresh, or boiled into a syrupy beverage.

By the Kettle Falls in May 1826, Douglas came across *Heuchera*. This may have been the *Heuchera cylindrica* grown today, with elegant pale greenish spikes instead of the more commonly known pink variety. *Heucheras* are part of the alum family; the pounded root, a powerful astringent, can be used as a poultice or infusion to treat wounds and sores.

When, in the same month, Douglas tracked down the gunsmith

Jacques Rafael Finlay to have his gun mended, he wrote that Finlay and his family had been living on

> the roots of *Phalangium Quamash* (called by the natives all over the country Camas) and a species of black lichen which grows on the pines. The manner of preparing it is as follows; it is gathered from the trees and all the small dead twigs taken out of it, and then immersed in water until it becomes perfectly flexible, and afterwards placed on a heap of heated stones with a layer of grass or leaves between it and the stones to prevent its being burned; then covered over with the same material and a thin covering of earth and allowed to remain until cooked which generally takes a night. Then before it cools it is compressed into thin cakes and is fit for use.

The 'black lichen' was probably *Bryoria fremontii*, or edible horse-hair, a dangling lichen that suspends itself from the branches of Douglas fir and other pines. It was used as a staple food, being readily available in even the worst of weather, as it could be plucked from the trees. After being washed thoroughly, as Douglas describes, it was pit-cooked, with wild onions, roots and bulbs, and then dried into cakes for storage. Before they were eaten, the cakes were boiled with berries, roots or meat.

At the Jackfish River in June 1827, Douglas saw plentiful drifts of perennial blue flax, *Linum perenne*, on dry, elevated places. Douglas wrote little about this plant, although it is listed as one he brought back. Its deep sky-blue flowers are a sight to remember. Curiously, although this sub-species of flax, which was originally named after Meriwether Lewis of Lewis and Clark fame, was much in evidence, it was little used by the native people, other than as a hair rinse, even though flax is one of the earliest crops grown for agriculture.

Lupins (*Lupinus*)

Douglas also discovered *Lupinus sulphureus*, yellow tree lupin, a shrub-like plant whose spurs of sweet-smelling yellow flowers reminded him of the broom and gorse that cover the hills of Scotland with glowing yellow. Douglas returned to London with some eighteen varieties of lupin, mainly blues and purples. However, it was *Lupinus polyphyllus* that became the foundation plant of the beloved lupins that only a few decades later were growing in gardens everywhere, from cottages to fashionable mansions.

The development of the rainbow colours now associated with the lupins plucked by Douglas in 1826 was the responsibility of an irasci-ble Englishman named George Russell. A jobbing gardener, he was struck by the vase of purple lupins in the home of his employer in York. In 1911, when he was fifty, he began to fill first one allotment, then two or three adjacent plots, with countless rows of lupins. From these he ruthlessly chose only the very best flowers – the best being essentially those he liked. From this unscientific base came dozens of multi-coloured flowers, and by 1925 the allotments had become a showplace. But George Russell refused to sell even one plant, until, ten years later, he was persuaded after much cajoling to part with his plants to James Baker, a seedsman and lupin fanatic. George Russell was an all-or-nothing character. He sold every plant, emptying his allotments in a couple of hours, and added just one condition to the sale. His assistant for twenty years had been a young lad called Sonny, who had been told that his infantile paralysis would mean that he would never walk or lead a 'normal' life. George Russell carried the child on his back, gradually encouraged him to move around in a limited way on his own, and taught him all he knew. Now, he extracted a promise from Baker that Sonny should be given a job for life with the lupins. In 1937, Baker exhibited the lupins at the Royal Horticultural Show and was awarded the Society's Gold Medal. Over 70,000 people visited Baker's Floral Farm to see the Russell lupins growing in the fields; when the first catalogue was published, over half the named varieties sold out.

So Douglas' lupins came full circle to the Royal Horticultural Society, a century after they arrived in Britain. In 1938, at the age of eighty-one, George Russell was awarded the Society's prized Veitch Medal.

Bear Grass (*Xerophyllum tenax*)

In August 1826, towards the end of his summer collecting trips on his first expedition to the Pacific North West, Douglas packed his sparse possessions into an 'Indian bag made of curious workmanship constructed of Indian hemp, *Apocynum* and *Helionas tenax*'. Douglas had encountered this last grass-like plant, which he took to be *Helionas tenax*, several times. Later, renamed *Xerophyllum tenax*, it was successfully introduced to Europe. One of the Indian peoples, the Ktunaxa, used its tough leaves to ornament their baskets and sold it to neighbouring tribes. The common name is bear grass, so called because bears are reputed to munch its fleshy base leaves in the spring. The real joy of the plant, and no doubt the reason Douglas was so fascinated when he found this unpromising clump of leaves, is the wonderful straight flower stems, which soar up to 5 feet (1.5 metres). Once only, when the plant is between five and ten years old, a spectacular mass of tiny, sweet-smelling white flowers appears. Thereafter, the flowering part of the plant dies.

Phlox and snowberry

Douglas stowed in his collecting box the perennial sweet pea, *Lathyrus*, which grows on the fertile river banks and produces deep purple-red flowers, *Solidago*, or golden rod, and varieties of *Liatris*, with its spikes of mauve-purple tufted flowers. Into his final collecting box also disappeared many species of penstemons, violas, yet more species of *Ribes* (currants), some with small brown flowers, others with racemes of yellow flowers, as well as the common *Sonchus* or cowthistle, and species of viburnums, cherries and willows, and carpets of *Monarda*, or bergamot. Then there was the pretty *Phlox hoodii*, not dissimilar to the pink rock phlox, *Phlox douglasii*, which Douglas is credited with introducing, a mound of leaves sporting lavender-blue flowers with attractive violet-blue markings like central 'eyes'.

A couple of well-known shrubs, wonderful for background filling in gardens, are also the result of Douglas' eagle-eyed observation. These are *Aruncus sylvester*, known in its home ground as goat's beard, and *Symphoricarpos albus*, or snowberry, with its glacial white pearl-like berries that birds consume with fervour in the chill of early winter.

California

Douglas spent two seasons collecting in California, from early 1831 until August 1832. He reaped a rich harvest, and the plants he found here were among the more colourful and exotic of his discoveries. The Monterey peninsula alone has a great diversity of flora, and Douglas applied himself initially in the forest of Del Monte with his usual zeal. He despatched seeds and roots by sea and across land.

Among the first plants he collected was the fuchsia-flowered gooseberry, *Ribes speciosum*, now amongst the showiest of the ornamental currants with bright red flowers born in clusters of three to four from April to June. The lilies pleased him enormously. He introduced six varieties of Mariposa lily or *Calochortus* – *alba*, *luteus*, *macrocarpus*, *pulchellus*, *splendens* and *venustus* – all with characteristic papery petals and delicate stems. Bright annuals such as *Collinsia grandiflora* and *parviflora* came from the north, and there was also a beauty commonly called Chinese houses, *Collinsia hetrophylla*. All have curiously shaped, lilac-lipped flowers.

Brilliant yellow-flowered plants included *Coreopsis atkinsoniana*, an annual with the doubtful common name of tickweed, curious since the daisy-like flowers have bright scarlet centres. There was the shrub *Dendromecon rigida*, which will spread up a wall to a height of 30 inches (3 metres), and is covered in glowing, buttery-yellow flowers; the tall *Sidalcea malviflora*, with its spikes of pink flowers, now available in all shades of pink; and the ever-popular tongue-twisting *Eschscolzia californica*, or Californian poppy. At the time of Douglas' explorations, the Spanish called it the 'drowsy one', perhaps because it spreads in sheets of colour over the hillsides up to 2000 feet (620 metres), the flowers opening from February to September in the heat of the sun. *Clarkias*, named after the American William Clark, who had crossed the Rockies with Meriwether Lewis and nicknamed 'farewell to spring' flowers, together with their near-twins *Godetias*, have invaded the hanging baskets, allotments, public spaces and private acres of Britain. So too have *Gaillardias*, or blanket flowers, with their concentric circles of colour on a daisy-like face, and ever-increasing varieties of penstemons, gathered both north and south on the western seaboard; Douglas' innumerable varieties have spawned the wide selection available today.

Two Californian plants for which Douglas should be fondly remembered are the curiously but precisely named poached eggs, *Limnanthes douglasii*, and baby blue eyes, *Nemophila menziesii*. The latter retained its name and colour for many years, until a new colour type emerged recently. This was christened 'Pennie Black', and sports flowers of such deep purple that they appear black; the edge of the petals retains the traditional frill of scalloped white. *Mentzelia lindleyi*, blazing star, is also accurately named. Its lemon-yellow petals have a cluster of ten to fifty gleaming stamens that shine through the rather scrawny, stiff-stemmed branches. The petals themselves form a perfect star and, as the name suggests, open in the heat of the midday sun. One shrub that also graces modern gardens is *Garrya elliptica*, named, like the Garry oak, after Nicholas Garry of the Hudson's Bay Company. *Garrya elliptica* has leathery leaves and produces dangling silvery-green catkins in the bleak winter months. Ever the Scot, Douglas would have cheered at such a bonus in a Highland January.

Appendix 3

PLANTS DISCOVERED, INTRODUCED OR NAMED BY DAVID DOUGLAS

David Douglas discovered thousands of plants, mosses and seaweeds. Many were not of interest to the Horticultural Society because they would not thrive in the British climate or were too fragile to succeed; and there was limited use of many of the mosses and seaweeds.

The list reproduced below has been compiled over many years at Glasgow Botanic Gardens, where many of Douglas' plants are grown grouped together. It details Douglas' better-known plants and does not attempt to be comprehensive or exhaustive.

The growth in botanical knowledge since Douglas' day means that many species have been reclassified and therefore claim new names. For example, Douglas gave the name *Lilium pudicum* to what we now know as *Fritillaria pudica*. The list names the plants as they are currently known.

The authors would like to thank Paul Matthews, Curator, Glasgow Botanic Gardens, for permission to reproduce this list.

Abies amabilis	Pacific silver fir, or lovely fir
– grandis	Grand fir, or white fir
– procera	Noble fir
– venusta	Santa Lucia fir
Abronia mellifera	Sand verbena
Acer circinatum	Vine maple
– macrophyllum	Broad-leaved maple
Agastache urticifolia	Grand hyssop or Giant hyssop
Amelanchier alnifolia	Saskatoon
– florida	
Amsinckia douglasiana	Fiddleneck
– lycopsoides	
Anemone hudsoniana	
– multifida	Cut-leafed anenome

Antirrhinum multiflorum	Sticky snapdragon
Arbutus menziesii – *procera* – *tomentosa*	Madrona
Arceutholobium douglasi	Western dwarf mistletoe
Arctostaphylos columbiana – *tomentosa*	Bearberry
Arenaria douglasii	Sandwort
Artemisia douglasii	
Aruncus americanus – *vulgaris*	Goat's beard
Aster chilensis – *douglasii*	Aster
Astragalus agrestis – *crassicarpus* – *douglasii* – *drummondii* – *lentiginosus* – *purshii* – *succulentus*	Milk-vetches (all species of Astragalus)
Audibertia incana	
Baccharis douglasii	
Bartonia aurea	
Benthamia lycopsoides	
Berberis glumacea – *nervosa*	
Boisduvalia densiflora	
Brassavola nodosa	Lady of the night
Brodiaea congesta	Wild hyacinths (all varieties of Broadiaea)
– *coronaria* – *douglasii*	
Brodiaea flava – *grandiflora*	

– hyacinthina
– laxa

Calandrinia ciliata var.	Redmaids
menziesii	
– discolor	
– speciosa	

Calliopsis athinsiniana

Calochortus albus	Mariposa lilies, cat's ears or
– barnardii	fairy lanterns
– elegans	
– luteus	
– macrocarpus	
– nitidus	
– pulchellus	
– pusillus	
– splendens	
– venustus	

Calycanthus occidentalis

Camassia esculenta	Camas lilies (all varieties of
	Camassia)
– quamash var. flora alba	

| *Carex douglasii* | Sedge |

Castilleja affinis	Paintbrush
– coccinea	
– miniata	
– parviflora	

| *Castanopsis chrysophylla* | Golden chestnut |

Ceanothus collinus
– velutinus
– – var. laevigatus

| *Celtis douglasii* | Hackberry or nettle tree |

| *Chaenactis douglasii* | Hoary false yarrow |

Cheiranthus capitatus

| *Chelone centranthifolia* | Turtle head |
| *– nemorosa* | |

| *Chorizanthe douglasii* | Douglas's water hemlock |

Cicuta douglasii
– *occidentalis*

Clarkia amoena
– *amoena*
– *elegans*
– *gauroides*
– *lepida*
– *pulchella*
– *purpurea*
– – ssp. *quadrivulnera*

Clarkia purpurea ssp.
– *viminea*
– *rhomboidea*

Clematis virginiana   Virginian clematis

Clintonia elegans   Corn lilies
– *pulchella*

Collinsia bicolor
– *grandiflora*
– *heterophylla*   Chinese houses
– *parviflora*   Blue-eyed Mary

Collomia bellidifolia
– *gracilis*
– *grandiflora*
– *heterophylla*
– *linearis*
– *pinnatifida*

Coreopsis atkinsoniana   Tickseed
– *douglasii*

Cornus stolonifera   Red-osier dogwood

Crataegus douglasii   Black hawthorn

Cryptantha flaccida

Cynoglossum grande   Hound's tongue

Cypripedium montanum

Delphinium menziesii   Menzies larkspur

Dendromecon rigida

Diplopappus incana	
Donia villosa	
Douglasia nivalis	Mountain pink
Downingia elegans *– pulchella*	
Draba douglasii	
Epilobium minumum	Small-flowered willowherb
Epipactis gigantea	
Erigeron speciosus	Showy fleabane
Eriogonum compositum *– – spp. nudum* *– douglasii* *– elatum* *– latifolium Sim* *– – ssp. nudum* *– sphaerocephalum*	Sulphur flower
Eriophyllum caespitosum *– lanatum (leucophyllum)*	Woolly sunflower
Erythronium grandiflorum	Glacier lily, or dog-toothed violet
Eschscholtzia caespitosa	
Eschscholtzia californica *– – var. dougl.*	California poppy
Frasera speciosa	
Fraxinus latifolia	
Fritillaria pudica	Yellow bell
Gaillardia aristata	Brown-eyed Susan or blanket flower
Garrya elliptica	Tassel bush
Gaultheria shallon	Salal
Gaura parviflora	
Geranium carolinianum	Carolina geranium

Gesneria douglasii

Gilia achillaeafolia (ssp. multicaulis)
– *aggregata*
– *androsaca*
– *capitata*
– *coronopifolia*
– *densiflora*
– *liniflora var. pharnaceoides*
– – *alba*
– *parviflora*
– *pungens*
– *sinuata*
– *splendens*
– *tenuiflora*
– *tricolor*

Godetia amoena rubicunda
– – *vinosa*
– *decumbens*
– *lindleyi*
– *quadivulnera*
– *viminea*

Gomesa planifolia

Greyia spinosa

Harkelia congesta	Stickseed
Helianthus annuus ssp. lenticularis	Sunflower

Helonias tenax

Hesperoscordon lacteum

Heuchera cylindrica – *micrantha*	Round-leaved alum root
Holodiscus discolor	Ocean spray
Hosackia bicolor capitatum – *crassifolia*	Pink bird-foot clover
Hydrophyllum capitatum	Baldhead waterleaf

Hyssopus urticifolius

Ipomopsis elegans

Iris douglasiana   Tough-leaved or beardless
– tenax Dougl.   iris

Lasthenia californica
– glabrata

Lathyrus californicus   Perennial sweet pea
– japonicus
– jepsonii ssp. californicus

Layia chrysanthemoides   Tidy tips

Leptosiphon androsaceus
– densiflorus

Lespedeza capitata

Limnanthes douglasii   Poached-egg plant

Linanthus liniflorus
– – ssp. pharnaceoides

Linum perenne ssp. Lewisii Wild blue flax
– sibiricum

Lithospermum ruderale

Lonicera ciliosa   Orange honeysuckle
– douglasii
– glaucescens
– hispidula
– hirsuta   Hairy honeysuckle

Lotus douglasii
– pinnatus

Lupinus albicaulis   Lupin
– albifons
– – var. douglasii
– arbustus
– argenteus
– – var. tenellus
– aridus
– benthamii
– bicolor
– chamissonis
– densiflorus
– flexuosus
– grandifolius

– hirsutissimus
– latifolius
– laxiflorus
– lepidus

Lupinus leptophyllus
– leucophyllus
– littoralis
– lucidus
– micranthus
– nanus
– obtusilobus
– ornatus
– plumosus
– polyphyllus
– – var. albiflorus
– rivularis
– sabinii
– sericeus
– succulentus
– sulphureus
– tristis

Madia elegans

Mahonia aquifolium   Oregon grape

Malus fissea   Pacific coast crab apple
– fusca

Malva coccinea   Mallow

Malvastrum coccineum

Meconella linearis

Mentzelia albicaulis   Small evening star
– laevicaulis (Dougl.)   Blazing star
– lindleyi   Blazing star

Microseris douglasii

Microsteris gracilis   Pink twink

Mikania scandens

Mimulus alsinoides   Monkey flowers
– cardinalis
– douglasii

– floribundus
– guttatus
– lewisii
– moschatus
– roseus

Montia linearis
– perfoliata
– spathulata

Myosotis hookeri   Forget me not

Navarretia squarrosa

Nemophila aurita

Nemophila insignis   Baby blue eyes
– menziesii
– parviflora
– pedunculata

Nicotiana multivalvis   Native tobacco

Oenothera albicaulis   Evening primrose (all varieties of Oenothera)

– biennis var. muricata
– boothii
– californica
– contorta
– densiflora
– dentata
– lepida
– lindleyi
– speciosa
– triloba

Oncidium pubes

Paeonia brownii   Wild paeony

Pedicularis canadensis   Lousewort
– racemosa

Penstemon acuminatus
– attenuatus
– breviflorus
– caeruleo-purpurea
– centranthifolius

– confertus	Yellow penstemon
– deustus	
– diffusus	
– digitatifolius	
– fruticosus	Shrubby penstemon
– – var. scouleri	
– glandulosus	
– gracilis	
– heterophyllus	
– nemorosus	
– ovatus	
– procerus	Small-flowered pentstemon
– pruinosus	
– richardsonii	
– serrulatus	
– speciosus	
– staticifolius	
– triphyllus	
– venustus	
Phacelia divaricata	Heliotrope
– douglasii	
– hastata	
– linearis	
– ramosissima	
– tanacetifolia	
– viscida	
Phlox douglasii	Phlox
– longifolia	
– sabinii	
– speciosa	
Pholistoma auritum	
Picea sitchensis	Sitka spruce
Pinus contorta	Lodgepole pine
– coulteri	Big-cone pine
– lambertiana	Sugar pine
– monticola	Western white pine
– ponderosa	Western yellow pine
– radiata	Monterey pine
– sabiniana	Digger pine
Platystemon californicus	Cream cups

Plectris congesta

Poa douglasii   Bluegrass

Pogogyne douglasii

Pogonia pendula

Polygonum douglasii

Potentilla arachnoidea   Cinquefoil (all varieties of Potentilla)
– arguta
– congesta
– effusa
– glandulosa   Sticky cinquefoil
– gracilis   Graceful cinquefoil
– hippiana
– obscura
– ontopoda
– pectinata
– pectinsecta
– pennsylvanica   Prairie cinquefoil
– var strigosa

Prunus emarginata   Bitter cherry
– pumila

Pseudotsuga menziesii   Douglas fir
– taxifolia

Psoralea macrostachya
– orbicularis
– physodes

Purshia tridentata   Antelope bush

Pyrus rivularis

Quercus douglasii   Blue oak
– garryana   Garry or Oregon white oak

Ribes aureum   Golden currant
– bracteosum   Stink currant
– cereum   Squaw currant
– divaricatum   Straggly gooseberry
– echinatum
– glutinosum
– gracile   Pasture gooseberry

– irriguum
– lacustre   Swamp currant
– malvaceum   Chaparral currant
– menziesii   Swamp gooseberry, prickly currant

– niveum
– petiolare   Western black currant
– sanguineum   Flowering currant
– – var. glutinosum Winter currant
– setosum   Red-shoot gooseberry
– speciosum   Fuschia-flowered gooseberry
– tenuiflorum
– viscosissimum   Sticky currant

Rubus leucodermis   Black raspberry
– leucostachys   Black raspberry
– longipetalus
– macropetalus
– nutkanus
– parviflorus   Thimbleberry
– spectabilis   Salmonberry

Salvia dorrii var. camosa Grey ball sage
– pachyphylla

Sanicula bipinnatifida

Satureja douglasii

Selaginella douglasii

Senecio douglasii

Sida hederacea

Sidalcea malvaeflora   Marsh hollyhock

Silene douglasii   Douglas' campion
– inamoena
– ramossima

Sinningia helleri

Sisyrinchium douglasii   Blue-eyed grass
– grandiflorum

Solanum douglasii

Spergula arvensis

Sperula ramosissima	
Sphaeralcea munroana	False mallow
Spiraea ariaefolia *– douglasii*	Pink spirea or hardhack
Stylomecon hederophylla	Flaming poppy
Symphoria racemosa	
Symphoricarpus rivularis	Snowberry
Synthyris reniformis	
Tanacetum boreale *– douglasii*	
Tellima grandiflora	Fringecup
Thermopsis fabacea *– montana*	
Trifolium fucatum *– macrocephalum* *– tridentatum*	
Triteleia laxa	
Vaccinuum membr anceum *– ovatum*	Huckleberry
Valerianella congesta	
Verbena bracteata *– bracteosa*	
Viola douglasii *– praemorsa*	
Xerophyllum tenax	Bear grass

Appendix Four

THE DAVID DOUGLAS
TRAIL IN SCOTLAND

A casual stroll through any British suburban garden will reveal to the keen observer the range of Douglas introductions, from the ubiquitous flowering currant, mahonias and lupins through to sunflowers, penstemons and *Mimulus* (monkey flowers). Drive or walk in the countryside of Britain, and you will inevitably come across trees introduced by Douglas. In some places, the impact is dramatic because of the scale of the planting or the size of the trees. But, inevitably, it is in his native Scotland that you can find the most important sites linked to Douglas. Here is a selection of sites worth visiting.

The David Douglas memorial and Scone Palace and grounds

Scone has many links with Douglas, although no descendants of the family remain in the area. The memorial to Douglas was erected in 1841 in the grounds of Scone Old Parish Church at the southern end of the 'new' village of Scone, 2 miles from Scone Palace. The stone monument is an impressive 23 feet tall and is inscribed with a tribute to Douglas and a list of the various plants he introduced (see page 183). (Interestingly, Douglas's father, a stonemason with a reputation for first-class workmanship, was often given the task of putting up tombstones in churchyards.) According to contemporary accounts, a portrait and biographical notice listing Douglas's achievements were inserted into a cavity in the stone, where they must presumably still lie.

The memorial is signposted from the A94 road through Scone. There is ample car parking next to the church.

Scone Palace, the ancient coronation site of the Scottish monarchs, is located just outside Perth on the A93 road to Braemar. Together with the gardens and grounds, the Palace is one of Scotland's premier tourist attractions. The estate belongs to the Earls of Mansfield, who have traditionally taken a keen interest in forestry and horticulture. Douglas was born in the 'old' village of Scone, yards from the Palace, and you can still see the outline of the village and the village cross today, although the village was moved to its present site – 'new' Scone – in the early nineteenth century.

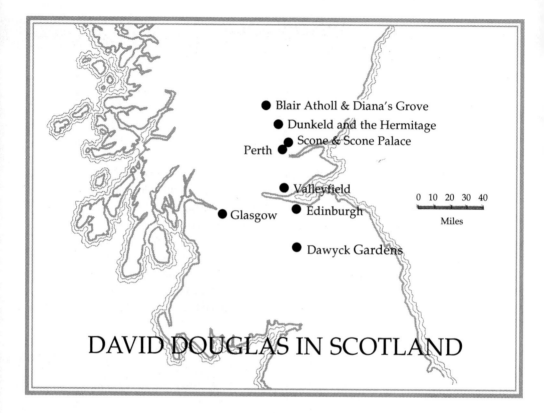

Blair Atholl & Diana's Grove
Dunkeld and the Hermitage
Scone & Scone Palace
Perth
Valleyfield
Glasgow Edinburgh
Dawyck Gardens

0 10 20 30 40
Miles

DAVID DOUGLAS IN SCOTLAND

In the Palace grounds, the fine pinetum includes magnificent specimens of conifers introduced by Douglas. The specimen noble firs, grand firs, and Sitka spruce are particularly impressive; there are also examples of Oregon maple and vine maple, Monterey pine, big-cone pine, western white and western yellow pines. There is also a fine original Douglas fir grown from seed collected by Douglas himself. Recently, the estate has grown many of the plants and flowers introduced by Douglas for display in flower beds around the grounds; one area is dedicated to Douglas introductions.

The house and grounds at Scone Palace are normally open from Good Friday to mid-October; tours are available in winter by prior appointment. Admission fees are charged.

A pleasant footpath through Quarrymill Woodland Park links the Memorial and the Palace.

Dunkeld and The Hermitage

The area around Dunkeld, Perthshire, is one of the richest in Europe in terms of tree heritage, and is often called 'the cradle of the Scottish

forest renaissance' on account of the pioneering tree planting undertaken by the Dukes of Atholl in the eighteenth and early nineteenth
centuries. There are many renowned trees and also a number of champion trees in terms of size and growth. These include the Birnam Oak,
a remnant ancient oak from the forest mentioned in Shakespeare's
Macbeth ('till Birnam wood remove to Dunsinane'), the first 'parent'
larch tree in Scotland, and huge specimen conifers. One of these, an
original Douglas fir from Douglas' own seed collection, stands in the
grounds between Dunkeld Cathedral and Dunkeld House Hotel.

All these sites are accessible on foot from the village of Dunkeld,
which is just off the A9 about 13 miles north of Perth. An excellent
leaflet available from the tourist office in the village describes a variety
of signposted walks taking in the trees and woodlands.

Close by is The Hermitage, where reputedly the tallest tree in the
British Isles, a Douglas fir, can be seen. Now owned by the National
Trust for Scotland, The Hermitage has been a popular tourist attraction for nearly 250 years because of its mix of turbulent waterfalls,
huge trees and dramatic views. The Douglas fir stands on Forestry
Commission land on the opposite side of the River Braan from The
Hermitage, but is best viewed from the National Trust side. When it
was last measured in 1994 it was some 212 feet (65 metres) tall, which
is pretty impressive for a 'youngster' not much more than a century old,
though it will have to go some to improve on the tallest Douglas fir in
the Pacific North West, in Oregon, which stands over 329 feet (100
metres) high.

The Hermitage is situated just under 1 mile north of Dunkeld
and is well-signposted off the A9. There is a small charge for parking.

If you turn off the main A9 road and drive 2 or 3 miles north on
the B898 back road to Dalguise and Grantully, you will see next to the
roadside a stand of grand fir (*Abies grandis*) in Craigvinean Forest.
These have been measured as the fastest-growing stand of trees in
Britain. The trees are visible also from the A9.

Valleyfield Wood

Valleyfield Wood in Fife has a long history of informal recreational
access and was acquired a few years ago by the local authority, now
Fife Council, as an important countryside facility. The remodelling of
the grounds around Valleyfield House was the only commission
carried out in Scotland by Humphrey Repton, the famous English
landscape architect. His proposals were implemented by Sir Robert
Preston, Valleyfield's owner, in 1802. Preston was a renowned
gardener and encouraged Douglas to study in his extensive library.

Today, much effort is going into restoring what had become a rather derelict woodland site. There are several pleasant walks through the woodlands, which have some fine specimen trees. Guided walks are organized by Fife Council Ranger Service during the summer.

The entrance to Valleyfield Wood is in Valleyfield village on the B9037 road from Culross to Dunfermline. Parking is available, and admission is free.

Glasgow Botanic Garden

Founded in 1817, the Garden flourished under the direction of Professor William Hooker in the 1820s and 1830s, receiving new plants sent by collectors from around the world, including many from Douglas. Hooker and his son Joseph subsequently became famous for transforming Kew Gardens into the centre of horticultural excellence it remains to this day. Douglas worked at the Glasgow Botanic Garden from 1820 to 1823, coming under Hooker's benevolent influence, attending lectures and accompanying him on field trips to the Highlands. It was Hooker who recommended Douglas to the Horticultural Society as a plant-collector.

Glasgow City Council manages the Garden as an important botanical tourist attraction as well as a centre for education, conservation and research. The Garden contains a diverse range of hardy and non-hardy species, and specializes in orchids, ferns and begonias. There is a Visitors' Centre, and educational material is available. An interpretative trail and dedicated flower beds are planned to commemorate the link with Douglas.

The Garden is in the west end of Glasgow by the River Kelvin and close to the junction of Great Western Road and Queen Margaret Drive. Entry is free; opening hours are 7.00 a.m. until dusk throughout the year. Parking is available in the surrounding streets but can be difficult during the working week.

Dawyck Botanic Gardens Arboretum

Dawyck Arboretum, near Peebles in the Scottish Borders, has a long and distinguished history and is now an outstation of the Royal Botanic Garden Edinburgh. The Gardens were given the woodland policies in 1978 by the Balfour family, who had themselves acquired many tree specimens. In the early nineteenth century, the estate subscribed to many of the great plant-hunting expeditions, including Douglas' journeys. The estate has one of the best collections of Douglas firs raised from Douglas' original seed, and this now forms a magnificent backdrop to the grounds. There are many other fine

North American conifers as well as original collections from China, including a number of champion specimens.

The Gardens are open from March to the end of October. They are on the B712 about 8 miles west of Peebles. An admission fee is charged.

Other 'big-tree' sites

The British Isles are very fortunate in that many different types of tree from all over the world can be grown here. Favourable conditions – soil fertility, rainfall, length of the growing season – mean that growth rates are excellent and allow new species to grow to their full potential quickly. Thus 'big trees' are a feature of a number of particularly favoured localities. These include Perthshire, Argyll and the Great Glen in Inverness-shire in Scotland; the Welsh Marches, Gloucestershire and the south-west of England and Wales; and the sheltered glens of Ireland. Some of the best Scottish examples associated with David Douglas introductions are listed below.

Diana's Grove
Located next to Blair Castle at Blair Atholl in Perthshire, Diana's Grove is a spectacular two-acre plot of 'big trees'. Especially notable are the conifers from the Pacific North West, including the full range of 'Douglas' species and champion trees as well as giant redwoods and one of the original 'parent' larches from the first introduction of this species into Scotland in 1738.

Diana's Grove is in the grounds of Blair Castle, just off the A9 some 35 miles north of Perth. The grounds and Castle are open from the beginning of April to the end of October. There is an admission charge.

Reelig Glen
The spectacular wooded glen at Reelig, near Inverness, is owned and managed by the Forestry Commission. The big trees, including many original introductions, were planted by the Fraser family, who formerly owned the glen. An excellent walk leads through huge specimen conifers, including big Douglas, grand and noble firs.

Reelig Glen is 1 mile south of the A862 Inverness to Beauly road, 8 miles west of Inverness. Turn from the A862 on to the side road signed 'Moniack and Clunes'. The car park is by the bridge which crosses the Moniack Burn. Admission is free.

Drumlanrig Castle
Drumlanrig Castle, the Dumfriesshire home of the Duke of Buccleuch,

is one of the ancient strongholds of the Douglas clan. John Douglas, David's brother, served here as Clerk of Works, corresponding with his brother. Douglas also sent some of his early seed collections, and one huge original Douglas fir survives in the woodlands around the house. The current Duke is particularly interested in forestry and is a past President of the Royal Scottish Forestry Society. Buccleuch Estates is now one of the largest private woodland managers in Britain.

The sandstone castle, a unique example of late seventeenth-century Renaissance architecture, contains a celebrated collection of paintings. There are also woodland walks around the grounds, a visitor centre, and ranger service.

Drumlanrig Castle is on the A76, 3 miles north of Thornhill in Dumfriesshire. There is an admission charge.

Ardkinglas Woodland Garden

The 25 acres of this woodland garden at the head of Loch Fyne contain several excellent specimen champion trees as well as a number of huge Douglas introductions. Outstanding among these is the grand fir, standing more than 200 feet (60 metres) tall. Alongside several notable mature noble and Douglas firs are a number of recently introduced plants with Douglas associations, including *Ribes sanguineum* (flowering currant), *Rubus spectabilis* (salmonberry) and *Garrya elliptica* (tassel brush); there are plans to introduce more.

Ardkinglas Woodland Garden lies just off the A83 at Cairndow in Argyll, about 8 miles north-east of Inverary, and forms part of the 'Glorious Gardens of Argyll and Bute' promotion. The woodland garden is open all year during daylight. A 'Tree Shop' sells specialist plants and books and craft items in wood. Admission is charged.

Younger Botanic Garden Benmore and Puck's Glen

The Younger Botanic Garden in Argyll, a specialist outlier of the Royal Botanic Garden Edinburgh, has a spectacular avenue of giant redwoods and many other huge specimen conifers. Close by is the spectacular Puck's Glen, a Forestry Commission woodland with gorge walks among giant trees. In summer, guided walks link the Gardens and the Glen.

The Younger Botanic Garden is on the A815, 7 miles north of Dunoon in Argyll. There is an admission charge for the Garden, but not for Puck's Glen. Walks are available all year round.

The Commission's Kilmun Arboretum is only 3 miles away from Benmore and is well worth a visit for those interested in trees. Contact the Forest Enterprise office at Kilmun for full details.

KEY EVENTS IN THE LIFE
OF DAVID DOUGLAS

1799
Born 25 June at Scone, Perthshire, the son of a stonemason.

1802
Starts at the village school. Subsequently attends Kinnoull School near Perth where he is a less than willing pupil.

1810
Leaves school to be apprenticed as a gardener at Scone Palace. Pursues his botanical interests through walking, climbing and evening study.

1818
Takes up position as under gardener at Valleyfield, Fife, home of Sir Robert Preston.

1820
Appointed to a post at the Botanic Garden, Glasgow, and becomes pupil and friend of Dr William Hooker, Professor of Botany. Attends lectures and botanizes in the Highlands.

1823
On Hooker's recommendation, accepted by the Horticultural Society as a botanical collector.
June: Departs on first botanizing expedition, to north-eastern United States and Canada to collect specimens of fruit trees.

1824
9 January: Returns from successful first expedition.
25 July: Departs for the Pacific North West of America.

1825
7 April: Arrives at the mouth of the Columbia River to begin serious botanizing along the river and its tributaries. Over-winters at Fort Vancouver.

1826

End March: Resumes botanizing, travelling to Grand Rapids, Walla Walla, Kettle Falls, and Spokane and the Upper Columbia River.
September: Travels up the Willamette and Umpqua Rivers in Oregon in search of the sugar pine.
26 October: Finds the sugar pine. Over-winters at Fort Vancouver.

1827

20 March: Leaves Fort Vancouver to cross continent to Hudson's Bay via the Athabasca Pass. *En route* climbs peaks in the northern Rockies (the first person known to do so) and meets Thomas Drummond, fellow Scot and plant-collector.
28 August: Arrives at York Factory on Hudson Bay and sails for London.
11 October: Arrives in London and is welcomed as a celebrity by the Horticultural Society. Awarded fellowships of the Geological, Linnean and Zoological Societies.

1828

Remains in London, becoming frustrated with the Horticultural Society, but tending specimens from his own collections in the Society's gardens.

1829

31 October: Leaves England to return to the Pacific North West, travelling via Hawaii.

1830

3 June: Arrives at the Columbia River and resumes botanizing, sending back seeds of the noble and grand firs.
December: Travels to California.

1831

Botanizes around Monterey and tours Franciscan missions south to Santa Barbara and north to San Francisco. Visits the coast redwood forests.

1832

August: Leaves California and sails to Hawaii. Botanizes and makes astronomical observations.
9 September: Resigns from Horticultural Society on hearing of Joseph Sabine's resignation as Secretary.
14 October: Returns to the Columbia River.

1833

March: Journeys north to Fort St James on Stuart Lake, with the intention of travelling on to Alaska and Siberia.
13 June: Canoe wrecked at Fort George Canyon with loss of specimens and diary.
August: Returns to Fort Vancouver.
October: Departs for Hawaii via California.

1834

2 January: Arrives on Hawaii Island. Climbs to the summits of Mauna Kea, Kilauea, and Mauna Loa volcanoes.
12 July: Killed on the slopes of Mauna Kea after falling into a bull pit.
4 August: Buried in Honolulu.

1835

February: News of Douglas' death reaches London.

1836

William Hooker publishes his 'Brief Memoir' of Douglas.

1841

Memorial to Douglas erected in the grounds of the Old Parish Church, Scone.

1855

Memorial tombstone erected on Douglas grave at Kawaiahao Church, Honolulu.

1914

Douglas' journal published by the Royal Horticultural Society.

BIBLIOGRAPHY

Allen, J.L. *Lewis and Clark and the Image of the American Northwest*, Dover, New York, 1975.

American Forests. 'National Register of Big Trees, 1998–99', Spring 1998.

Anonymous. 'Monument in Memory of the Botanist Douglas', *Gardener's Magazine*, XVII (1842), pp. 289–301.

Balfour, F.R.S. *The History of Conifers in Scotland and their Discovery by Scotsmen*, Report of the Conifer Conference, 'Conifers in Cultivation', Royal Horticultural Society, London, 1932.

—. 'David Douglas', *Journal of the Royal Horticultural Society*, LXVII (1942), pp. 121–28, 153–62.

Barnston, George. 'Abridged Sketch of the Life of Mr David Douglas, Botanist, with a few details of his travels and discoveries', *Canadian Naturalist and Geologist*, V (1860), pp. 120–32, 200–8, 267–78, 329–49.

Bernhardson, W., *et al* (eds.). *South America on a Shoestring*, 5th edition, Lonely Planet, London, 1994.

Brickell, Christopher (ed.). *New Royal Horticultural Society Encyclopedia of Gardening*, Dorling Kindersley, London, 1992.

Bryson, Bill. *A Walk in the Woods*, Doubleday, London, 1997.

Calder, J. (ed.). *The Enterprising Scot*, Royal Museum of Scotland/HMSO, Edinburgh, 1986.

Coates, Alice M. *Flowers and their Histories*, A. & C. Black, London, 1968.

—. *The Quest for Plants: A History of the Horticultural Explorers*, Studio Vista, London, 1969.

Cunningham, L. 'David Douglas: Botanist', *Journal of the Caledonian Society of Hawaii*, 1984.

David Douglas Society of Western North America. Newsletters, published annually since 1989. Available from the Editor, 6401 Conconi Place, Victoria, British Columbia, Canada U87 527.

Davies, John. *Douglas of the Forests*, Harris, Edinburgh, 1980.

Desmond, Ray. *Dictionary of British and Irish Botanists and Horticulturalists*, Taylor and Francis, London, 1994.

Dictionary of American Biography, revised edition, Scribner, New York, 1963.

Douglas, David. 'An Account of some new, and little known Species of the Genus Ribes', *Transactions of the Horticultural Society*, vol. VIII (1830), pp. 508–18.

—. *Journal Kept by David Douglas During His Travels in North America*, William Wesley and Son, London, 1914.

Encyclopaedia Americana, Grolier, New York, 1986.

Fletcher, Alan. 'Some Notes on Original Douglas Fir Trees', personal communication, 1997.

Fletcher, H.R. *The Story of the Royal Horticultural Society 1804–1968*, Oxford University Press, London, 1969.

Grant Roger, J. 'George Don, 1764–1814', *Journal of the Botanical Society of Edinburgh*, 1986.

Grescoe, Audrey. *Giants: the Colossal Trees of Pacific North America*, Raincoast Books, Vancouver, 1997.

Harvey, A.G. 'David Douglas in British Columbia', *British Columbia Historical Quarterly*, IV (1940), pp. 221–43.

—. *Douglas of the Fir*, Harvard University Press, Cambridge, Mass., 1947.

Henderson, D.M., and Faulkner, R. (eds.). *Proceedings of the Sitka Spruce Symposium*, The Royal Society of Edinburgh, Edinburgh, 1987.

Heward, Edward. *The Earl of Mansfield*, Barry Rose, London, 1979.

Hooker, W.J. 'Brief Memoir of the Life of Mr David Douglas, with Extracts from His Letters', Companion to *The Botanical Magazine*, II (1836), pp. 79–182.

Hunter, James. *A Dance Called America*, Mainstream, Edinburgh, 1994.

Hunter, Thomas. *Woods, Forests and Estates of Perthshire*, Henderson, Robertson and Hunter, Perth, 1883.

Hoyles, Martin. *The Story of Gardening*, Journeyman Press, London, 1991.

Jacob, Irene and Walter. *Gardens of North America and Hawaii*, Timber Press, Portland, Oregon, 1985.

Johnson, Robert C. *John McLoughlin, Father of Oregon*, Bindfords & Mort, Portland, Oregon, 1935.

Keay, John and Julia. *Collins Encyclopedia of Scotland*, HarperCollins, London, 1994.

Lancaster, Roy. 'The Trail Blazer', *Gardeners' World*, September 1996, pp. 32–37.

Logan, William Bryant, and Ochshorn, Susan. *Smithsonian Guide to Historic America: The Pacific States*, Stewart, Tabori and Chang, New York, 1989.

MacDonald, R., *et al* (eds.). *Exotic Forest Trees in Britain*, Forestry Commission Bulletin Number 30, HMSO, London, 1957.

MacDonald, Robert. *The Owners of Eden*, Ballantrae Foundation, Calgary, 1974.

McFeat, Tom. *Indians of the North Pacific Coast*, Carleton University Press, Ottawa, 1995.

Mackenzie, Alexander. *Voyages from Montreal on the River St Lawrence through the Continent of North America to the Frozen Pacific Oceans in the years 1789 and 1793*, facsimile of the 1801 edition, Hurtig, Edmonton, 1971.

McCubbin, Robert P., and Peter Martin. 'Eighteenth Century Life – British and American Gardens', special issue of *Eighteenth Century* Life, vol. 8, part 2, 1983, Colonial Williamsburg Foundation, College of William and Mary, Sussex, New Jersey.

McKelvey, Susan Delano. *Botanical Exploration of the Trans-Mississippi West 1790–1850*, Arnold Arboretum, Jamaica Plain, Mass., 1955.

McMillan, Alan. *Native Peoples and Cultures of Canada*, Douglas and McIntyre, Vancouver, second edition, 1995.

Marshall, William. *Historical Scenes in Perthshire*, Oliphant, Anderson & Ferrier, Edinburgh, 1881.

Mitchell, A. (ed.). *Conifers in the British Isles*, Forestry Commission Booklet Number 33, HMSO, London, 1975.

Mitchell, A., *et al* (eds.). 'Champion Trees in the British Isles', Forestry Commission Technical Paper 7, Edinburgh, 1994.

Mitchell, A.F. *Field Guide to the Trees of Britain and Northern Europe*, Collins, London, 1975.

Morison, S.E. *The Oxford History of the United States 1783–1917*, Oxford University Press, Oxford, 1927.

Morwood, W. *Traveller in a Vanished Landscape: The Story of David Douglas*, Gentry Books, London, 1973.

Muir, John. *The Yosemite: reprinted from original articles in the Magazine*, the Sierra Club, San Francisco, 1988.

Newman, Peter C. *Caesars of the Wilderness*, Penguin, Toronto, 1987.

—. *Company of Adventurers*, Penguin, Toronto, 1985.

Ogilvie, J.F. 'A Pilgrimage up the Athabasca Pass', *Scottish Forestry*, vol. 38, no. 2, 1984, pp. 106–154.

—. 'A Portrait of David Douglas', *Arboricultural Journal*, vol. 4, no. 2, 1980, pp. 119–25.

Parish, Roberta, Coupe, Ray, and Lloyd, Dennis. *Plants of the Southern Interior, British Columbia*, Lone Pine Publishing, Vancouver, 1996.

Peterson, Roger, and McKenny, Margaret. *Field Guide to Wildflowers in Northeastern/Northcentral and North America*, Audubon Society and National Wildlife Federation with Houghton Mifflin, Boston, Mass., 1968.

Ray, Mary Helen, and Robert Nicholls. *Guide to Significant and Historical Gardens of America*, Agree Publishing, New York, 1982.

Scone Archives (held at Scone Palace). 'Garden Accounts of W. Beattie', box 108.

—. *Loudon's Treatise*, 1803.

—. 'Memorandum of Planting at Scone 1804', volume 115.

—. 'Minutes of Planting at Scone 1804–1833', volume 114.

—. 'Papers Relating to Garden, List of Plants', box 105, 1817–18.

—. 'Statistical Account of Scone, 1791–1799', 1796.

Strang, R. M. 'Douglas Fir and the Scots Connection', *The Forestry Chronicle*, vol. 68, no. 2, 1992, pp. 246–48.

Tait, A.A. *The Landscape Garden in Scotland, 1735 to 1835*, 1980.

Venning, Frank D. *Guide to the Field Identification of Wildflowers of North America*, Golden Press, New York, 1984.

Van Doren, Charles, and McHenry, Robert. *Websters Guide to American History*, G. & C. Merrian, Mass. 1971.

Wallace, R. *Hawaii*, Time Life Books, Amsterdam, 1973.

Whitney, S. *Western Forests*, Audubon Society Nature Guides, Knopf, New York, 1985.

Wilson, Ernest. *Smoke that Thunders*, 1927, reprinted Waterstone, London, 1985.

Wood, R.F. *Studies of North-Western American Forests in Relation to Silviculture in Great Britain*, Forestry Commission Bulletin Number 25, HMSO, London, 1955.

INDEX